ARAÑA

NIGHT OF THE HUNTER

ARAÑA

NIGHT OF THE HUNTER

Writer
Fiona Kai Avery

Pencils
Roger Cruz, Francis Portella & Jonboy Meyers

Inks
Victor Olazaba, John Stanisci & Mark Irwin

Letters
Virtual Calligraphy's Rus Wooton

Colors
Udon's Jeannie Lee (and her awesome team)
& SotoColor's Larry Molinar

Cover Art
Takeshi Miyazawa, Mark Brooks & Roger Cruz

Assistant Editor
Nathan Cosby

Editors
Jennifer Lee & Mark Paniccia

Creative Consultant
J. Michael Straczynski

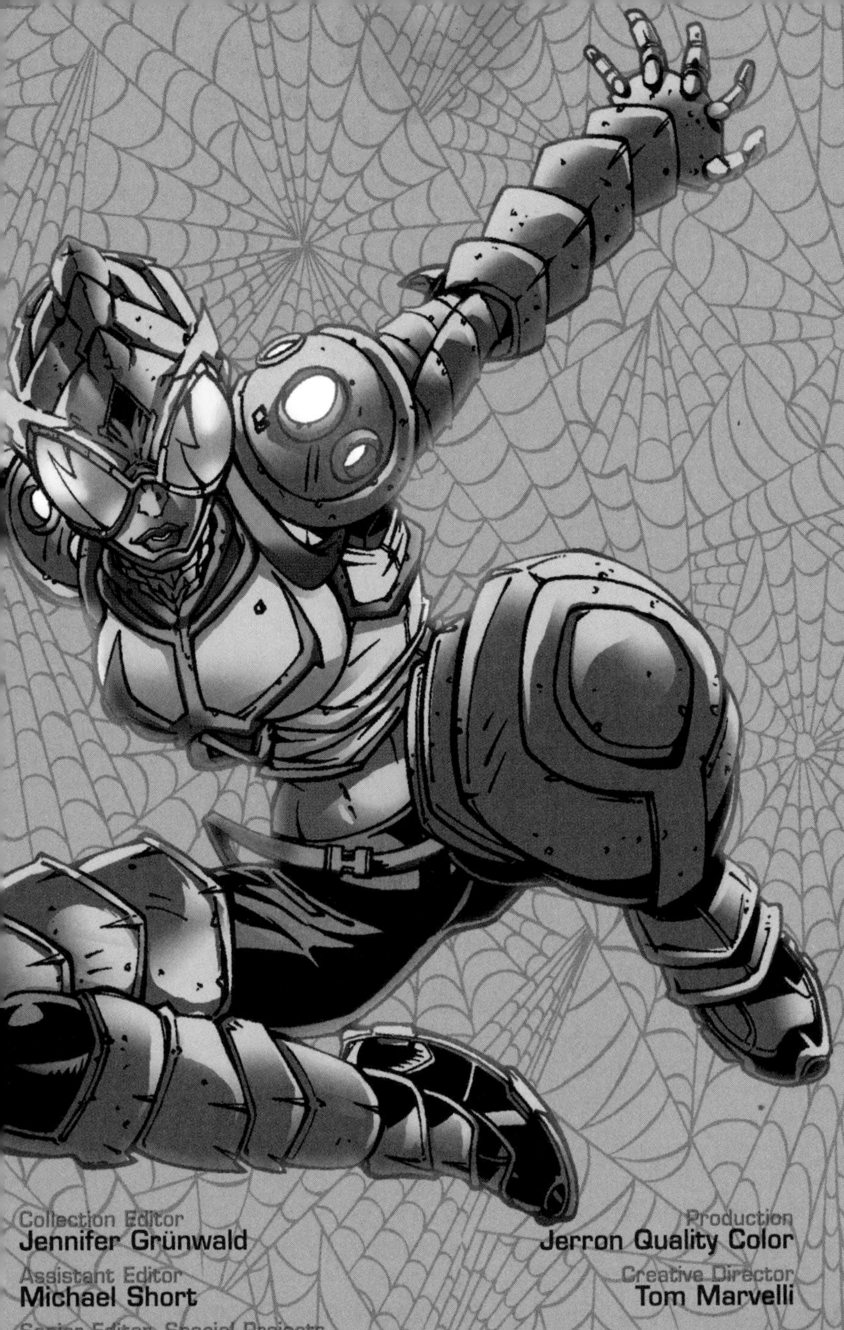

Collection Editor
Jennifer Grünwald
Assistant Editor
Michael Short
Senior Editor, Special Projects
Jeff Youngquist
Vice President of Sales
David Gabriel

Production
Jerron Quality Color
Creative Director
Tom Marvelli
Editor in Chief
Joe Quesada
Publisher
Dan Buckley

PREVIOUSLY

Araña. Anya Corazon. Last in a nine-hundred-year line of hunters, touched by blood and magic, protecting the world from equally ancient enemies striving towards a new Dark Age where they will rule supreme. She must stop them...and bring her grades up to at least a B+ or her dad won't let her go for her driver's test next year.

So one day you're having coffee with your best friend and her current crush. Pretty normal day, right? Unless you're Araña, and Lynn (your friend) is making googly eyes at Amun—the assassin hired to kill you! Great! Like it wasn't awkward enough...

Then a fight breaks out and Araña's gotta protect Lynn, and make a tough decision to save Amun's life. Super-heroing sucks sometimes.

So then Amun and Vincent try to kill a weakened Miguel. Araña saves the day, but she's left with a sense of uncertainty. Did her mother know how hard it is to be a normal fifteen-year-old with spider powers?

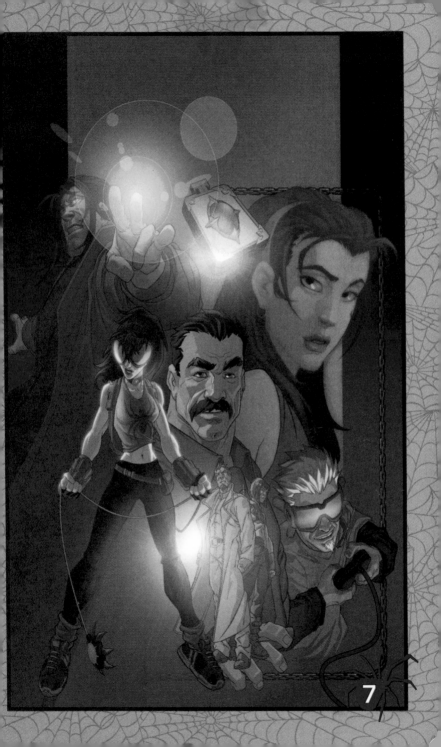

7

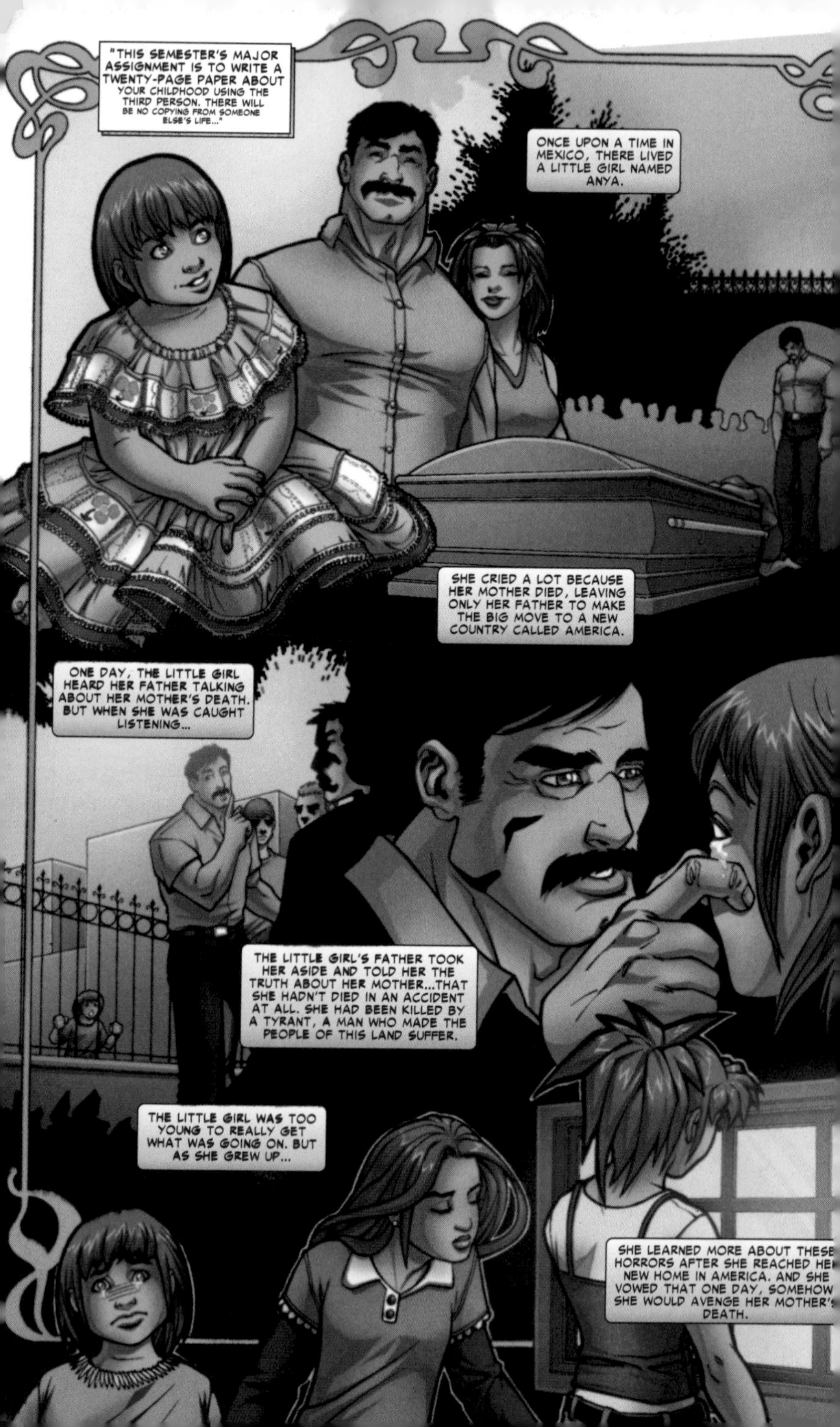
"THIS SEMESTER'S MAJOR ASSIGNMENT IS TO WRITE A TWENTY-PAGE PAPER ABOUT YOUR CHILDHOOD USING THE THIRD PERSON. THERE WILL BE NO COPYING FROM SOMEONE ELSE'S LIFE..."
ONCE UPON A TIME IN MEXICO, THERE LIVED A LITTLE GIRL NAMED ANYA.
SHE CRIED A LOT BECAUSE HER MOTHER DIED, LEAVING ONLY HER FATHER TO MAKE THE BIG MOVE TO A NEW COUNTRY CALLED AMERICA.
ONE DAY, THE LITTLE GIRL HEARD HER FATHER TALKING ABOUT HER MOTHER'S DEATH. BUT WHEN SHE WAS CAUGHT LISTENING...
THE LITTLE GIRL'S FATHER TOOK HER ASIDE AND TOLD HER THE TRUTH ABOUT HER MOTHER...THAT SHE HADN'T DIED IN AN ACCIDENT AT ALL. SHE HAD BEEN KILLED BY A TYRANT, A MAN WHO MADE THE PEOPLE OF THIS LAND SUFFER.
THE LITTLE GIRL WAS TOO YOUNG TO REALLY GET WHAT WAS GOING ON. BUT AS SHE GREW UP...
SHE LEARNED MORE ABOUT THESE HORRORS AFTER SHE REACHED HER NEW HOME IN AMERICA. AND SHE VOWED THAT ONE DAY, SOMEHOW SHE WOULD AVENGE HER MOTHER'S DEATH.

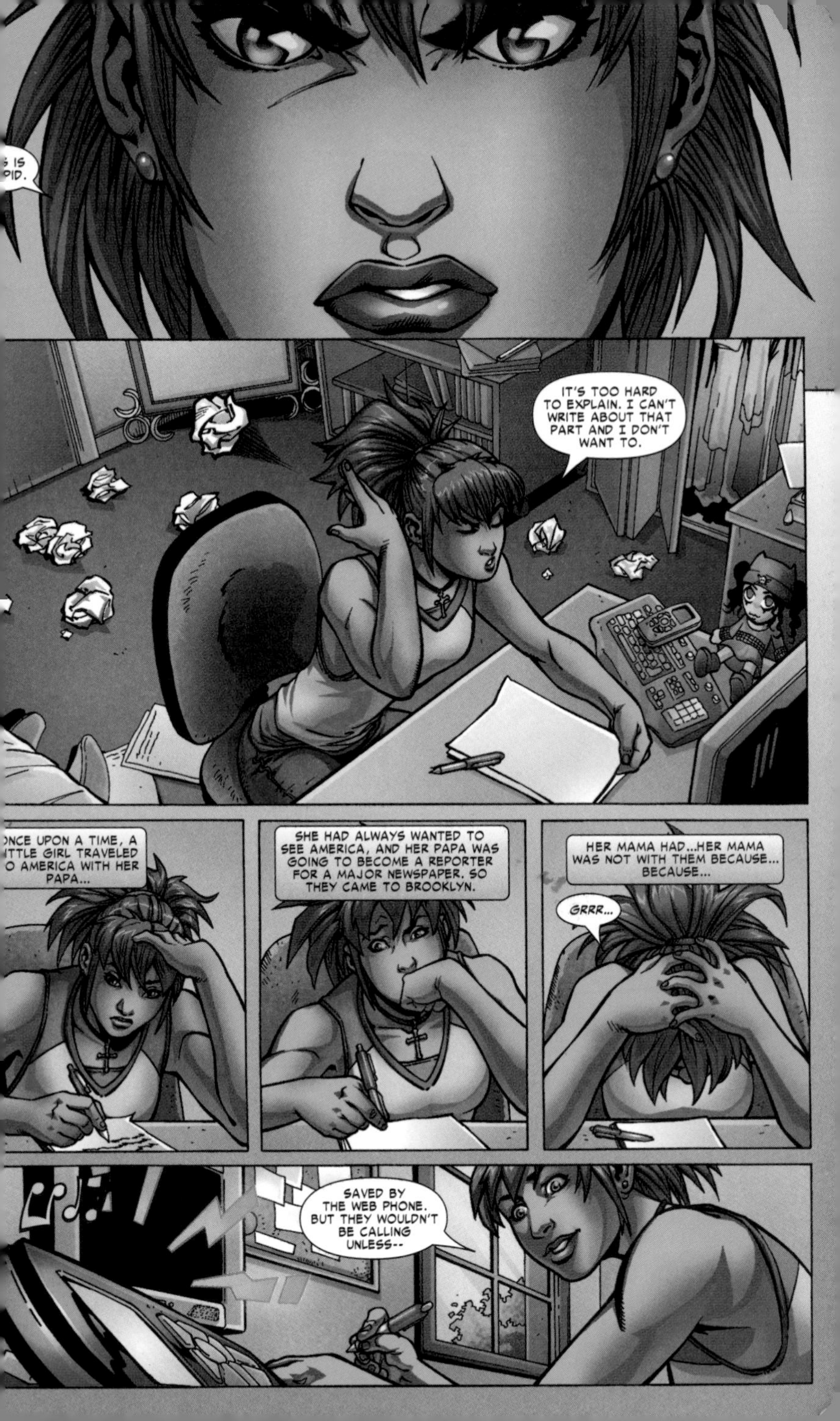
G IS
PID.
IT'S TOO HARD TO EXPLAIN. I CAN'T WRITE ABOUT THAT PART AND I DON'T WANT TO.
ONCE UPON A TIME, A LITTLE GIRL TRAVELED TO AMERICA WITH HER PAPA...
SHE HAD ALWAYS WANTED TO SEE AMERICA, AND HER PAPA WAS GOING TO BECOME A REPORTER FOR A MAJOR NEWSPAPER. SO THEY CAME TO BROOKLYN.
HER MAMA HAD...HER MAMA WAS NOT WITH THEM BECAUSE... BECAUSE...
GRRR...
SAVED BY THE WEB PHONE. BUT THEY WOULDN'T BE CALLING UNLESS--

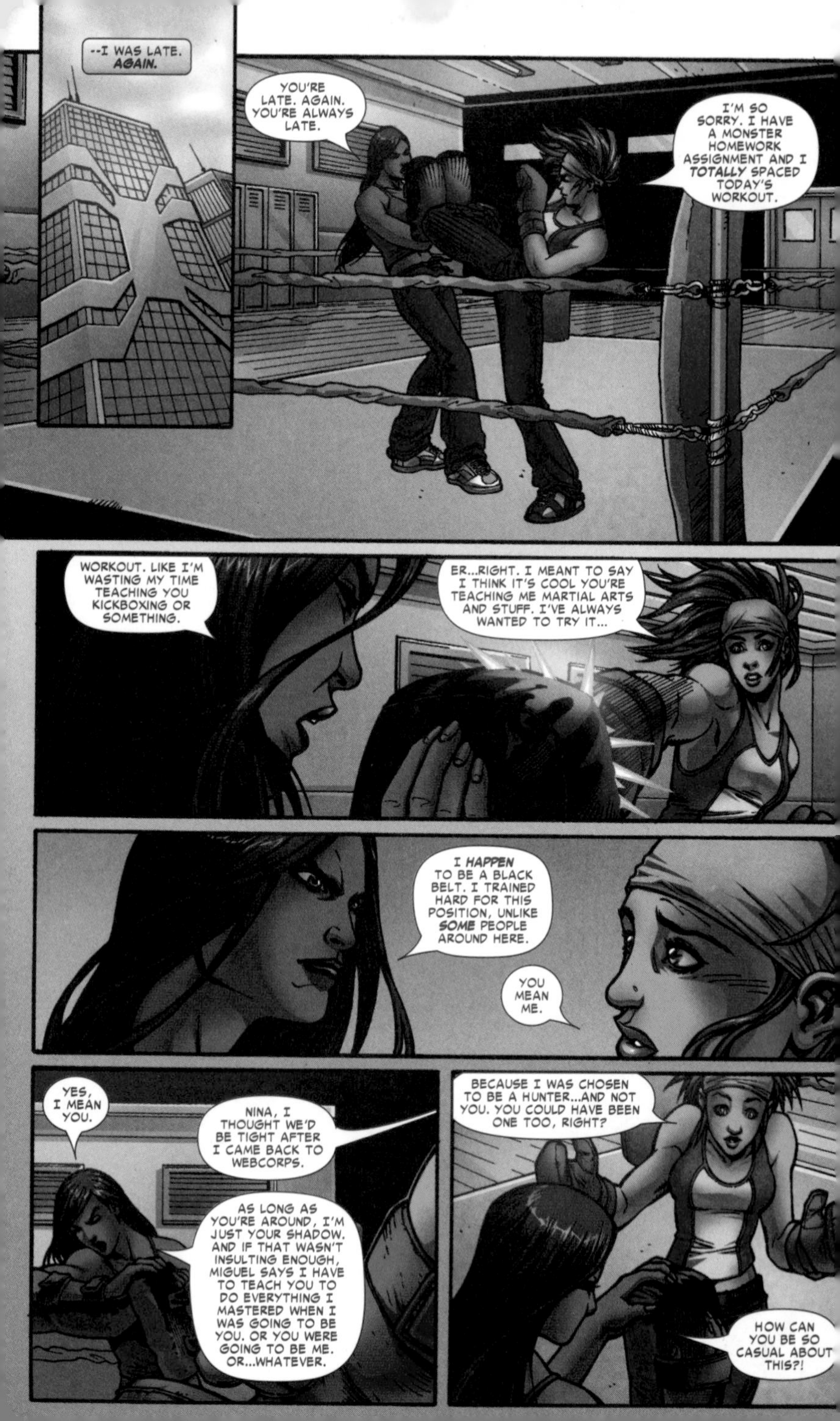
--I WAS LATE. AGAIN.
YOU'RE LATE. AGAIN. YOU'RE ALWAYS LATE.
I'M SO SORRY. I HAVE A MONSTER HOMEWORK ASSIGNMENT AND I TOTALLY SPACED TODAY'S WORKOUT.
WORKOUT. LIKE I'M WASTING MY TIME TEACHING YOU KICKBOXING OR SOMETHING.
ER...RIGHT. I MEANT TO SAY I THINK IT'S COOL YOU'RE TEACHING ME MARTIAL ARTS AND STUFF. I'VE ALWAYS WANTED TO TRY IT...
I HAPPEN TO BE A BLACK BELT. I TRAINED HARD FOR THIS POSITION, UNLIKE SOME PEOPLE AROUND HERE.
YOU MEAN ME.
YES, I MEAN YOU.
NINA, I THOUGHT WE'D BE TIGHT AFTER I CAME BACK TO WEBCORPS.
AS LONG AS YOU'RE AROUND, I'M JUST YOUR SHADOW. AND IF THAT WASN'T INSULTING ENOUGH, MIGUEL SAYS I HAVE TO TEACH YOU TO DO EVERYTHING I MASTERED WHEN I WAS GOING TO BE YOU. OR YOU WERE GOING TO BE ME. OR...WHATEVER.
BECAUSE I WAS CHOSEN TO BE A HUNTER...AND NOT YOU. YOU COULD HAVE BEEN ONE TOO, RIGHT?
HOW CAN YOU BE SO CASUAL ABOUT THIS?!

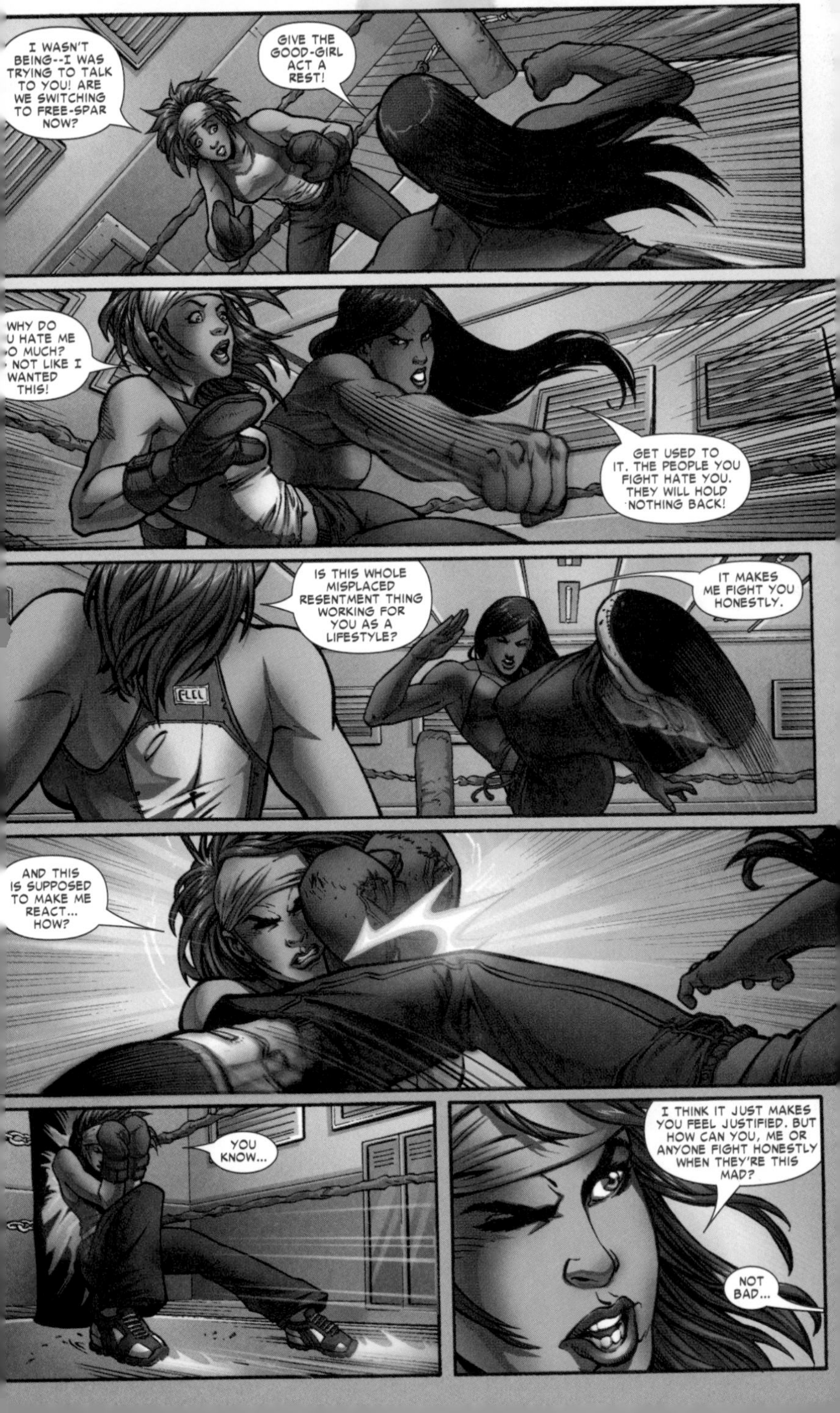

I WASN'T BEING--I WAS TRYING TO TALK TO YOU! ARE WE SWITCHING TO FREE-SPAR NOW?
GIVE THE GOOD-GIRL ACT A REST!
WHY DO U HATE ME O MUCH? NOT LIKE I WANTED THIS!
GET USED TO IT. THE PEOPLE YOU FIGHT HATE YOU. THEY WILL HOLD NOTHING BACK!
IS THIS WHOLE MISPLACED RESENTMENT THING WORKING FOR YOU AS A LIFESTYLE?
IT MAKES ME FIGHT YOU HONESTLY.
AND THIS IS SUPPOSED TO MAKE ME REACT... HOW?
YOU KNOW...
I THINK IT JUST MAKES YOU FEEL JUSTIFIED. BUT HOW CAN YOU, ME OR ANYONE FIGHT HONESTLY WHEN THEY'RE THIS MAD?
NOT BAD...

MIGUEL!

YO...

STANDING UP TO AN ASSAULT FROM NINA. YOUR FIGHTING IS COMING ALONG WELL, ANYA.

EXCUSE THE INTERRUPTION, BUT THEY WANT TO GO OVER THE LATEST INFORMATION ON THE TRIADS AND THEIR SERPENT.

THAT'S FINE. WE'LL BE RIGHT IN.

RIGHT-- KICK BUTT TIME! I'LL GET CLEANED UP AND JOIN YOU GUYS IN A MINUTE.

NINA, PLEASE TRY TO REMEMBER THAT ANYA'S NOT IN FULL CONTROL OF HER POWER YET. IF YOU GO TOO HARD AGAINST HER, YOU MIGHT--

GET HURT? OR HURT *HER*?

LOOK, I KNOW HOW FAR TO PUSH HER. I KNOW WHAT I'M DOING, OKAY?

FAIR ENOUGH.

NOTHING IS FAIR ABOUT IT. BUT YOU ASKED ME TO TEACH HER, AND I WILL.

WITH THIS GATHERING OF CRIME LORDS, AND LADY CHI IN THE MIX, WE HAVE TO DO WHATEVER WE CAN TO STOP THIS ALLIANCE, DISRUPT IT, AND THAT'S DANGEROUS.

AND I'M IN NO CONDITION TO HELP HER RIGHT NOW. SO...I APPRECIATE IT.

I DON'T WANT PITY FROM ANY OF YOU. DON'T EVEN PRETEND YOU CARE WHEN YOU'RE STILL THE SAME COLD JERK.

"IT WAS AN ILL-TIMED REMARK."

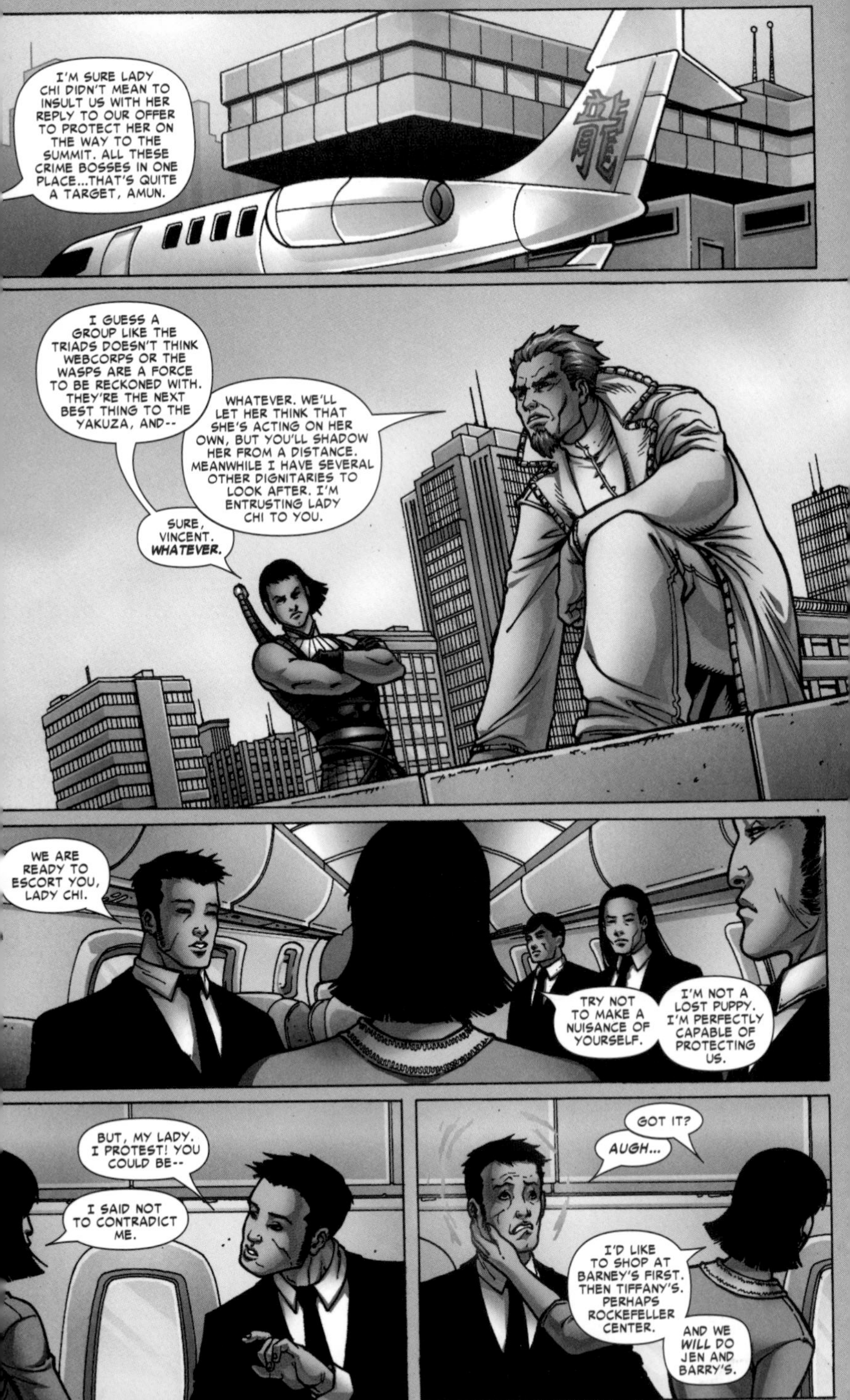
I'M SURE LADY CHI DIDN'T MEAN TO INSULT US WITH HER REPLY TO OUR OFFER TO PROTECT HER ON THE WAY TO THE SUMMIT. ALL THESE CRIME BOSSES IN ONE PLACE...THAT'S QUITE A TARGET, AMUN.
I GUESS A GROUP LIKE THE TRIADS DOESN'T THINK WEBCORPS OR THE WASPS ARE A FORCE TO BE RECKONED WITH. THEY'RE THE NEXT BEST THING TO THE YAKUZA, AND--
WHATEVER. WE'LL LET HER THINK THAT SHE'S ACTING ON HER OWN, BUT YOU'LL SHADOW HER FROM A DISTANCE. MEANWHILE I HAVE SEVERAL OTHER DIGNITARIES TO LOOK AFTER. I'M ENTRUSTING LADY CHI TO YOU.
SURE, VINCENT. WHATEVER.
WE ARE READY TO ESCORT YOU, LADY CHI.
TRY NOT TO MAKE A NUISANCE OF YOURSELF.
I'M NOT A LOST PUPPY. I'M PERFECTLY CAPABLE OF PROTECTING US.
BUT, MY LADY. I PROTEST! YOU COULD BE--
I SAID NOT TO CONTRADICT ME.
GOT IT?
AUGH...
I'D LIKE TO SHOP AT BARNEY'S FIRST. THEN TIFFANY'S. PERHAPS ROCKEFELLER CENTER.
AND WE WILL DO JEN AND BARRY'S.

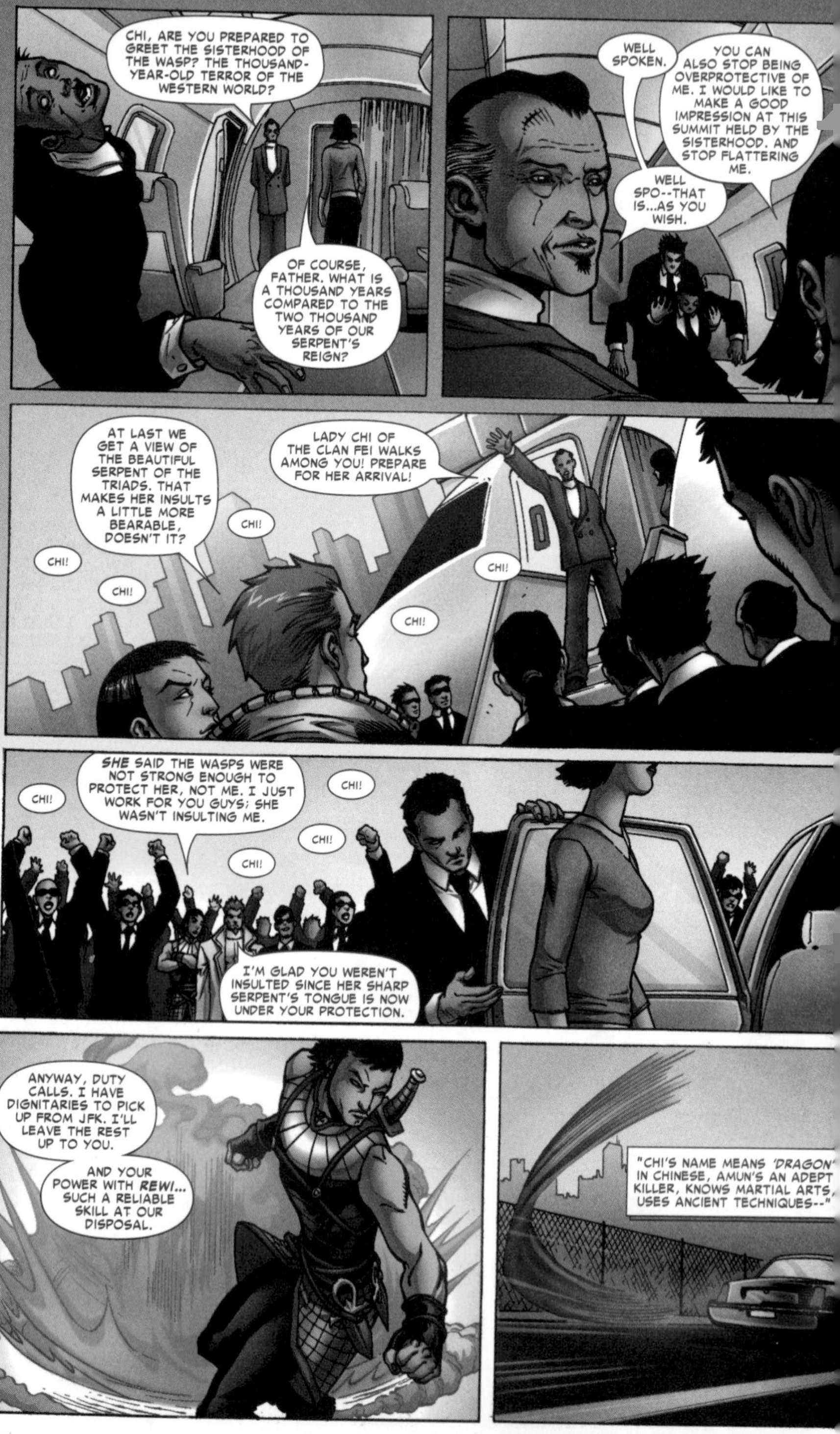
CHI, ARE YOU PREPARED TO GREET THE SISTERHOOD OF THE WASP? THE THOUSAND-YEAR-OLD TERROR OF THE WESTERN WORLD?
OF COURSE, FATHER. WHAT IS A THOUSAND YEARS COMPARED TO THE TWO THOUSAND YEARS OF OUR SERPENT'S REIGN?
WELL SPOKEN.
YOU CAN ALSO STOP BEING OVERPROTECTIVE OF ME. I WOULD LIKE TO MAKE A GOOD IMPRESSION AT THIS SUMMIT HELD BY THE SISTERHOOD. AND STOP FLATTERING ME.
WELL SPO--THAT IS...AS YOU WISH.
AT LAST WE GET A VIEW OF THE BEAUTIFUL SERPENT OF THE TRIADS. THAT MAKES HER INSULTS A LITTLE MORE BEARABLE, DOESN'T IT?
LADY CHI OF THE CLAN FEI WALKS AMONG YOU! PREPARE FOR HER ARRIVAL!
CHI!
CHI!
CHI!
CHI!
CHI!
SHE SAID THE WASPS WERE NOT STRONG ENOUGH TO PROTECT HER, NOT ME. I JUST WORK FOR YOU GUYS; SHE WASN'T INSULTING ME.
CHI!
CHI!
CHI!
CHI!
I'M GLAD YOU WEREN'T INSULTED SINCE HER SHARP SERPENT'S TONGUE IS NOW UNDER YOUR PROTECTION.
ANYWAY, DUTY CALLS. I HAVE DIGNITARIES TO PICK UP FROM JFK. I'LL LEAVE THE REST UP TO YOU.
AND YOUR POWER WITH REWI... SUCH A RELIABLE SKILL AT OUR DISPOSAL.
"CHI'S NAME MEANS 'DRAGON' IN CHINESE, AMUN'S AN ADEPT KILLER, KNOWS MARTIAL ARTS, USES ANCIENT TECHNIQUES--"

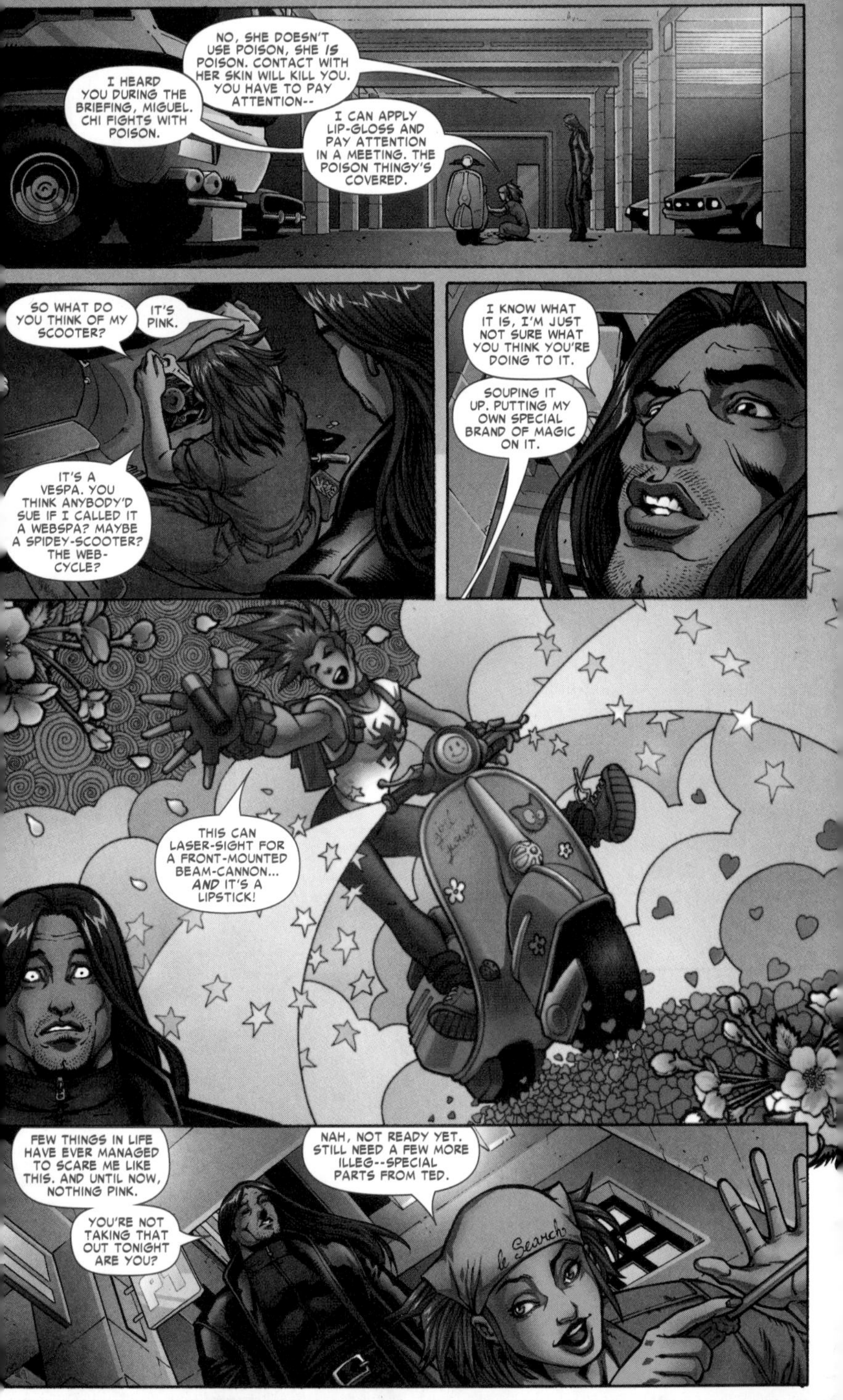

I HEARD YOU DURING THE BRIEFING, MIGUEL. CHI FIGHTS WITH POISON.
NO, SHE DOESN'T USE POISON, SHE *IS* POISON. CONTACT WITH HER SKIN WILL KILL YOU. YOU HAVE TO PAY ATTENTION--
I CAN APPLY LIP-GLOSS AND PAY ATTENTION IN A MEETING. THE POISON THINGY'S COVERED.
SO WHAT DO YOU THINK OF MY SCOOTER?
IT'S PINK.
IT'S A VESPA. YOU THINK ANYBODY'D SUE IF I CALLED IT A WEBSPA? MAYBE A SPIDEY-SCOOTER? THE WEB-CYCLE?
I KNOW WHAT IT IS, I'M JUST NOT SURE WHAT YOU THINK YOU'RE DOING TO IT.
SOUPING IT UP. PUTTING MY OWN SPECIAL BRAND OF MAGIC ON IT.
THIS CAN LASER-SIGHT FOR A FRONT-MOUNTED BEAM-CANNON... *AND* IT'S A LIPSTICK!
FEW THINGS IN LIFE HAVE EVER MANAGED TO SCARE ME LIKE THIS. AND UNTIL NOW, NOTHING PINK.
YOU'RE NOT TAKING THAT OUT TONIGHT ARE YOU?
NAH, NOT READY YET. STILL NEED A FEW MORE ILLEG--SPECIAL PARTS FROM TED.

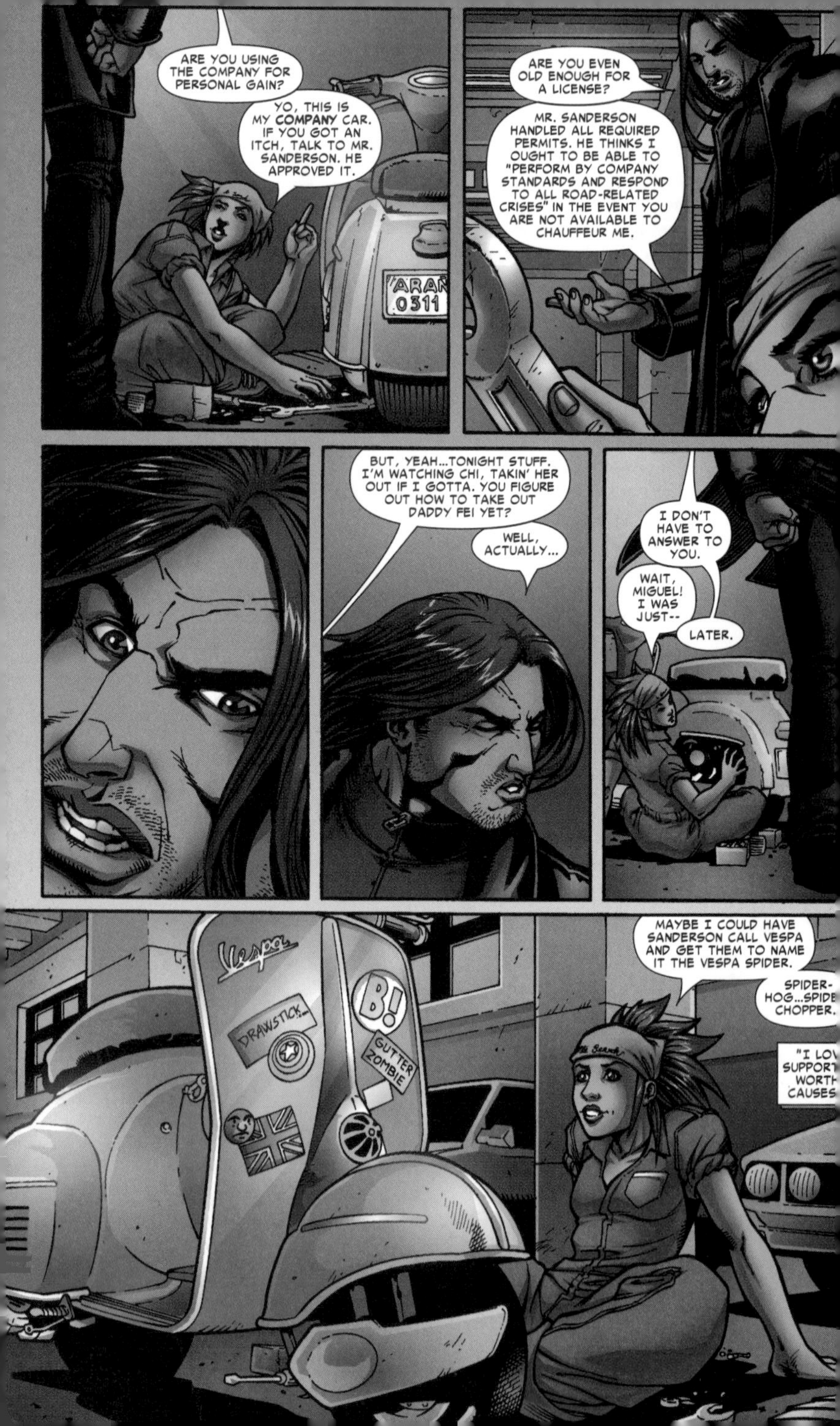
ARE YOU USING THE COMPANY FOR PERSONAL GAIN?
YO, THIS IS MY COMPANY CAR. IF YOU GOT AN ITCH, TALK TO MR. SANDERSON. HE APPROVED IT.
ARAN 0311
ARE YOU EVEN OLD ENOUGH FOR A LICENSE?
MR. SANDERSON HANDLED ALL REQUIRED PERMITS. HE THINKS I OUGHT TO BE ABLE TO "PERFORM BY COMPANY STANDARDS AND RESPOND TO ALL ROAD-RELATED CRISES" IN THE EVENT YOU ARE NOT AVAILABLE TO CHAUFFEUR ME.
BUT, YEAH...TONIGHT STUFF. I'M WATCHING CHI, TAKIN' HER OUT IF I GOTTA. YOU FIGURE OUT HOW TO TAKE OUT DADDY FEI YET?
WELL, ACTUALLY...
I DON'T HAVE TO ANSWER TO YOU.
WAIT, MIGUEL! I WAS JUST--
LATER.
Vespa
B!
DRAWSTICK
GUTTER ZOMBIE
MAYBE I COULD HAVE SANDERSON CALL VESPA AND GET THEM TO NAME IT THE VESPA SPIDER.
SPIDER-HOG...SPIDE CHOPPER.
"I LOV SUPPORT WORTH CAUSES

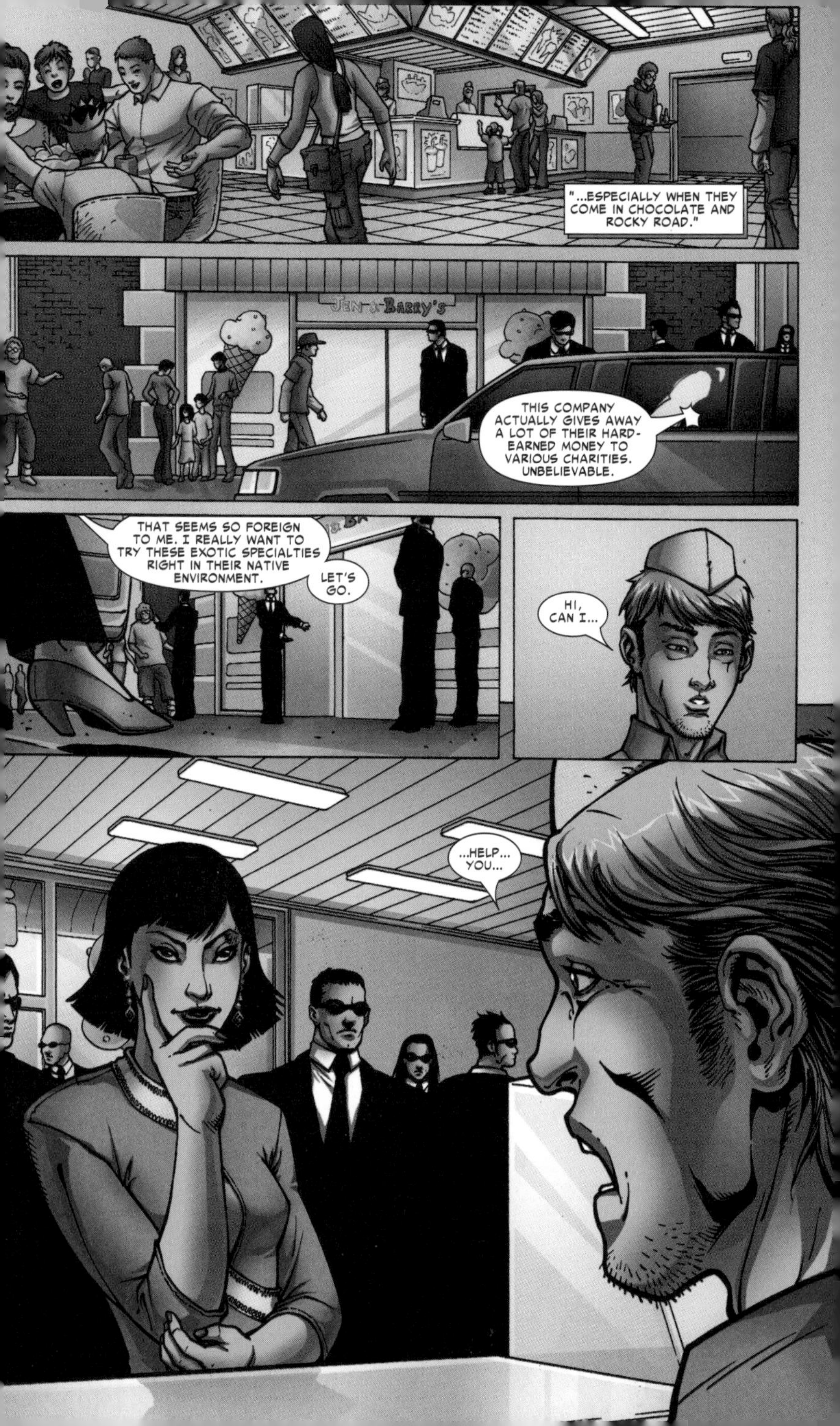
"...ESPECIALLY WHEN THEY COME IN CHOCOLATE AND ROCKY ROAD."
JEN & BARRY'S
THIS COMPANY ACTUALLY GIVES AWAY A LOT OF THEIR HARD-EARNED MONEY TO VARIOUS CHARITIES. UNBELIEVABLE.
THAT SEEMS SO FOREIGN TO ME. I REALLY WANT TO TRY THESE EXOTIC SPECIALTIES RIGHT IN THEIR NATIVE ENVIRONMENT.
LET'S GO.
HI, CAN I...
...HELP... YOU...

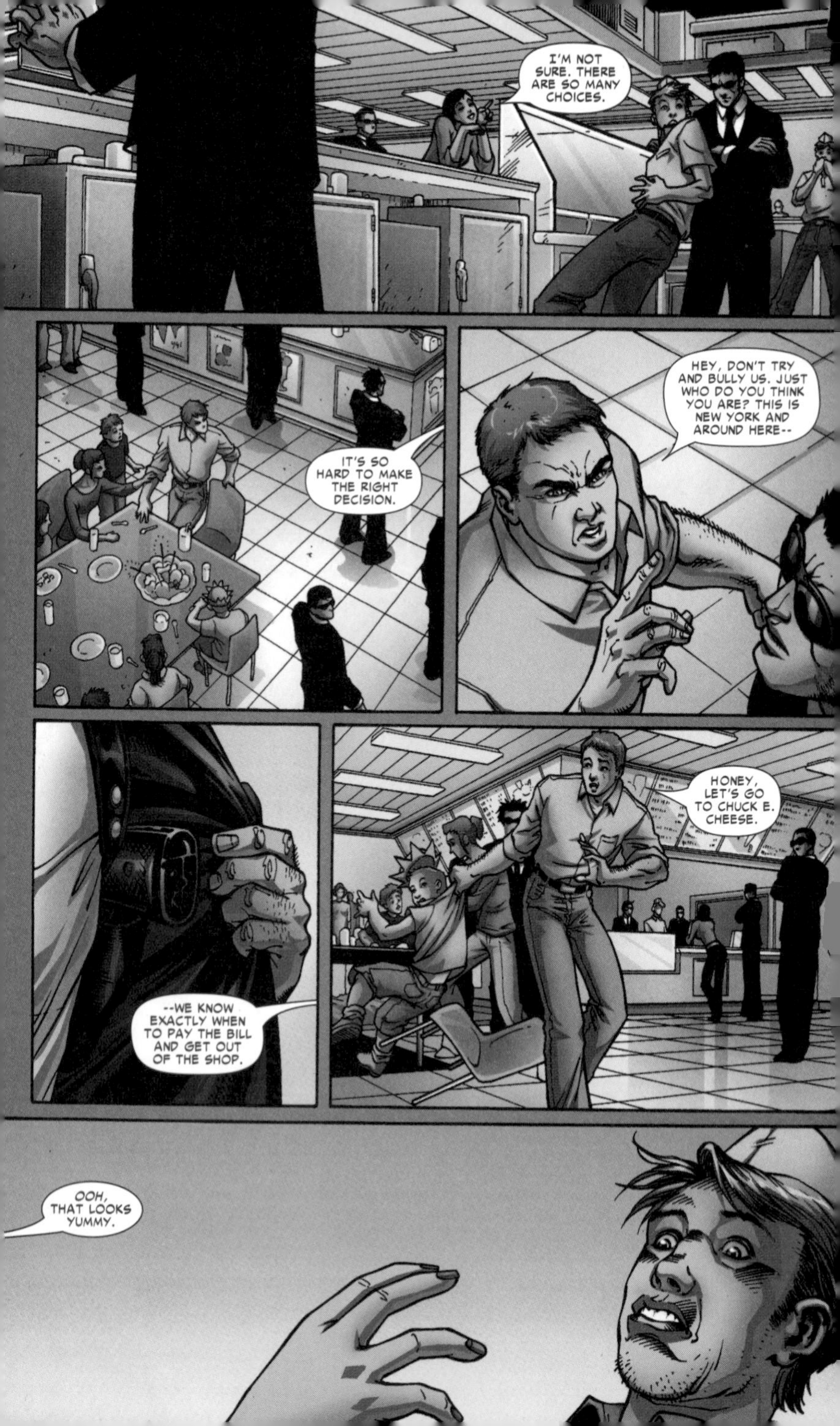
I'M NOT SURE. THERE ARE SO MANY CHOICES.
IT'S SO HARD TO MAKE THE RIGHT DECISION.
HEY, DON'T TRY AND BULLY US. JUST WHO DO YOU THINK YOU ARE? THIS IS NEW YORK AND AROUND HERE--
--WE KNOW EXACTLY WHEN TO PAY THE BILL AND GET OUT OF THE SHOP.
HONEY, LET'S GO TO CHUCK E. CHEESE.
OOH, THAT LOOKS YUMMY.

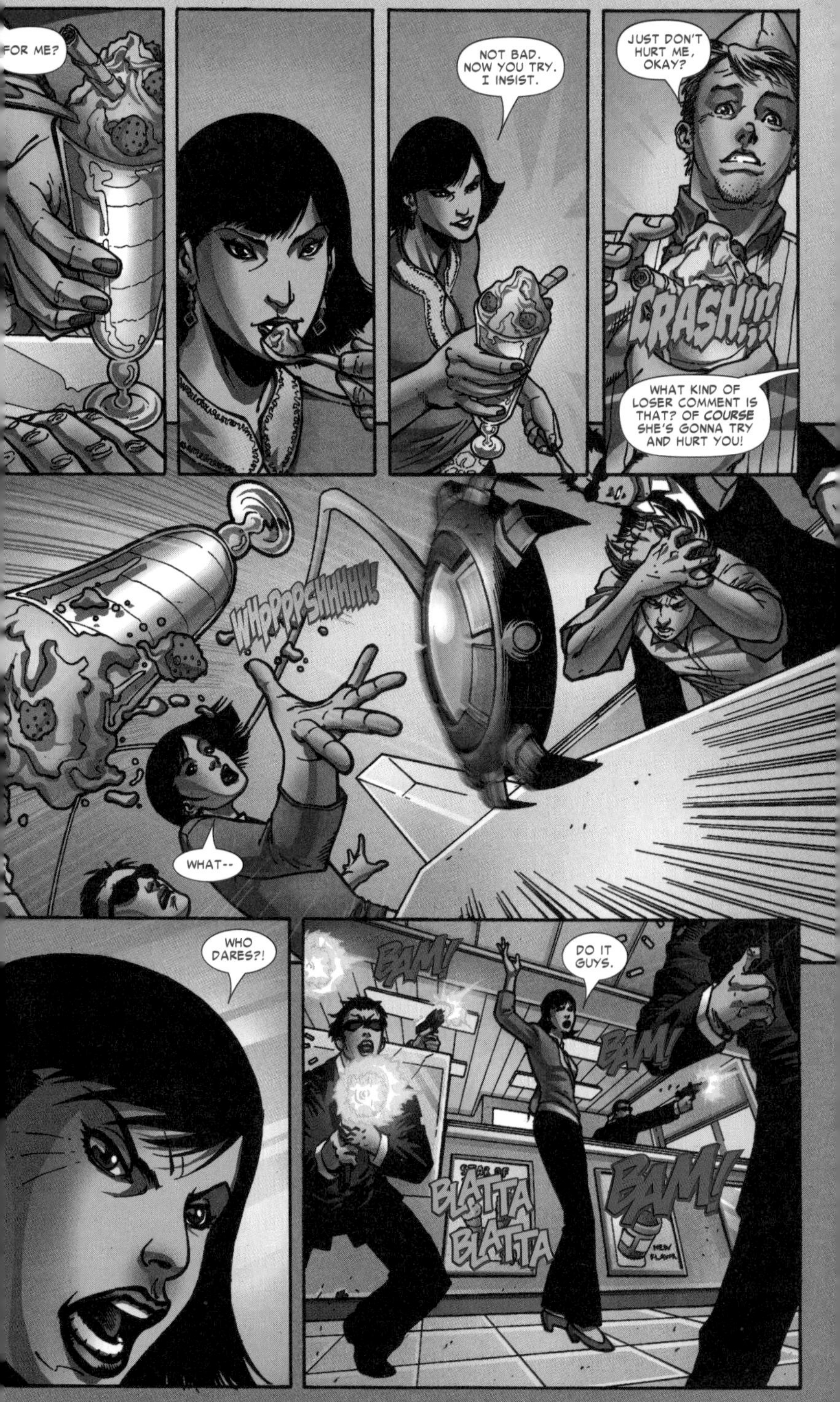
FOR ME?
NOT BAD. NOW YOU TRY. I INSIST.
JUST DON'T HURT ME, OKAY?
CRASH!!!
WHAT KIND OF LOSER COMMENT IS THAT? OF COURSE SHE'S GONNA TRY AND HURT YOU!
WHPPPSHHHH!
WHAT--
WHO DARES?!
BAM!
DO IT GUYS.
BAM!
BAM!
BLATTA BLATTA

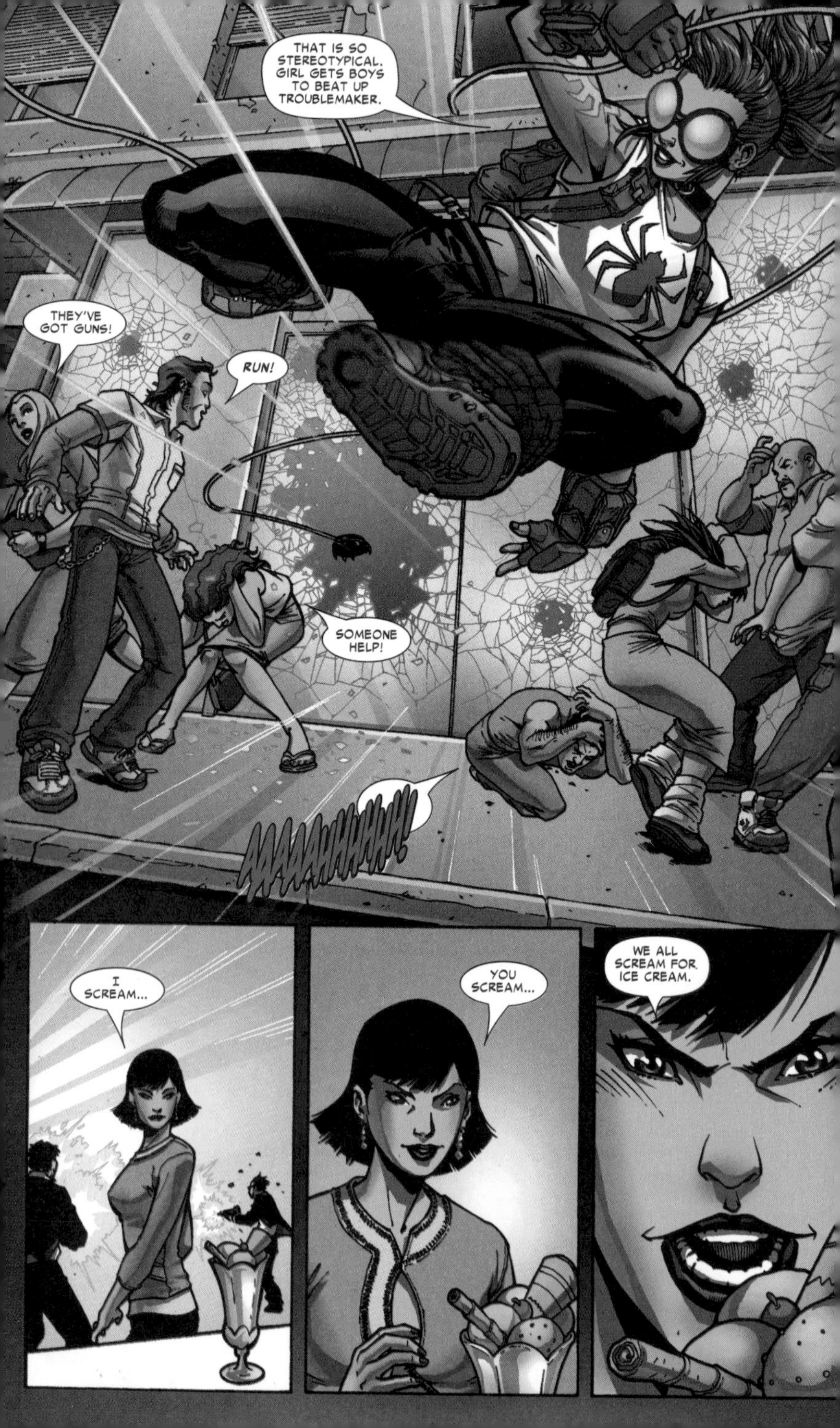

THAT IS SO STEREOTYPICAL. GIRL GETS BOYS TO BEAT UP TROUBLEMAKER.
THEY'VE GOT GUNS!
RUN!
SOMEONE HELP!
AAAAAHHHHH!
I SCREAM...
YOU SCREAM...
WE ALL SCREAM FOR ICE CREAM.

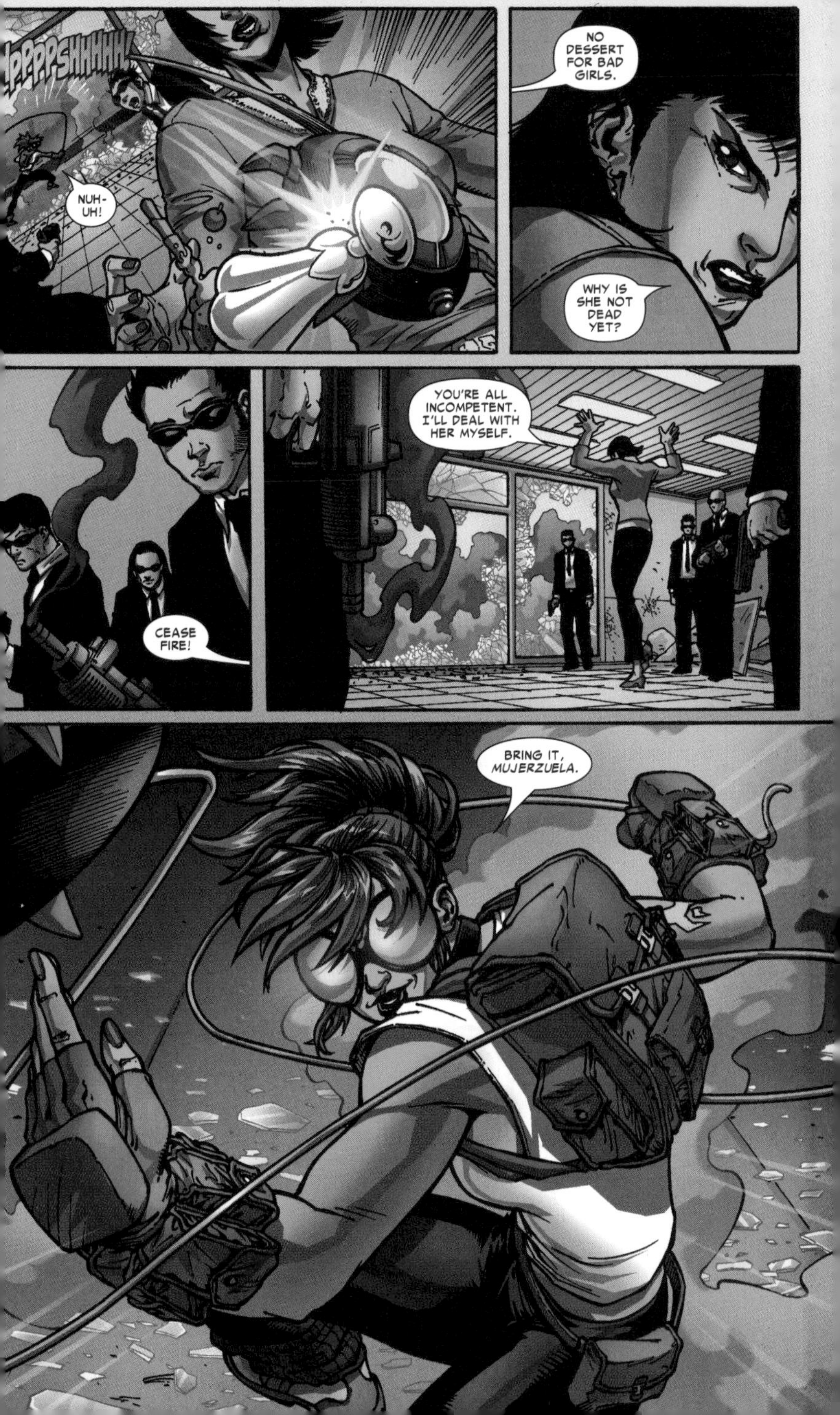
PPPPSHHHHH
NUH-UH!
NO DESSERT FOR BAD GIRLS.
WHY IS SHE NOT DEAD YET?
CEASE FIRE!
YOU'RE ALL INCOMPETENT. I'LL DEAL WITH HER MYSELF.
BRING IT, *MUJERZUELA.*

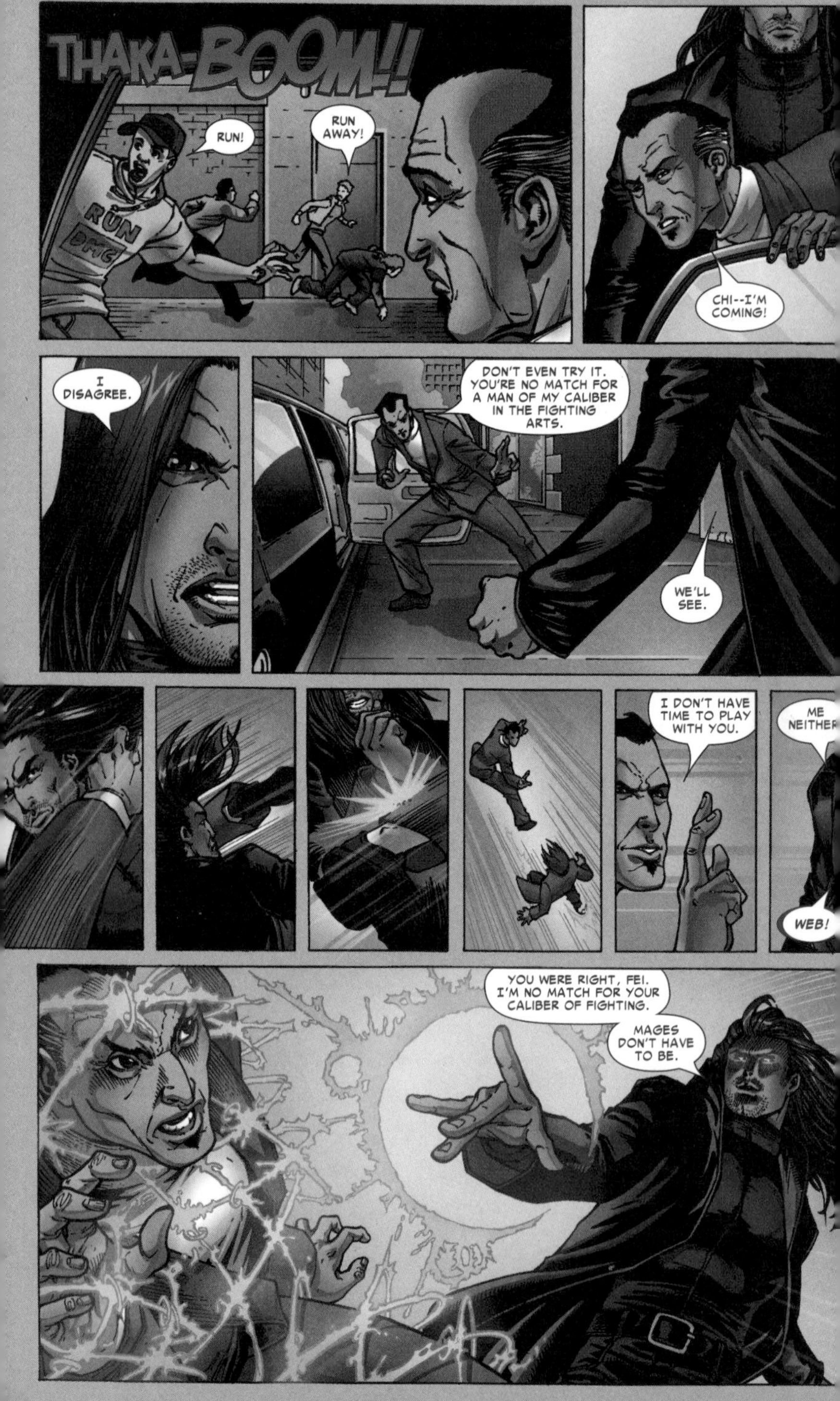
THAKA-BOOM!!
RUN!
RUN AWAY!
RUN DMC
CHI--I'M COMING!
I DISAGREE.
DON'T EVEN TRY IT. YOU'RE NO MATCH FOR A MAN OF MY CALIBER IN THE FIGHTING ARTS.
WE'LL SEE.
I DON'T HAVE TIME TO PLAY WITH YOU.
ME NEITHER
WEB!
YOU WERE RIGHT, FEI. I'M NO MATCH FOR YOUR CALIBER OF FIGHTING.
MAGES DON'T HAVE TO BE.

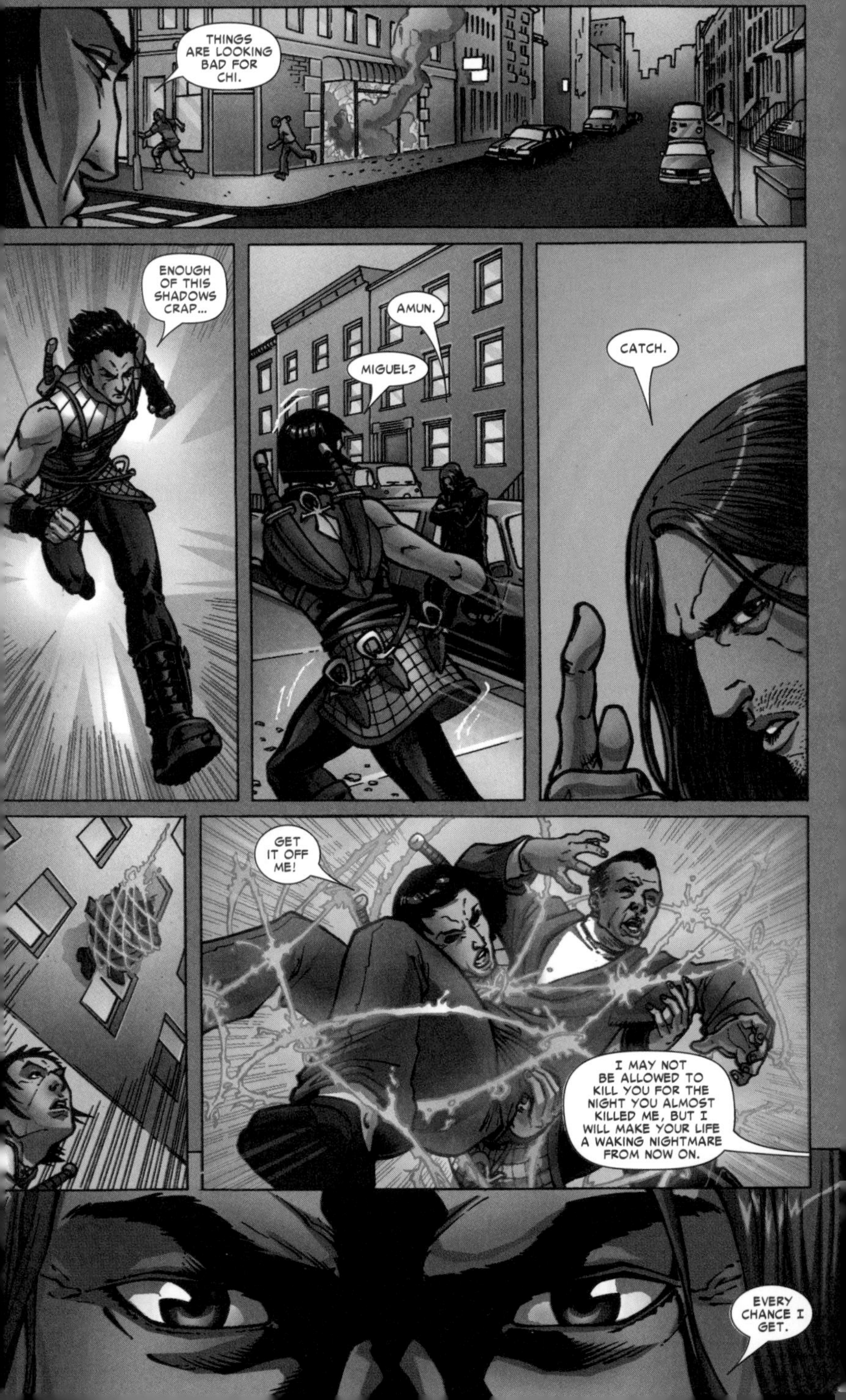
THINGS ARE LOOKING BAD FOR CHI.
ENOUGH OF THIS SHADOWS CRAP...
AMUN.
MIGUEL?
CATCH.
GET IT OFF ME!
I MAY NOT BE ALLOWED TO KILL YOU FOR THE NIGHT YOU ALMOST KILLED ME, BUT I WILL MAKE YOUR LIFE A WAKING NIGHTMARE FROM NOW ON.
EVERY CHANCE I GET.

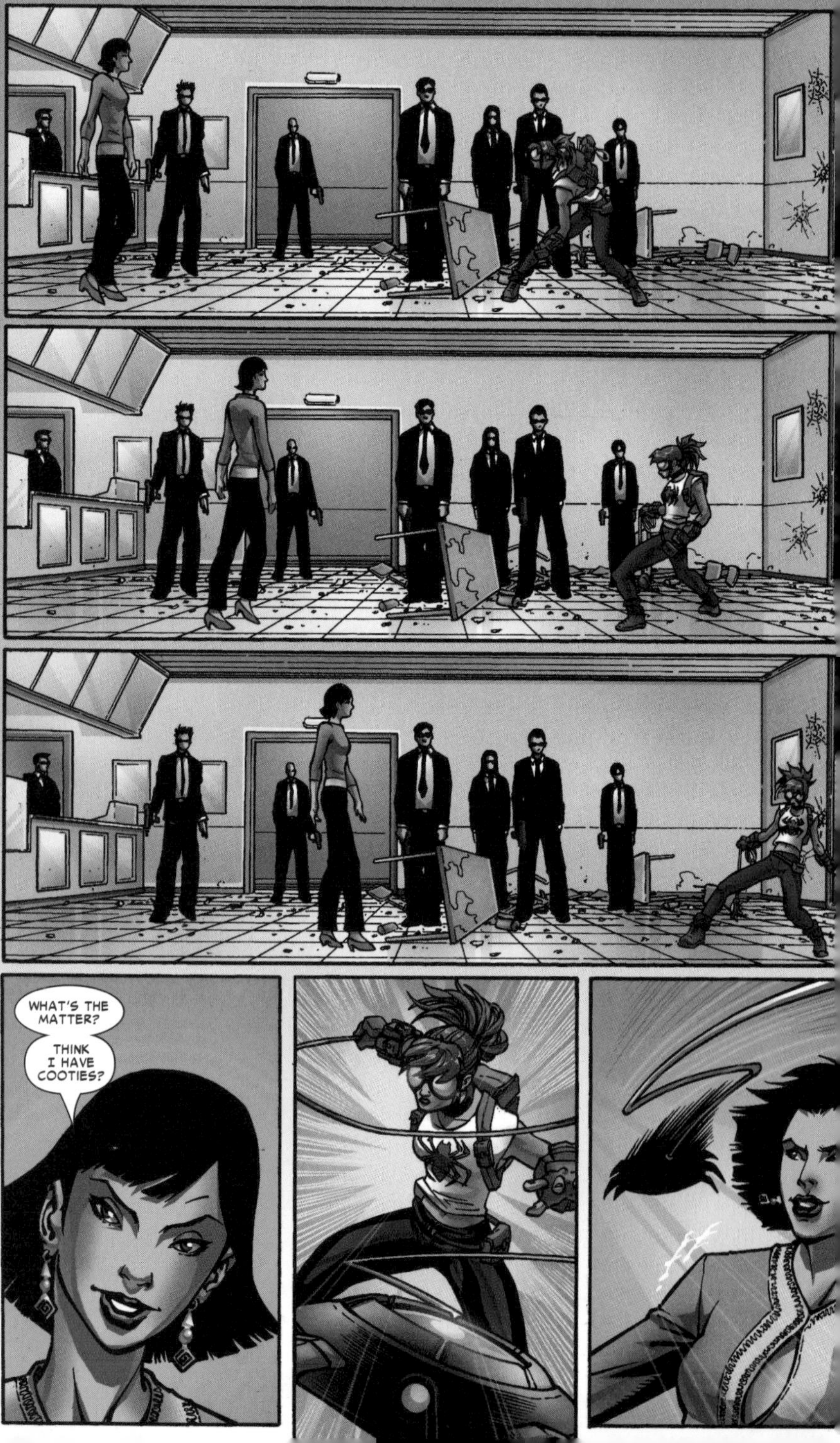
WHAT'S THE MATTER?
THINK I HAVE COOTIES?

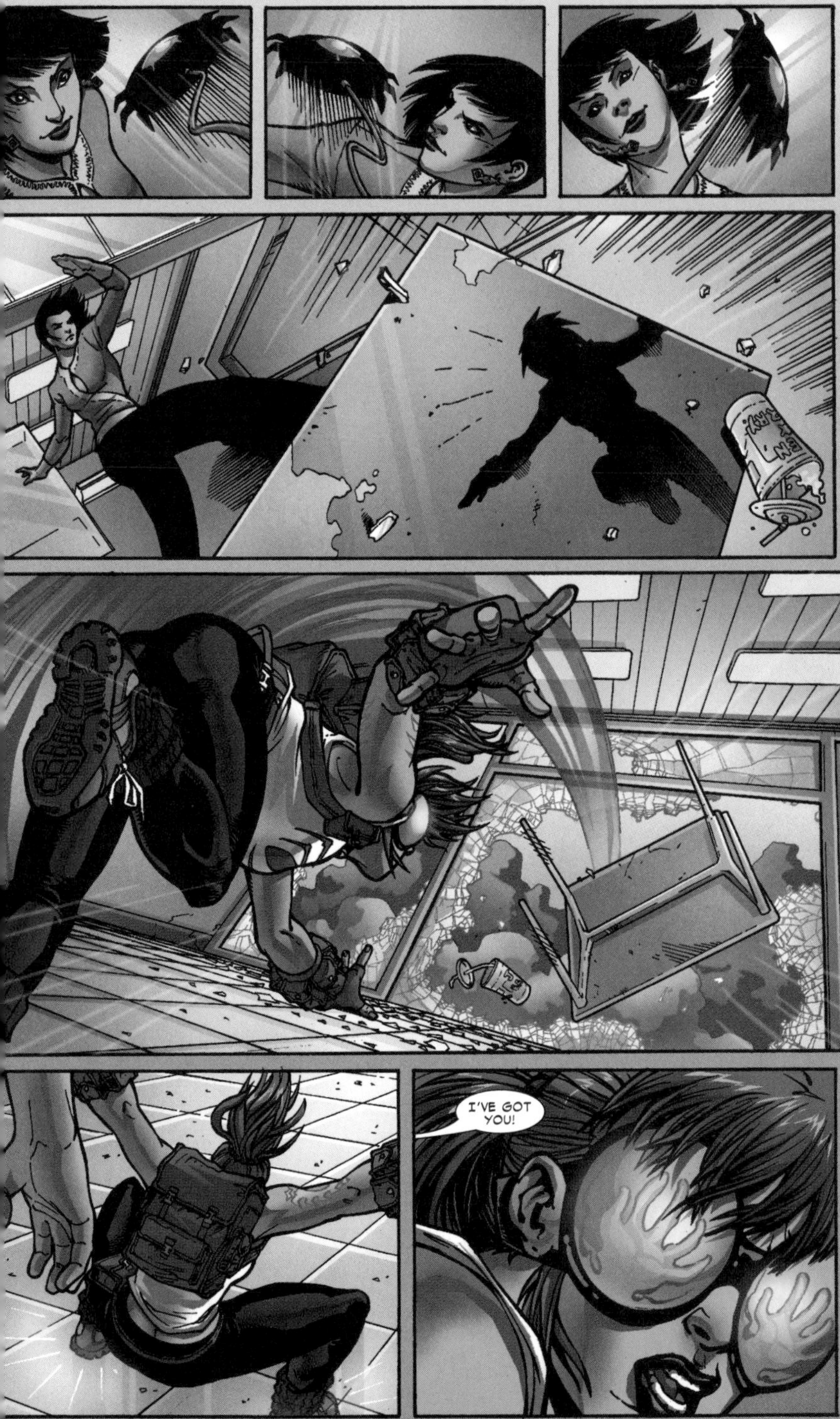
I'VE GOT YOU!

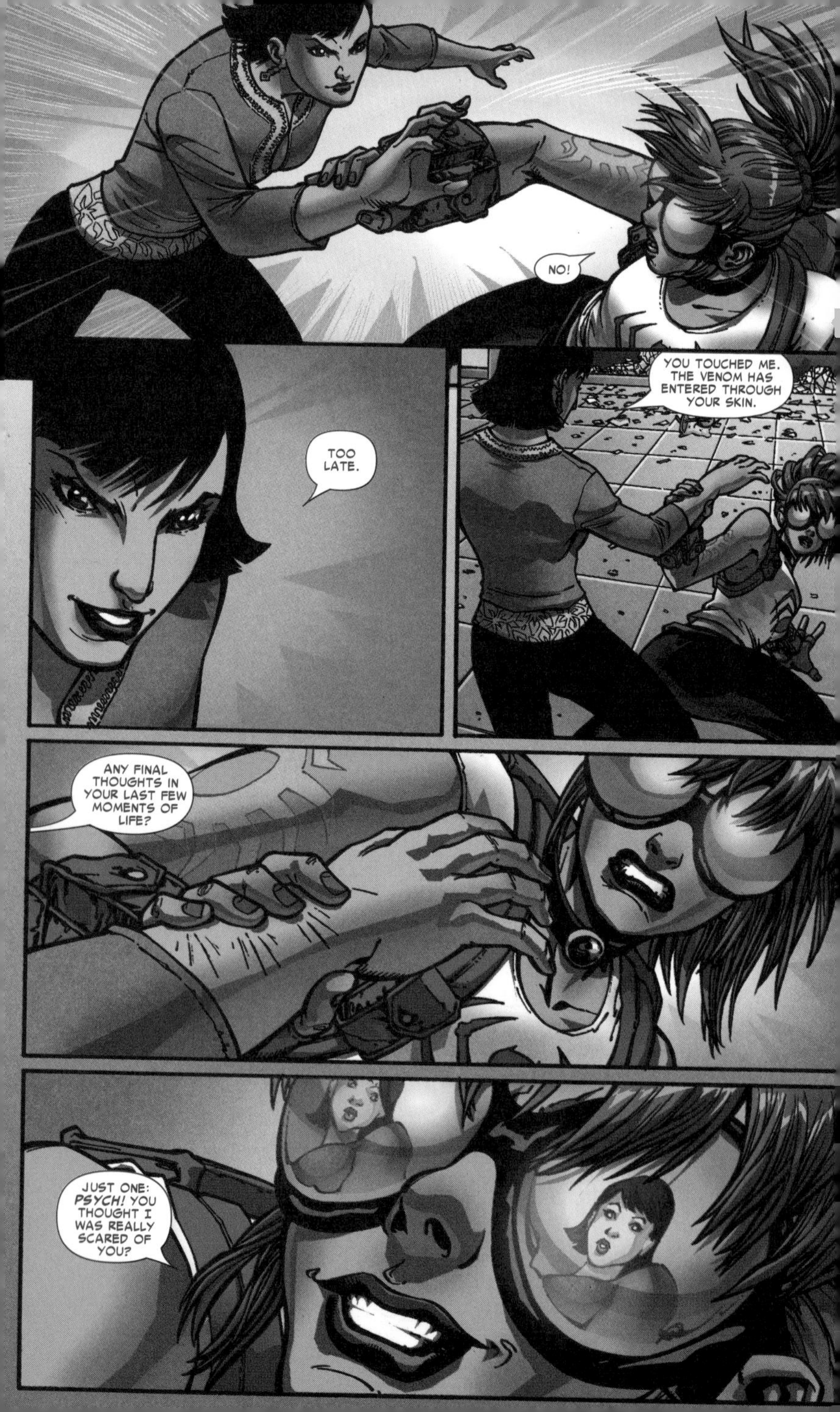
NO!
TOO LATE.
YOU TOUCHED ME. THE VENOM HAS ENTERED THROUGH YOUR SKIN.
ANY FINAL THOUGHTS IN YOUR LAST FEW MOMENTS OF LIFE?
JUST ONE: *PSYCH!* YOU THOUGHT I WAS REALLY SCARED OF YOU?

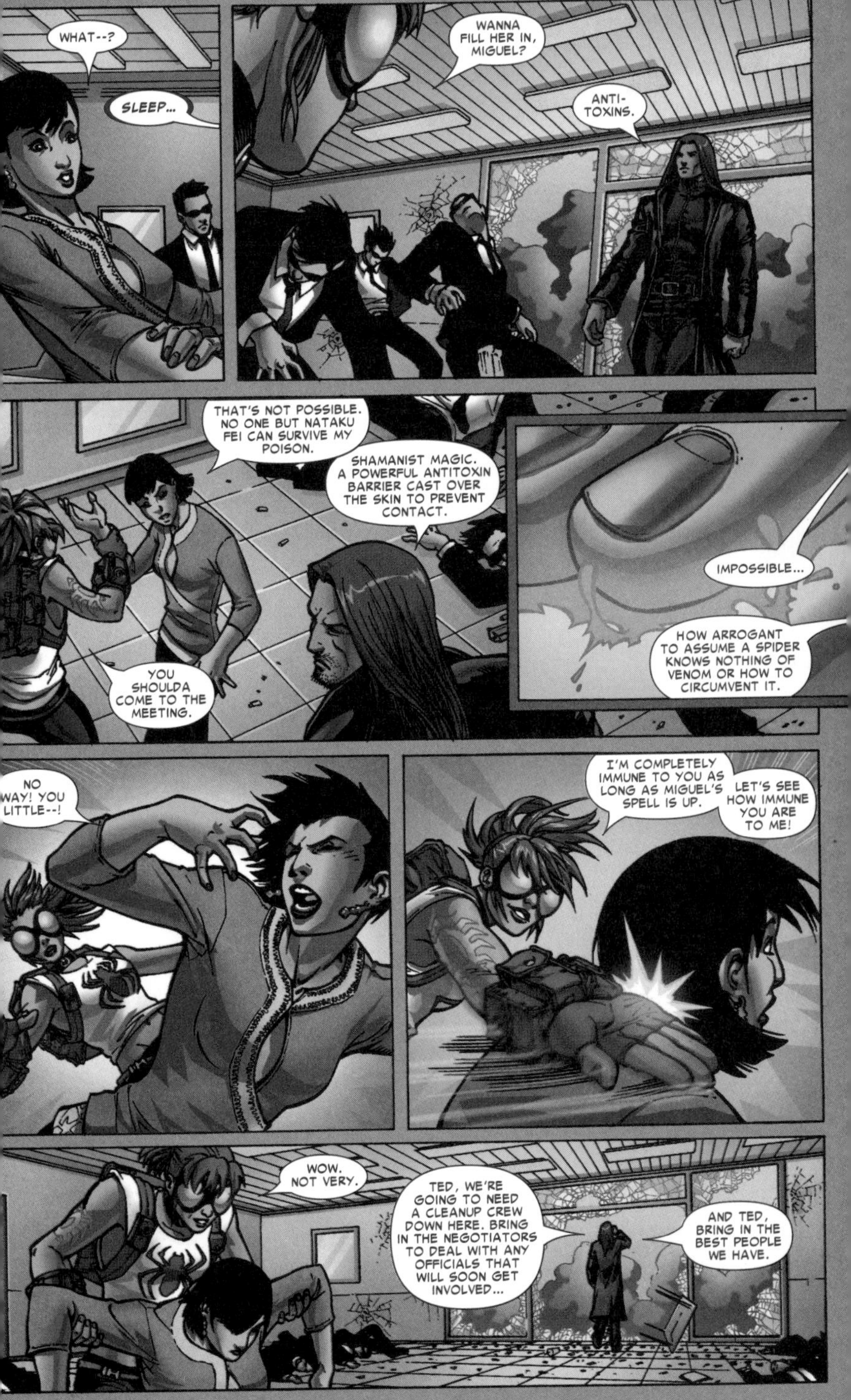
WHAT--?
SLEEP...
WANNA FILL HER IN, MIGUEL?
ANTI-TOXINS.
THAT'S NOT POSSIBLE. NO ONE BUT NATAKU FEI CAN SURVIVE MY POISON.
SHAMANIST MAGIC. A POWERFUL ANTITOXIN BARRIER CAST OVER THE SKIN TO PREVENT CONTACT.
YOU SHOULDA COME TO THE MEETING.
IMPOSSIBLE...
HOW ARROGANT TO ASSUME A SPIDER KNOWS NOTHING OF VENOM OR HOW TO CIRCUMVENT IT.
NO WAY! YOU LITTLE--!
I'M COMPLETELY IMMUNE TO YOU AS LONG AS MIGUEL'S SPELL IS UP.
LET'S SEE HOW IMMUNE YOU ARE TO ME!
WOW. NOT VERY.
TED, WE'RE GOING TO NEED A CLEANUP CREW DOWN HERE. BRING IN THE NEGOTIATORS TO DEAL WITH ANY OFFICIALS THAT WILL SOON GET INVOLVED...
AND TED, BRING IN THE BEST PEOPLE WE HAVE.

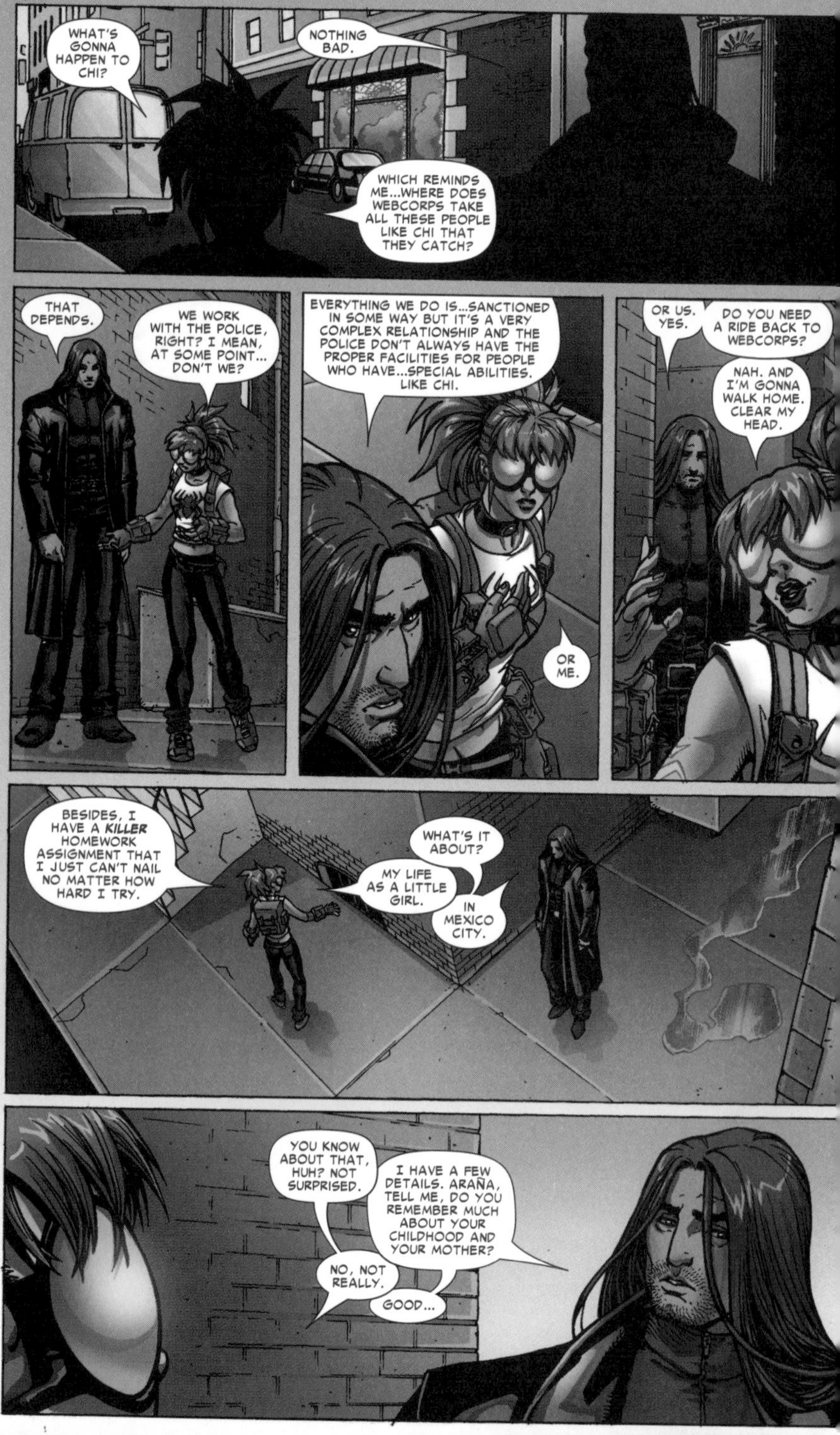

WHAT'S GONNA HAPPEN TO CHI?
NOTHING BAD.
WHICH REMINDS ME...WHERE DOES WEBCORPS TAKE ALL THESE PEOPLE LIKE CHI THAT THEY CATCH?
THAT DEPENDS.
WE WORK WITH THE POLICE, RIGHT? I MEAN, AT SOME POINT... DON'T WE?
EVERYTHING WE DO IS...SANCTIONED IN SOME WAY BUT IT'S A VERY COMPLEX RELATIONSHIP AND THE POLICE DON'T ALWAYS HAVE THE PROPER FACILITIES FOR PEOPLE WHO HAVE...SPECIAL ABILITIES. LIKE CHI.
OR ME.
OR US. YES.
DO YOU NEED A RIDE BACK TO WEBCORPS?
NAH. AND I'M GONNA WALK HOME. CLEAR MY HEAD.
BESIDES, I HAVE A **KILLER** HOMEWORK ASSIGNMENT THAT I JUST CAN'T NAIL NO MATTER HOW HARD I TRY.
WHAT'S IT ABOUT?
MY LIFE AS A LITTLE GIRL.
IN MEXICO CITY.
YOU KNOW ABOUT THAT, HUH? NOT SURPRISED.
I HAVE A FEW DETAILS. ARAÑA, TELL ME, DO YOU REMEMBER MUCH ABOUT YOUR CHILDHOOD AND YOUR MOTHER?
NO, NOT REALLY.
GOOD...

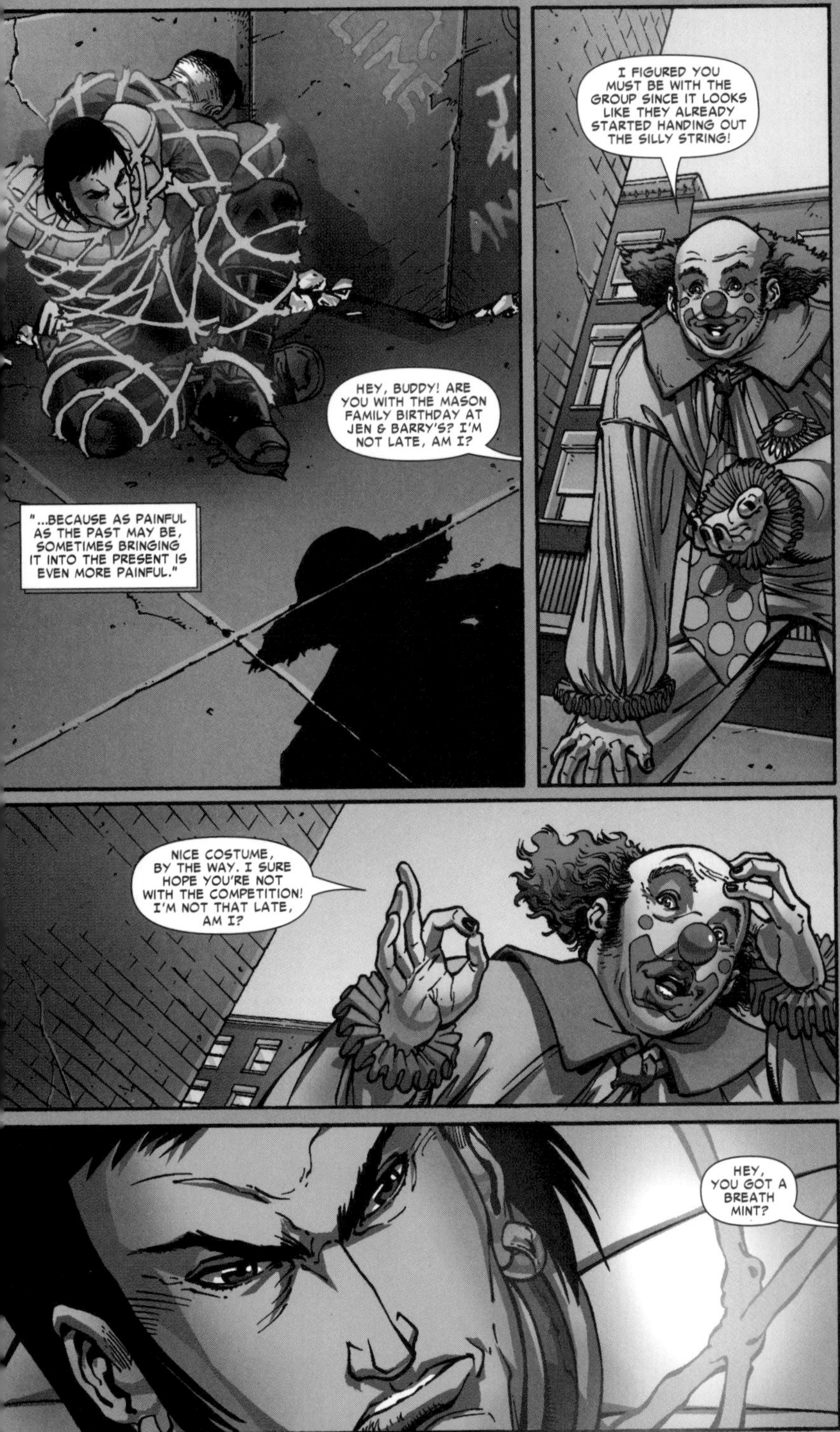
HEY, BUDDY! ARE YOU WITH THE MASON FAMILY BIRTHDAY AT JEN & BARRY'S? I'M NOT LATE, AM I?
"...BECAUSE AS PAINFUL AS THE PAST MAY BE, SOMETIMES BRINGING IT INTO THE PRESENT IS EVEN MORE PAINFUL."
I FIGURED YOU MUST BE WITH THE GROUP SINCE IT LOOKS LIKE THEY ALREADY STARTED HANDING OUT THE SILLY STRING!
NICE COSTUME, BY THE WAY. I SURE HOPE YOU'RE NOT WITH THE COMPETITION! I'M NOT THAT LATE, AM I?
HEY, YOU GOT A BREATH MINT?

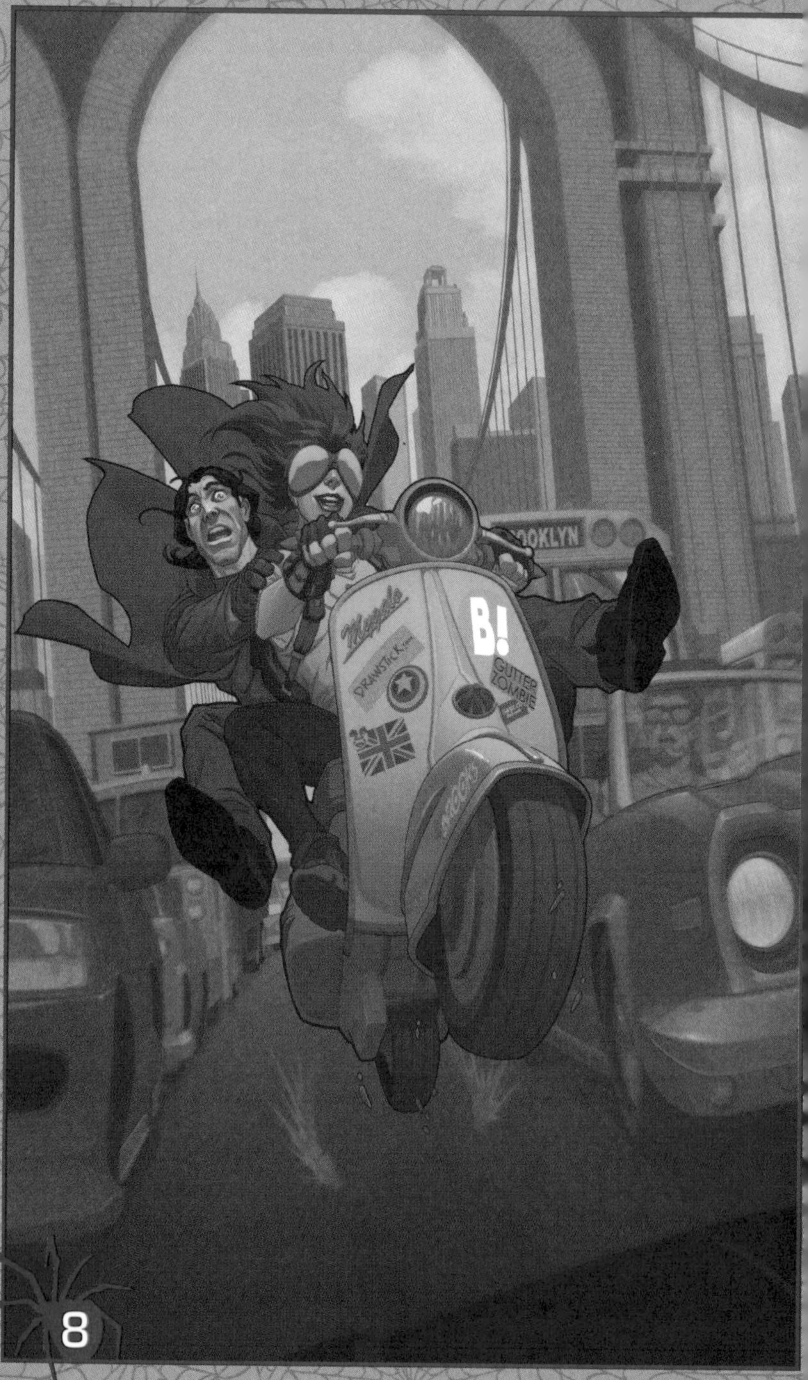
B!
GUTTER ZOMBIE

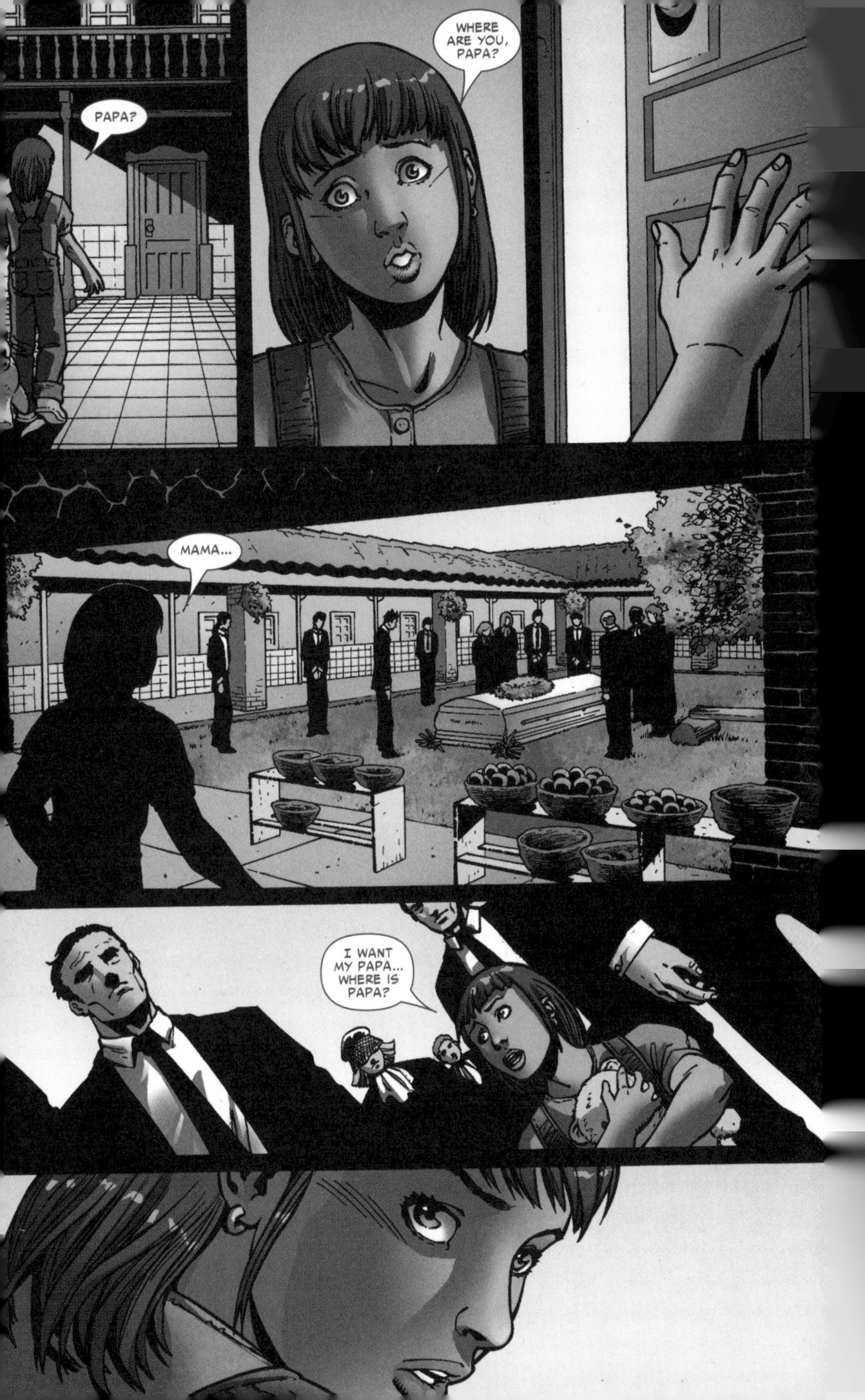
PAPA?
WHERE ARE YOU, PAPA?
MAMA...
I WANT MY PAPA... WHERE IS PAPA?

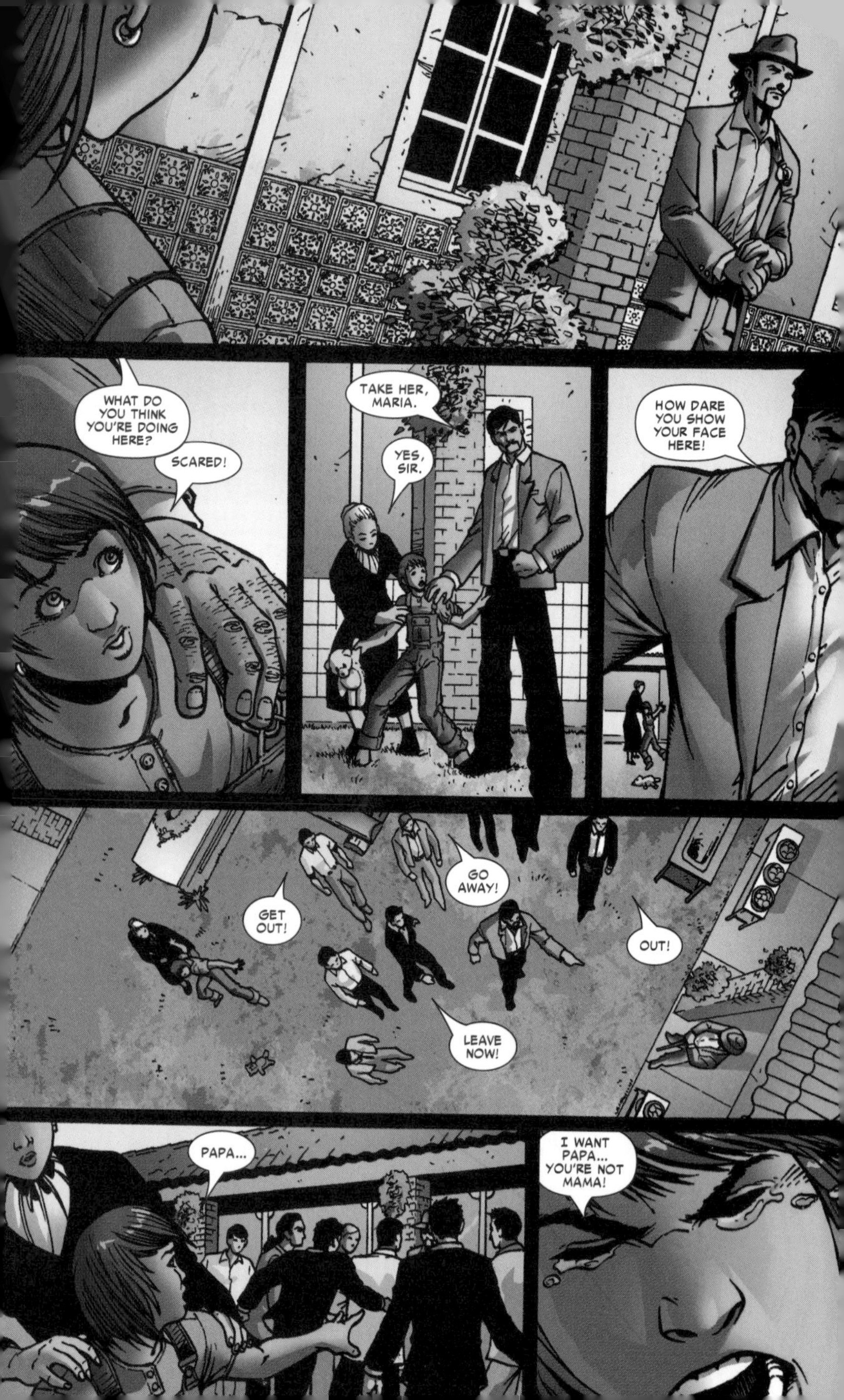
WHAT DO YOU THINK YOU'RE DOING HERE?
SCARED!
TAKE HER, MARIA.
YES, SIR.
HOW DARE YOU SHOW YOUR FACE HERE!
GO AWAY!
GET OUT!
OUT!
LEAVE NOW!
PAPA...
I WANT PAPA... YOU'RE NOT MAMA!

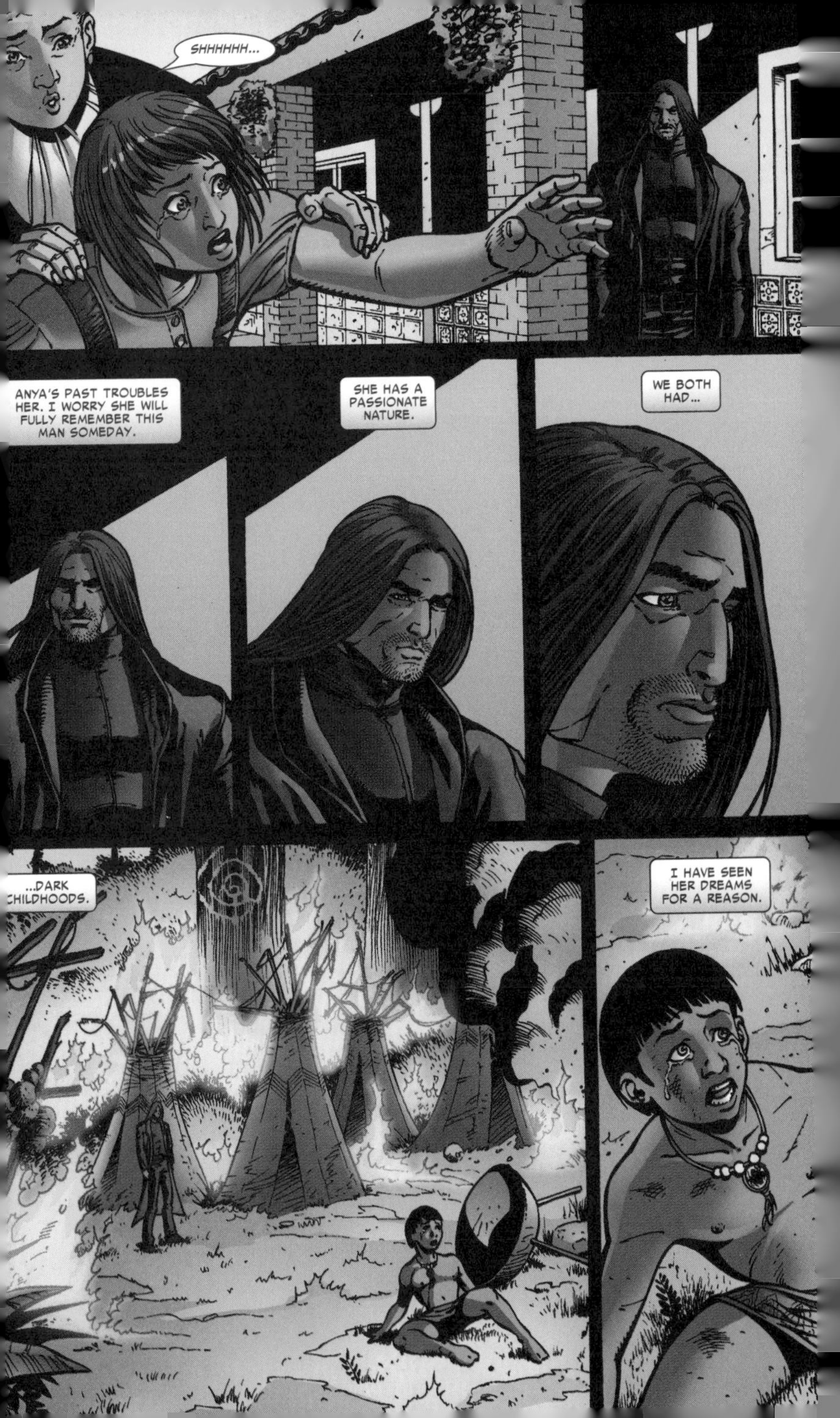
SHHHHHH...
ANYA'S PAST TROUBLES HER. I WORRY SHE WILL FULLY REMEMBER THIS MAN SOMEDAY.
SHE HAS A PASSIONATE NATURE.
WE BOTH HAD...
...DARK CHILDHOODS.
I HAVE SEEN HER DREAMS FOR A REASON.

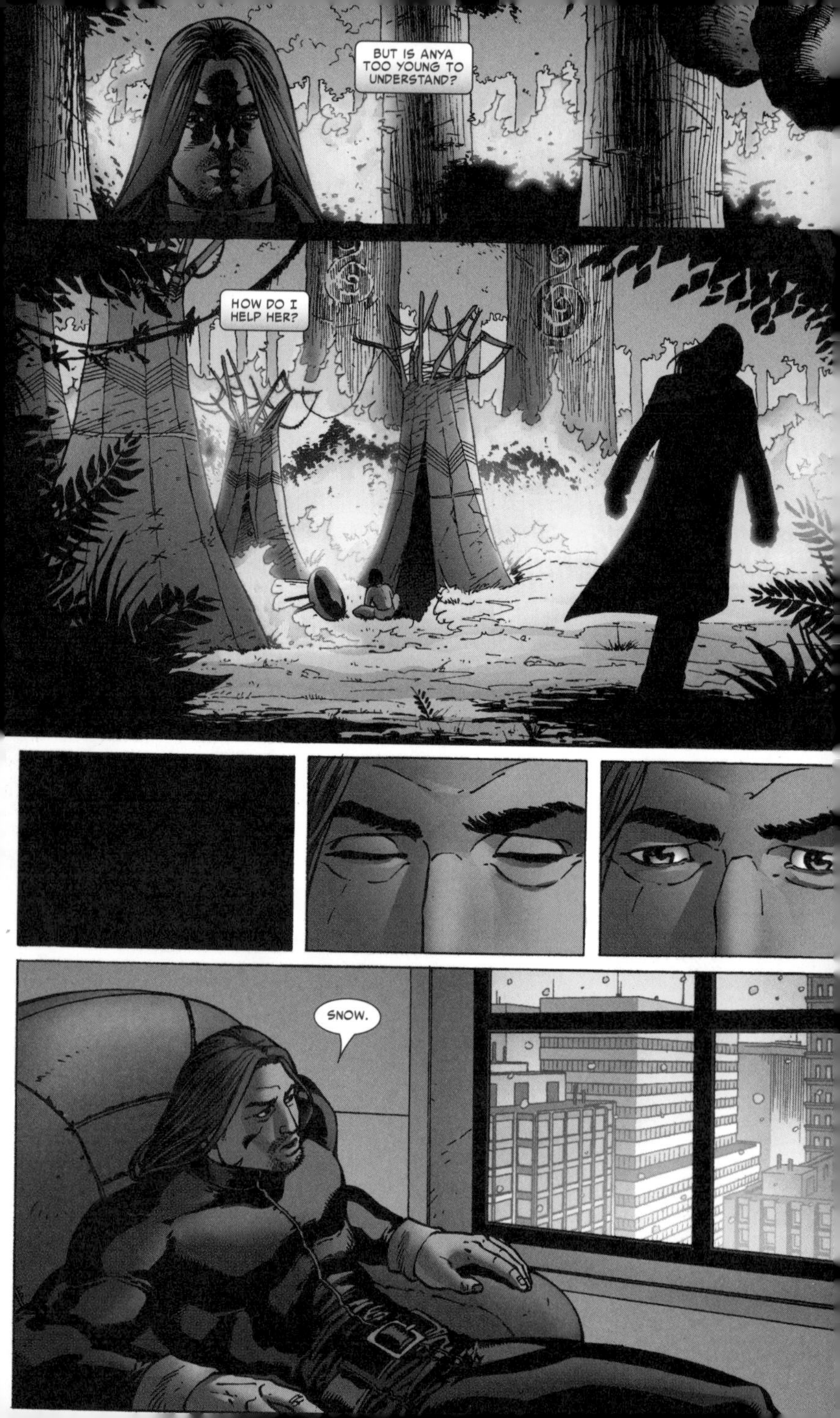
BUT IS ANYA TOO YOUNG TO UNDERSTAND?
HOW DO I HELP HER?
SNOW.

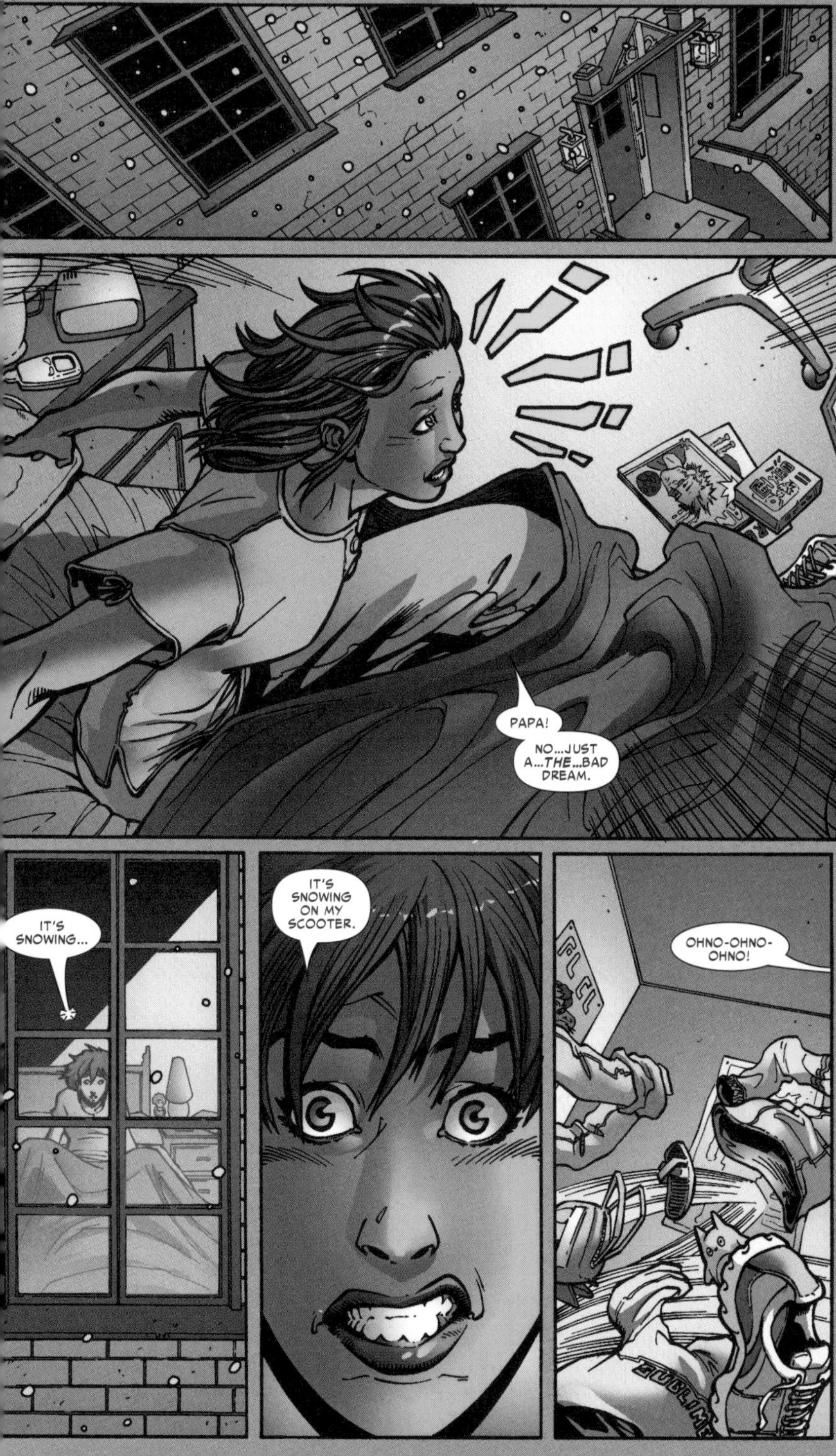
PAPA!
NO...JUST A...THE...BAD DREAM.
IT'S SNOWING...
IT'S SNOWING ON MY SCOOTER.
OHNO-OHNO-OHNO!

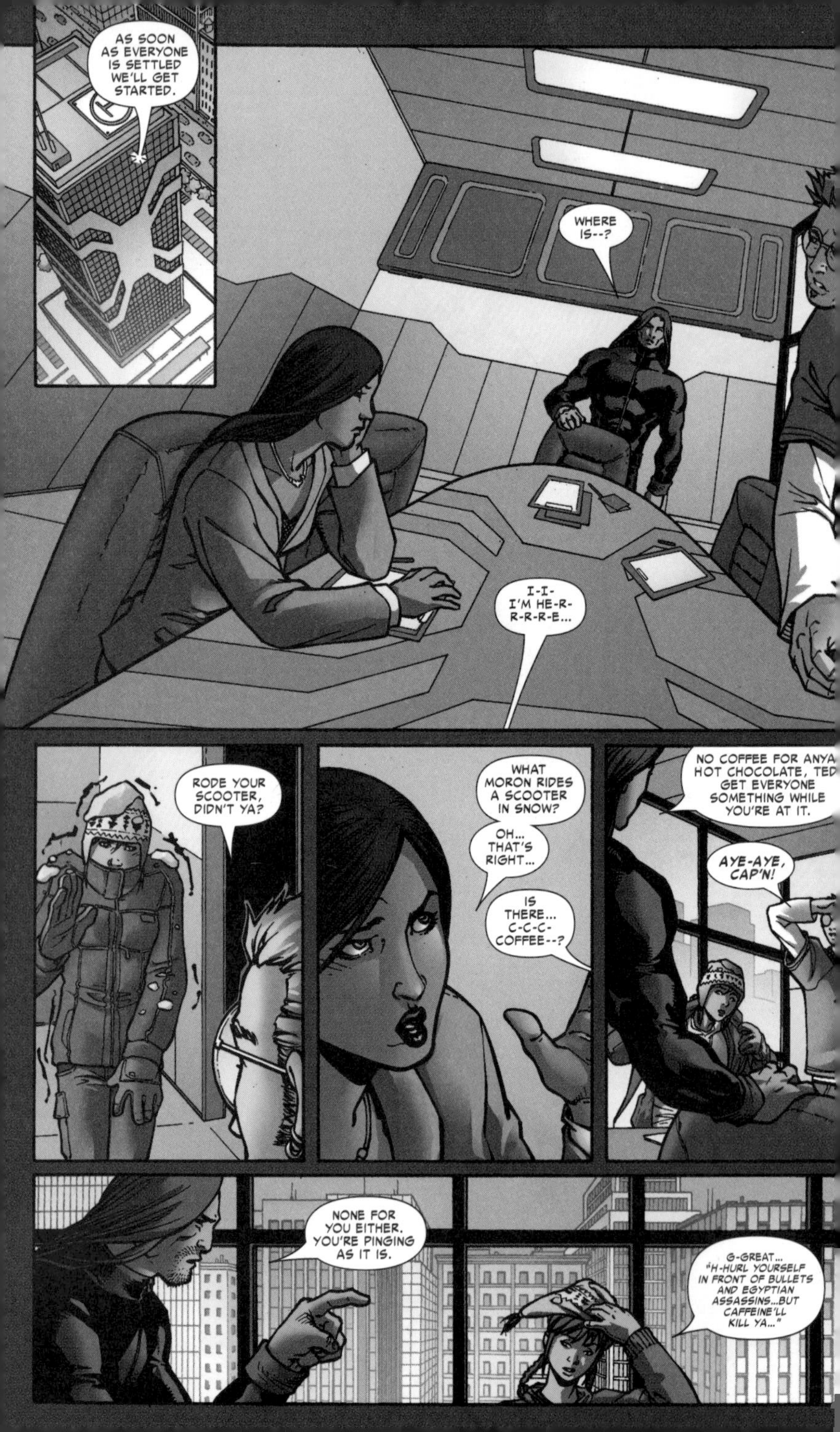
AS SOON AS EVERYONE IS SETTLED WE'LL GET STARTED.
WHERE IS--?
I-I- I'M HE-R-R-R-R-E...
RODE YOUR SCOOTER, DIDN'T YA?
WHAT MORON RIDES A SCOOTER IN SNOW?
OH... THAT'S RIGHT...
IS THERE... C-C-C-COFFEE--?
NO COFFEE FOR ANYA HOT CHOCOLATE, TED GET EVERYONE SOMETHING WHILE YOU'RE AT IT.
AYE-AYE, CAP'N!
NONE FOR YOU EITHER. YOU'RE PINGING AS IT IS.
G-GREAT... "H-HURL YOURSELF IN FRONT OF BULLETS AND EGYPTIAN ASSASSINS...BUT CAFFEINE'LL KILL YA..."

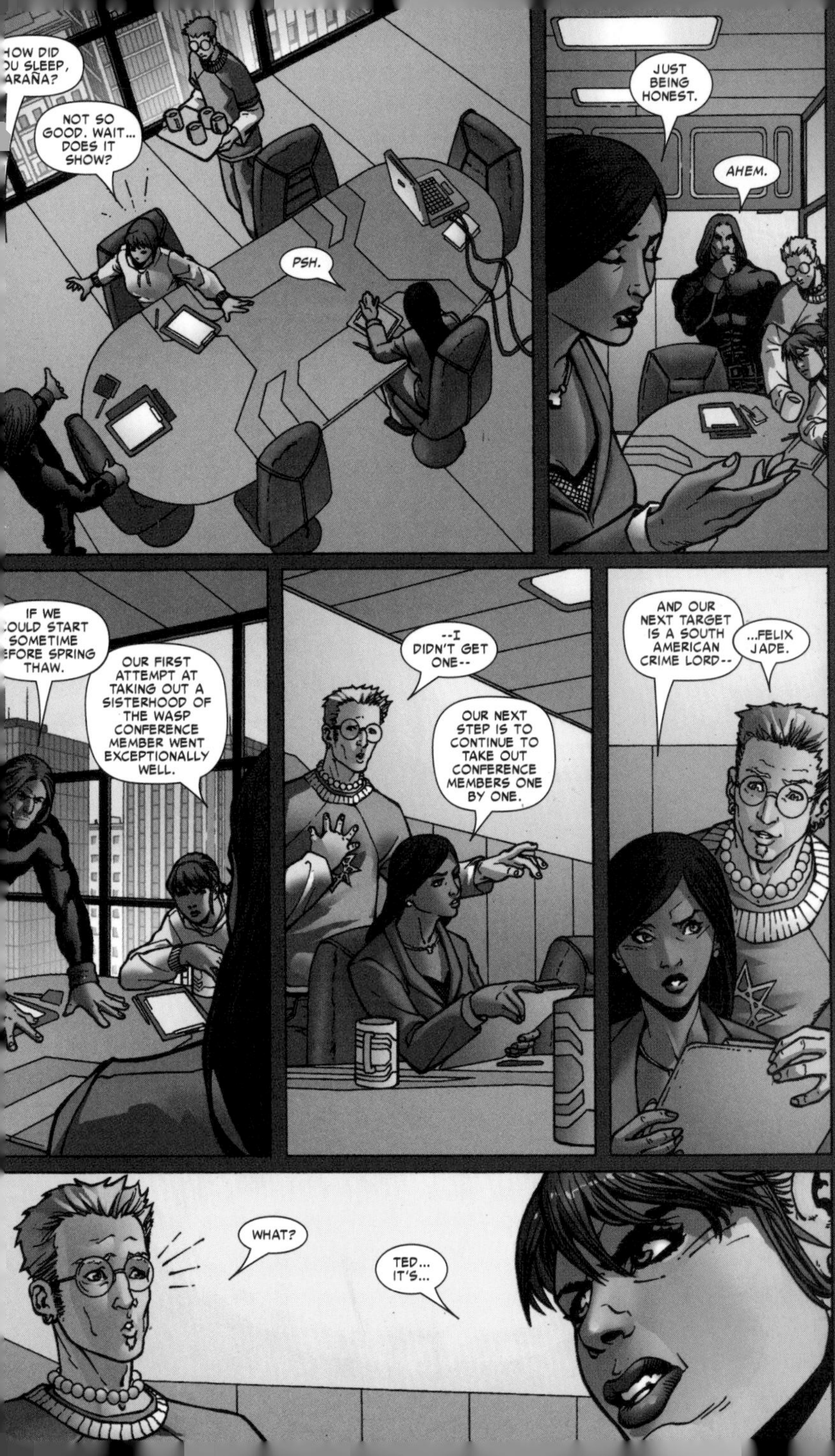
HOW DID
OU SLEEP,
ARAÑA?
NOT SO GOOD. WAIT... DOES IT SHOW?
PSH.
JUST BEING HONEST.
AHEM.
IF WE
OULD START SOMETIME
EFORE SPRING THAW.
OUR FIRST ATTEMPT AT TAKING OUT A SISTERHOOD OF THE WASP CONFERENCE MEMBER WENT EXCEPTIONALLY WELL.
--I DIDN'T GET ONE--
OUR NEXT STEP IS TO CONTINUE TO TAKE OUT CONFERENCE MEMBERS ONE BY ONE.
AND OUR NEXT TARGET IS A SOUTH AMERICAN CRIME LORD--
...FELIX JADE.
WHAT?
TED... IT'S...

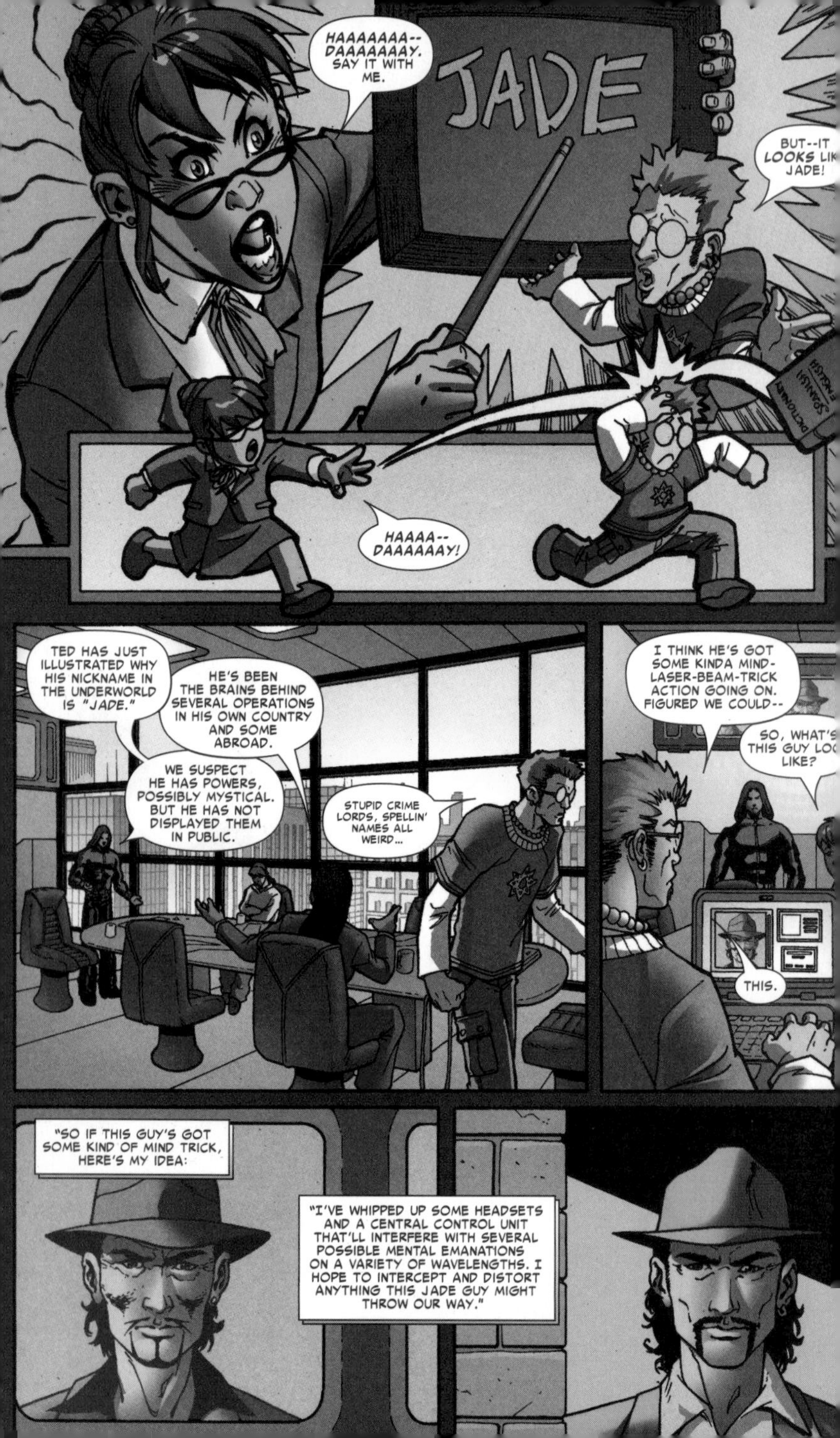
HAAAAAAA--
DAAAAAAAY.
SAY IT WITH
ME.
JADE
BUT--IT
LOOKS LIK
JADE!
HAAAA--
DAAAAAAY!
TED HAS JUST ILLUSTRATED WHY HIS NICKNAME IN THE UNDERWORLD IS "JADE."
HE'S BEEN THE BRAINS BEHIND SEVERAL OPERATIONS IN HIS OWN COUNTRY AND SOME ABROAD.
WE SUSPECT HE HAS POWERS, POSSIBLY MYSTICAL. BUT HE HAS NOT DISPLAYED THEM IN PUBLIC.
STUPID CRIME LORDS, SPELLIN' NAMES ALL WEIRD...
I THINK HE'S GOT SOME KINDA MIND-LASER-BEAM-TRICK ACTION GOING ON. FIGURED WE COULD--
SO, WHAT'S THIS GUY LOO LIKE?
THIS.
"SO IF THIS GUY'S GOT SOME KIND OF MIND TRICK, HERE'S MY IDEA:
"I'VE WHIPPED UP SOME HEADSETS AND A CENTRAL CONTROL UNIT THAT'LL INTERFERE WITH SEVERAL POSSIBLE MENTAL EMANATIONS ON A VARIETY OF WAVELENGTHS. I HOPE TO INTERCEPT AND DISTORT ANYTHING THIS JADE GUY MIGHT THROW OUR WAY."

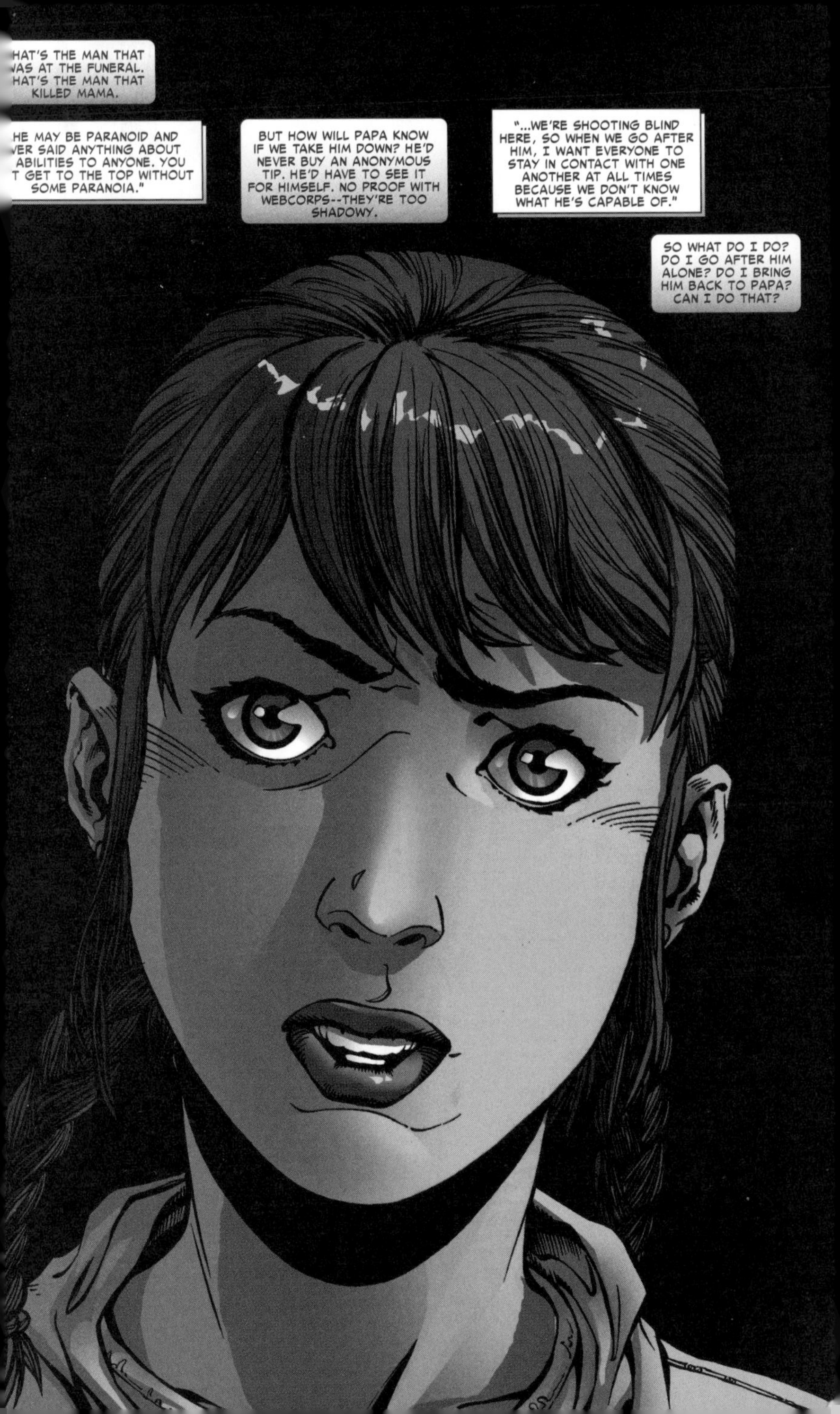
HAT'S THE MAN THAT
VAS AT THE FUNERAL.
HAT'S THE MAN THAT
KILLED MAMA.
HE MAY BE PARANOID AND
VER SAID ANYTHING ABOUT
ABILITIES TO ANYONE. YOU
T GET TO THE TOP WITHOUT
SOME PARANOIA."
BUT HOW WILL PAPA KNOW IF WE TAKE HIM DOWN? HE'D NEVER BUY AN ANONYMOUS TIP. HE'D HAVE TO SEE IT FOR HIMSELF. NO PROOF WITH WEBCORPS--THEY'RE TOO SHADOWY.
"...WE'RE SHOOTING BLIND HERE, SO WHEN WE GO AFTER HIM, I WANT EVERYONE TO STAY IN CONTACT WITH ONE ANOTHER AT ALL TIMES BECAUSE WE DON'T KNOW WHAT HE'S CAPABLE OF."
SO WHAT DO I DO? DO I GO AFTER HIM ALONE? DO I BRING HIM BACK TO PAPA? CAN I DO THAT?

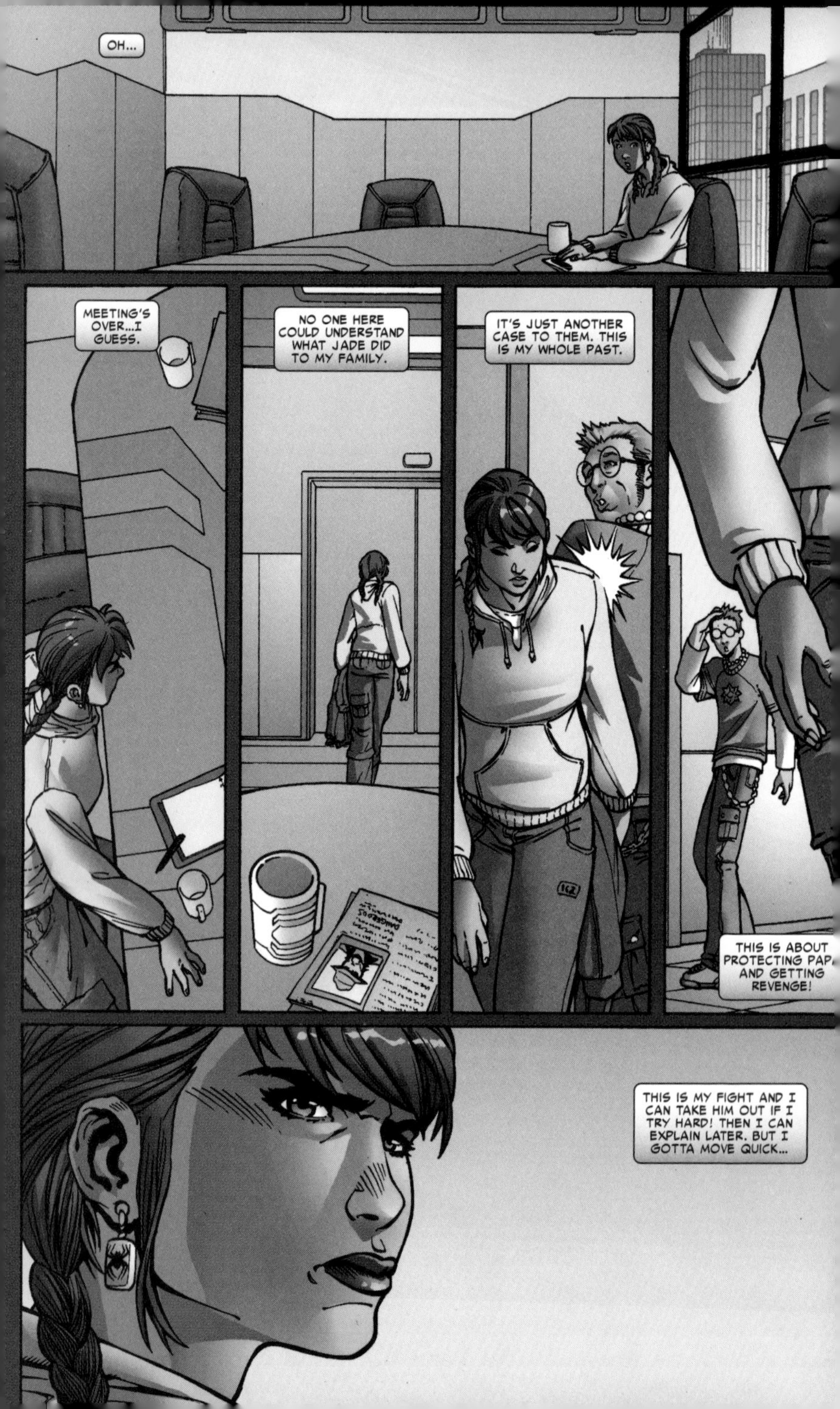
OH...
MEETING'S OVER...I GUESS.
NO ONE HERE COULD UNDERSTAND WHAT JADE DID TO MY FAMILY.
IT'S JUST ANOTHER CASE TO THEM. THIS IS MY WHOLE PAST.
THIS IS ABOUT PROTECTING PAPA AND GETTING REVENGE!
THIS IS MY FIGHT AND I CAN TAKE HIM OUT IF I TRY HARD! THEN I CAN EXPLAIN LATER. BUT I GOTTA MOVE QUICK...

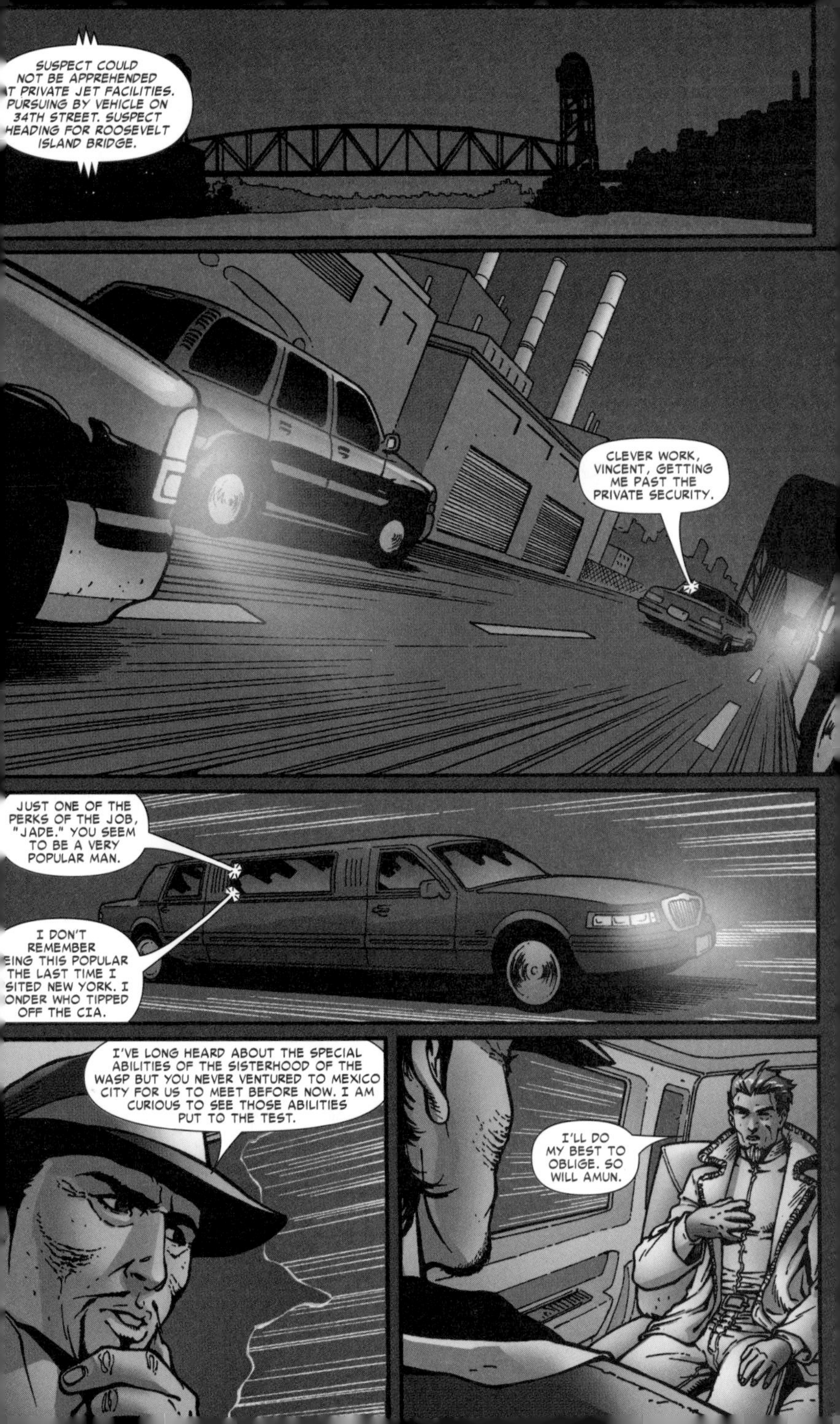
SUSPECT COULD NOT BE APPREHENDED AT PRIVATE JET FACILITIES. PURSUING BY VEHICLE ON 34TH STREET. SUSPECT HEADING FOR ROOSEVELT ISLAND BRIDGE.
CLEVER WORK, VINCENT, GETTING ME PAST THE PRIVATE SECURITY.
JUST ONE OF THE PERKS OF THE JOB, "JADE." YOU SEEM TO BE A VERY POPULAR MAN.
I DON'T REMEMBER BEING THIS POPULAR THE LAST TIME I VISITED NEW YORK. I WONDER WHO TIPPED OFF THE CIA.
I'VE LONG HEARD ABOUT THE SPECIAL ABILITIES OF THE SISTERHOOD OF THE WASP BUT YOU NEVER VENTURED TO MEXICO CITY FOR US TO MEET BEFORE NOW. I AM CURIOUS TO SEE THOSE ABILITIES PUT TO THE TEST.
I'LL DO MY BEST TO OBLIGE. SO WILL AMUN.

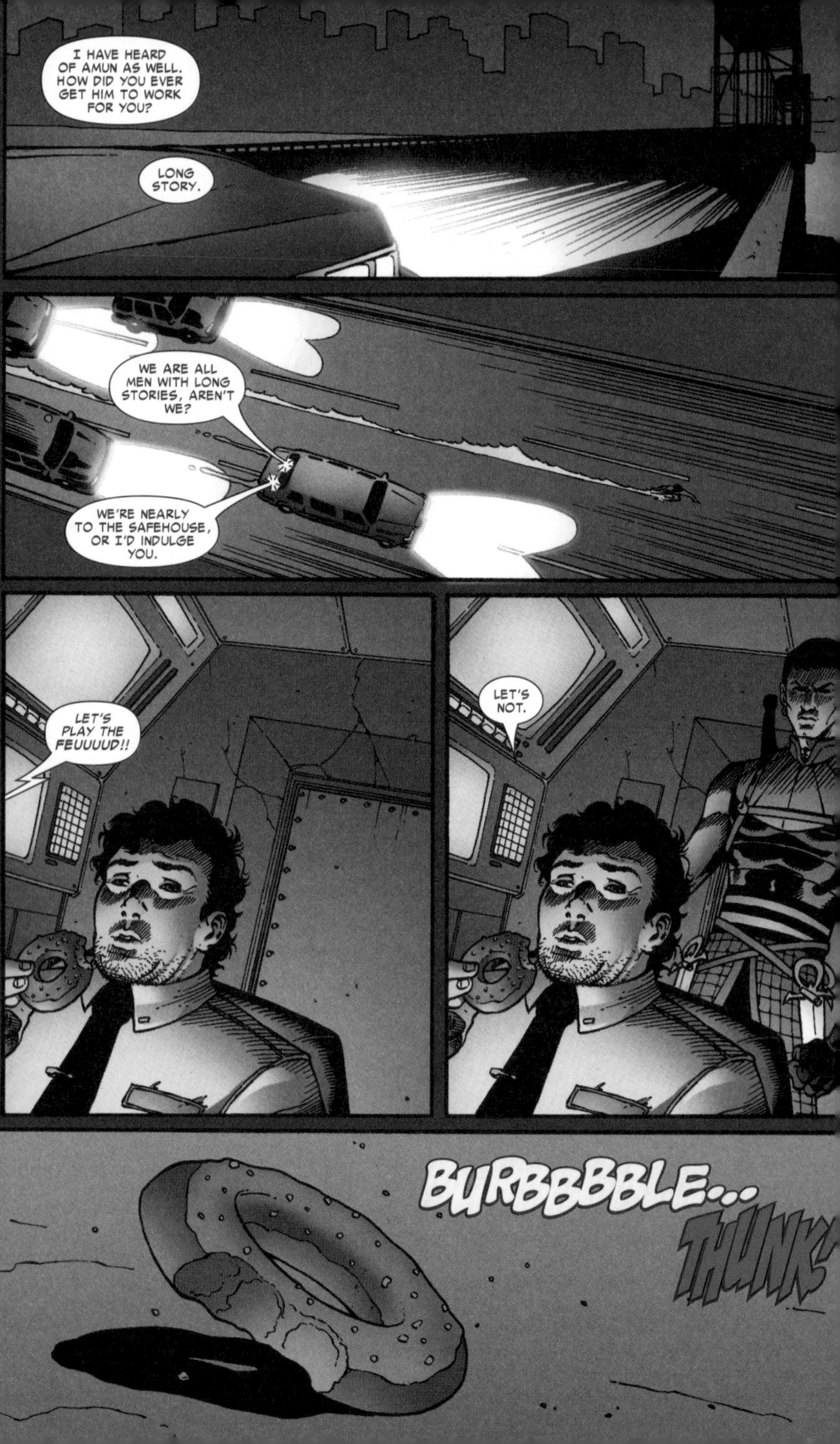
I HAVE HEARD OF AMUN AS WELL. HOW DID YOU EVER GET HIM TO WORK FOR YOU?
LONG STORY.
WE ARE ALL MEN WITH LONG STORIES, AREN'T WE?
WE'RE NEARLY TO THE SAFEHOUSE, OR I'D INDULGE YOU.
LET'S PLAY THE FEUUUUD!!
LET'S NOT.
BURBBBBLE...
THUNK!

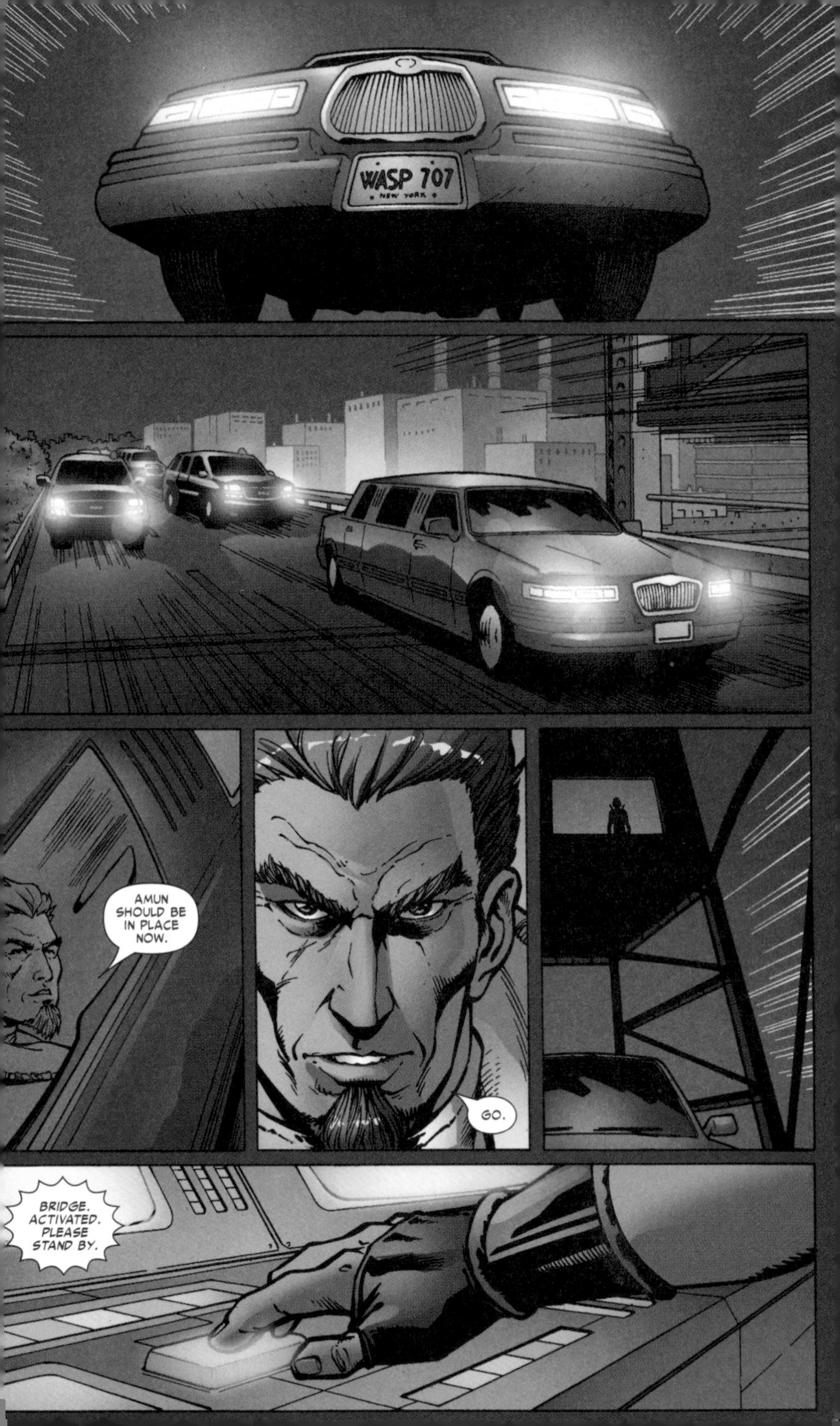
WASP 707
NEW YORK
AMUN SHOULD BE IN PLACE NOW.
GO.
BRIDGE. ACTIVATED. PLEASE STAND BY.

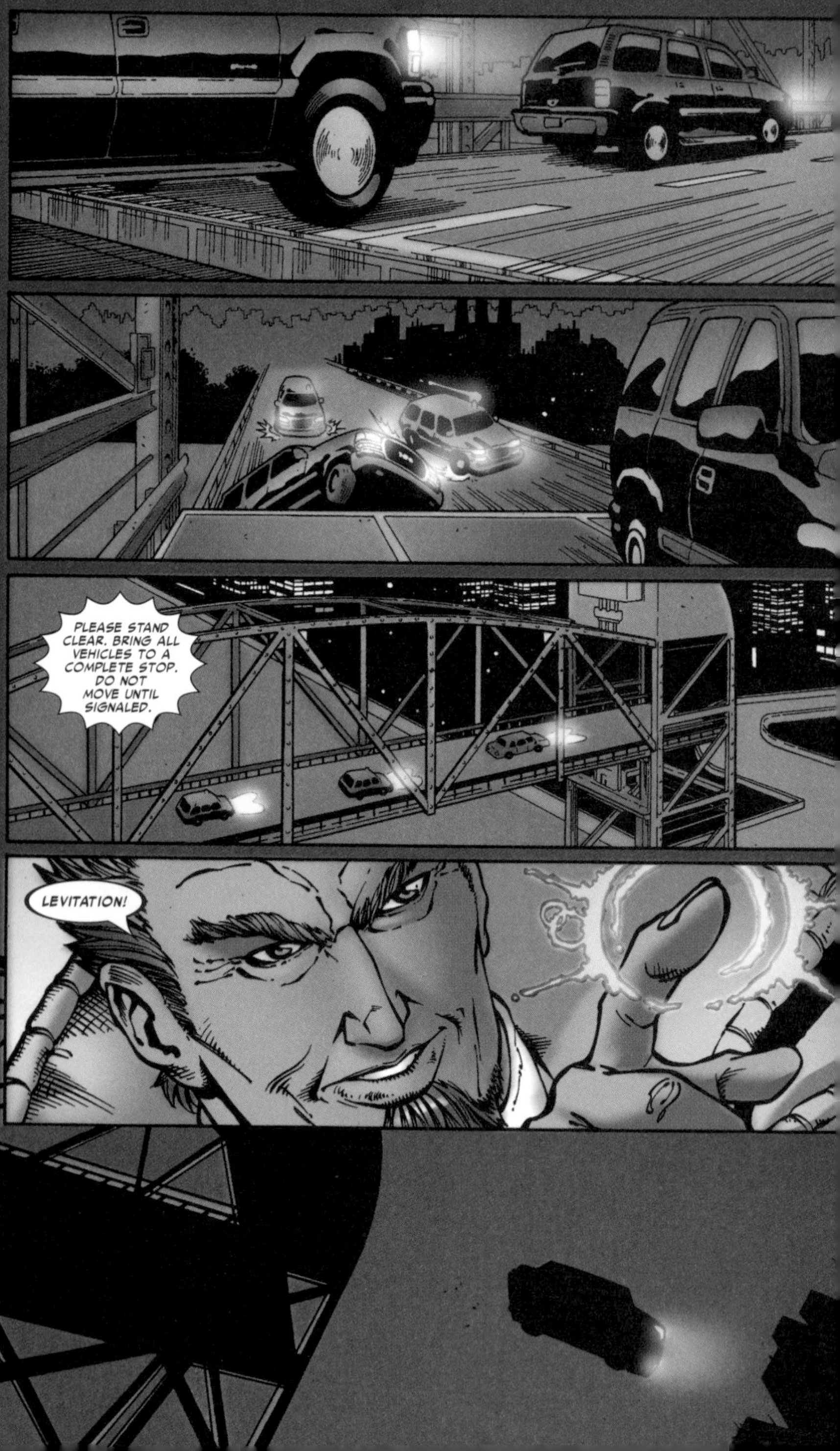
PLEASE STAND CLEAR. BRING ALL VEHICLES TO A COMPLETE STOP. DO NOT MOVE UNTIL SIGNALED.
LEVITATION!

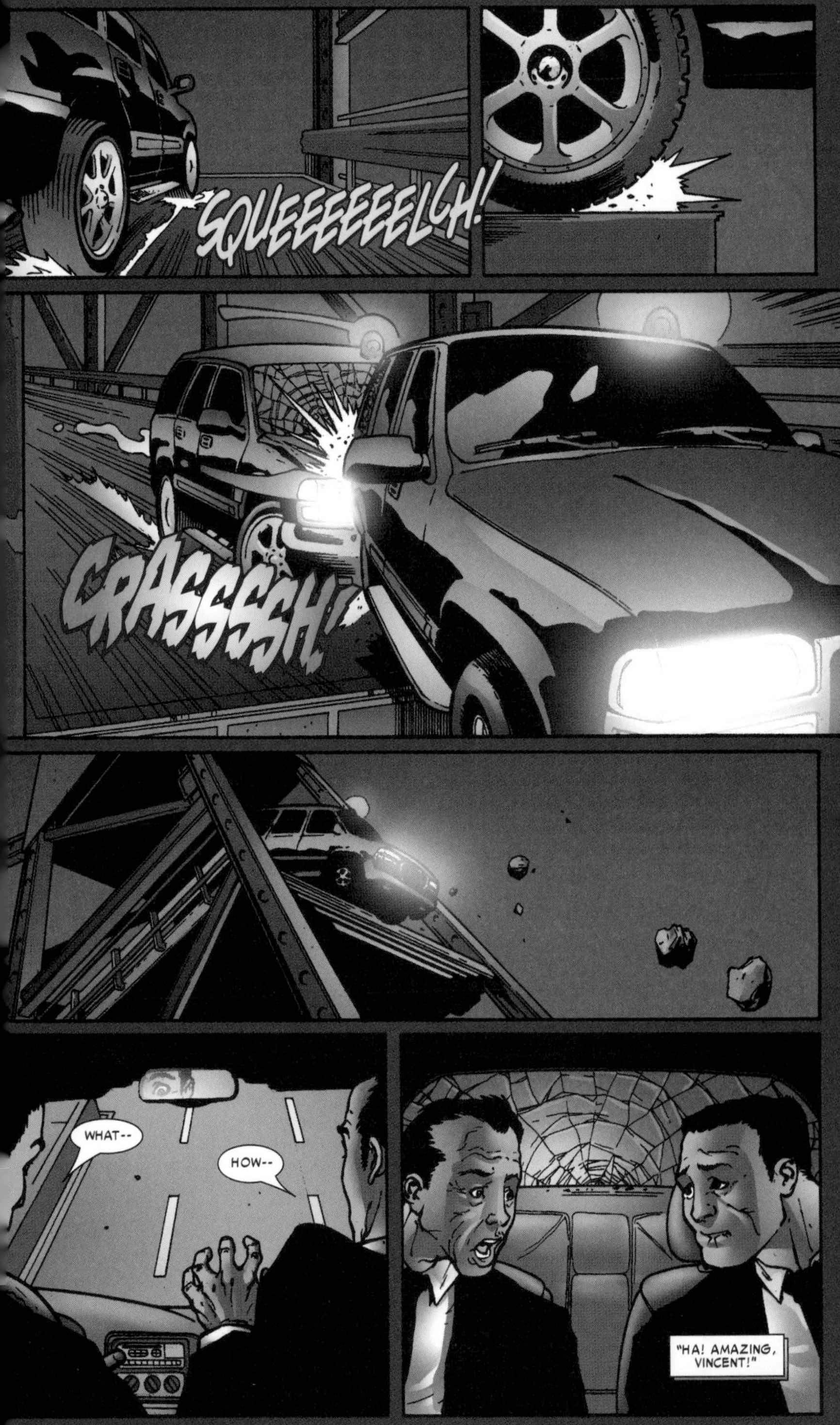
SQUEEEEEEELCH!
CRASSSSH!
WHAT--
HOW--
"HA! AMAZING, VINCENT!"

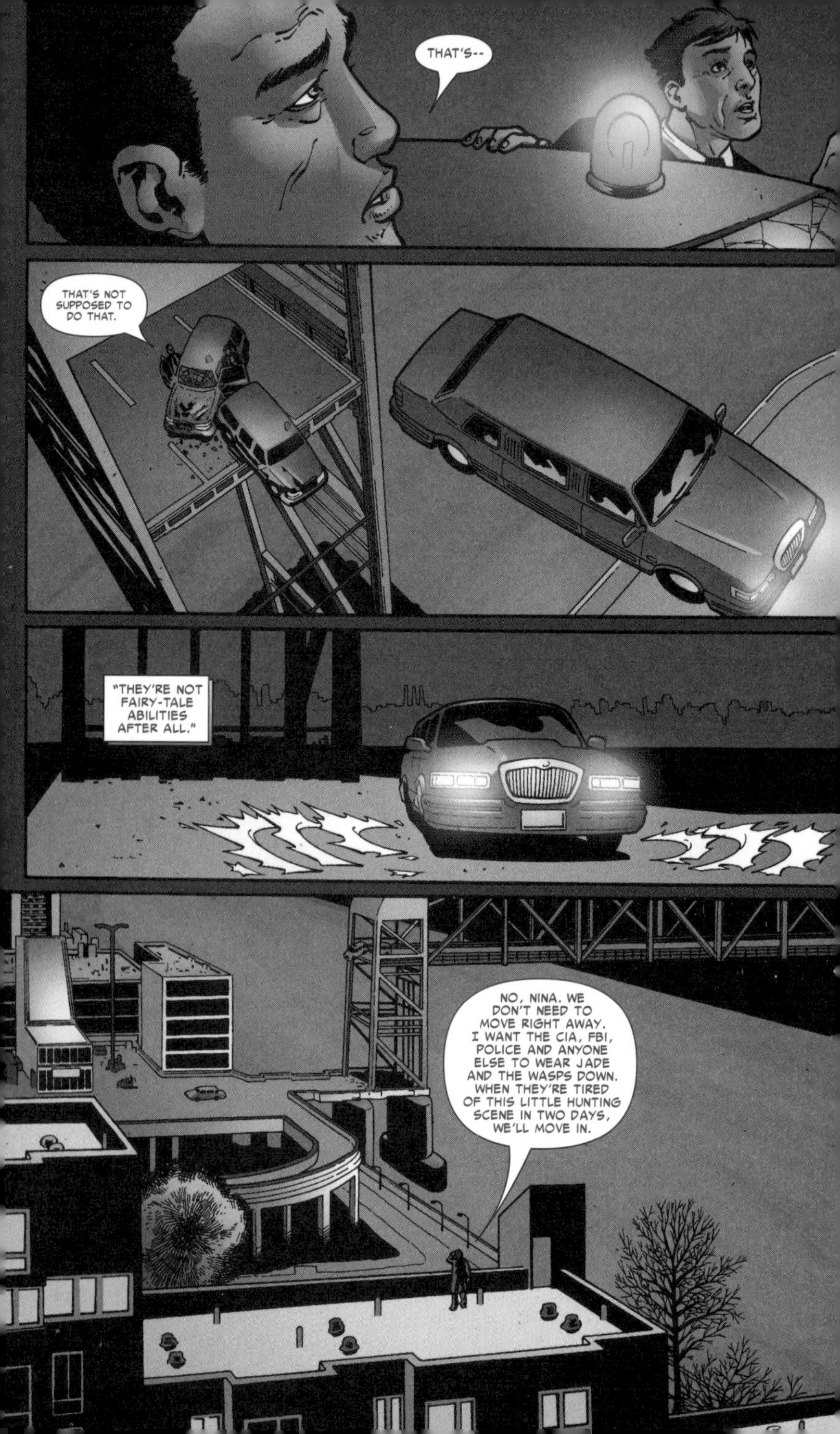
THAT'S--
THAT'S NOT SUPPOSED TO DO THAT.
"THEY'RE NOT FAIRY-TALE ABILITIES AFTER ALL."
NO, NINA. WE DON'T NEED TO MOVE RIGHT AWAY. I WANT THE CIA, FBI, POLICE AND ANYONE ELSE TO WEAR JADE AND THE WASPS DOWN. WHEN THEY'RE TIRED OF THIS LITTLE HUNTING SCENE IN TWO DAYS, WE'LL MOVE IN.

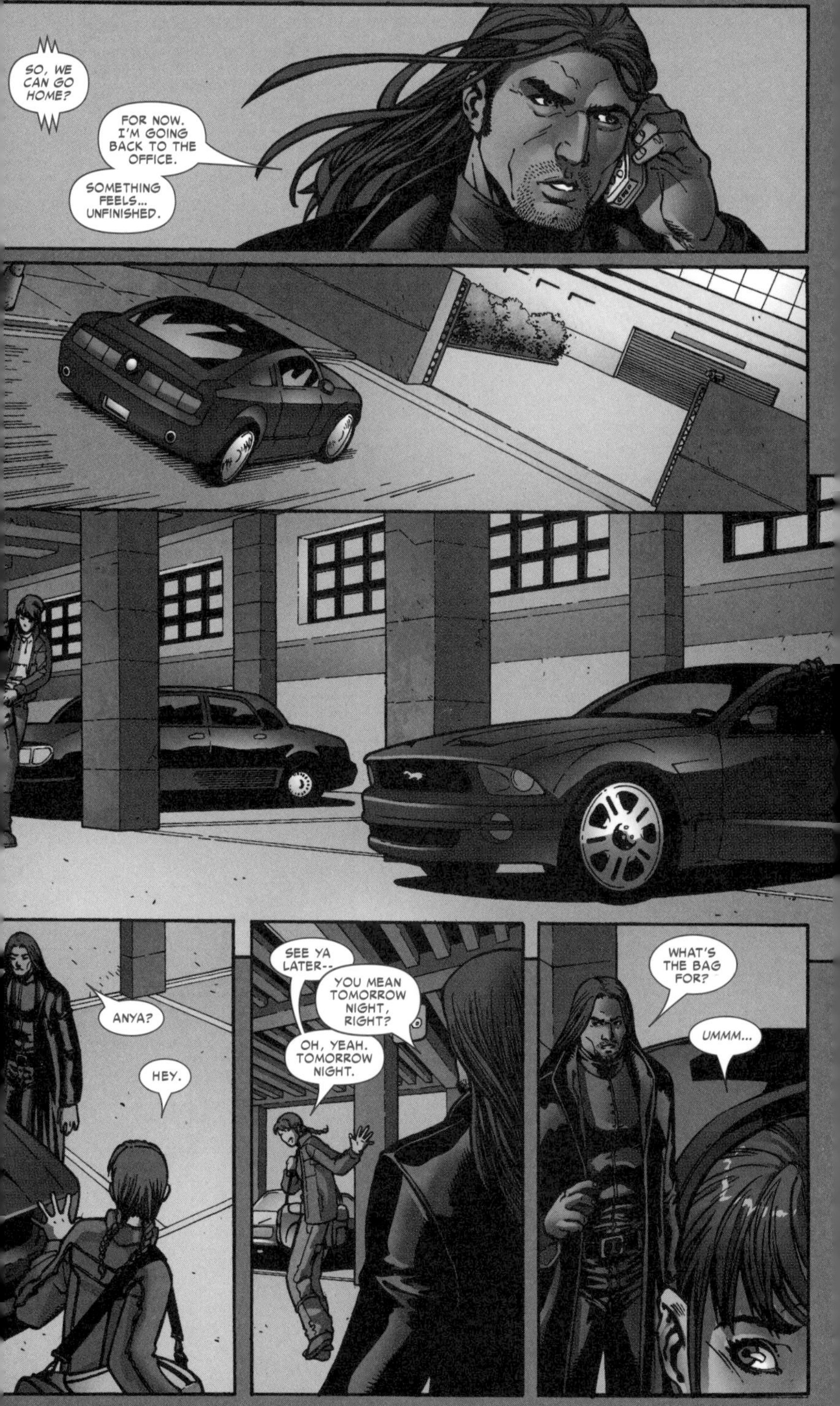
SO, WE CAN GO HOME?
FOR NOW. I'M GOING BACK TO THE OFFICE.
SOMETHING FEELS... UNFINISHED.
ANYA?
HEY.
SEE YA LATER--
YOU MEAN TOMORROW NIGHT, RIGHT?
OH, YEAH. TOMORROW NIGHT.
WHAT'S THE BAG FOR?
UMMM...

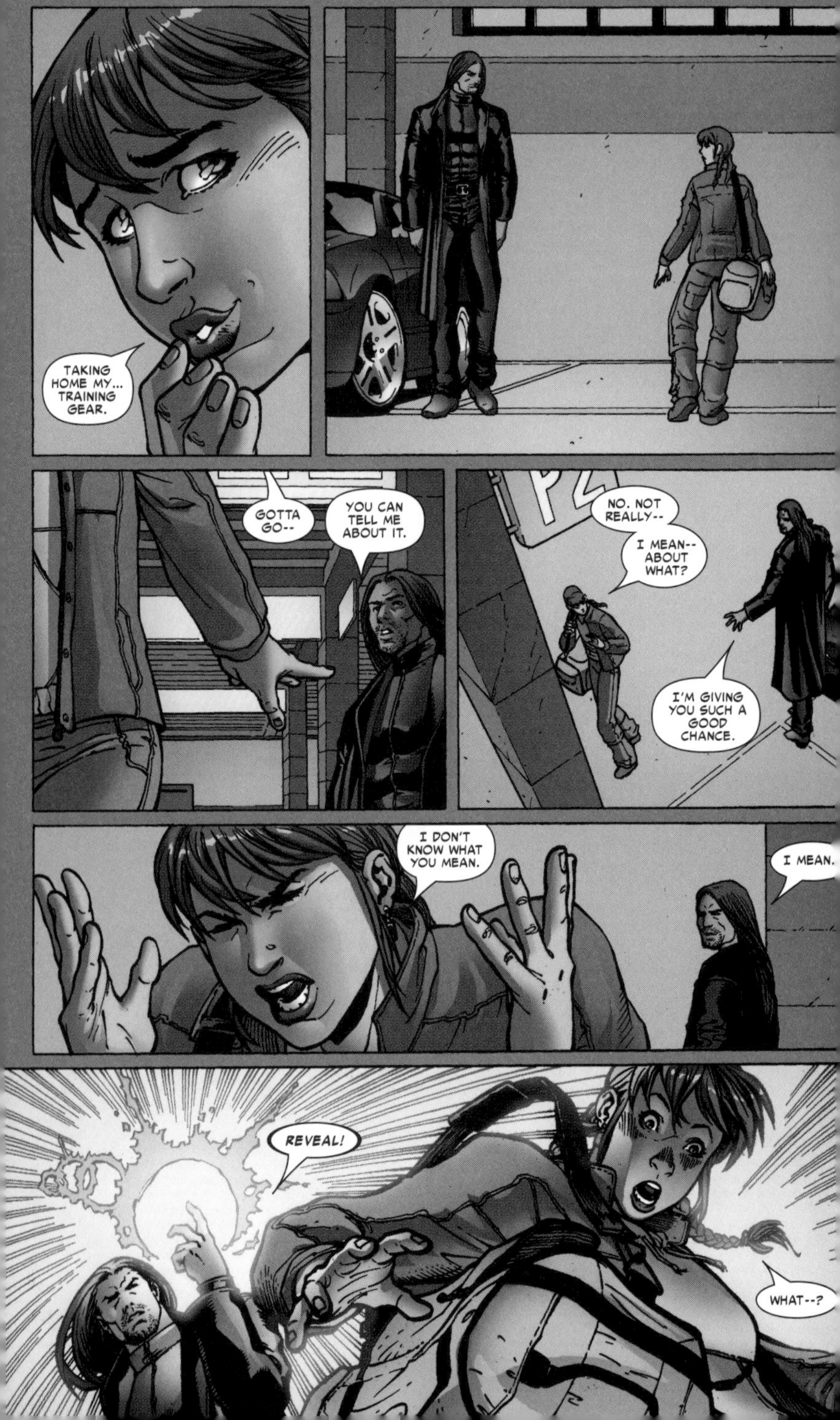

TAKING HOME MY... TRAINING GEAR.
GOTTA GO--
YOU CAN TELL ME ABOUT IT.
NO. NOT REALLY--
I MEAN-- ABOUT WHAT?
I'M GIVING YOU SUCH A GOOD CHANCE.
I DON'T KNOW WHAT YOU MEAN.
I MEAN.
REVEAL!
WHAT--?

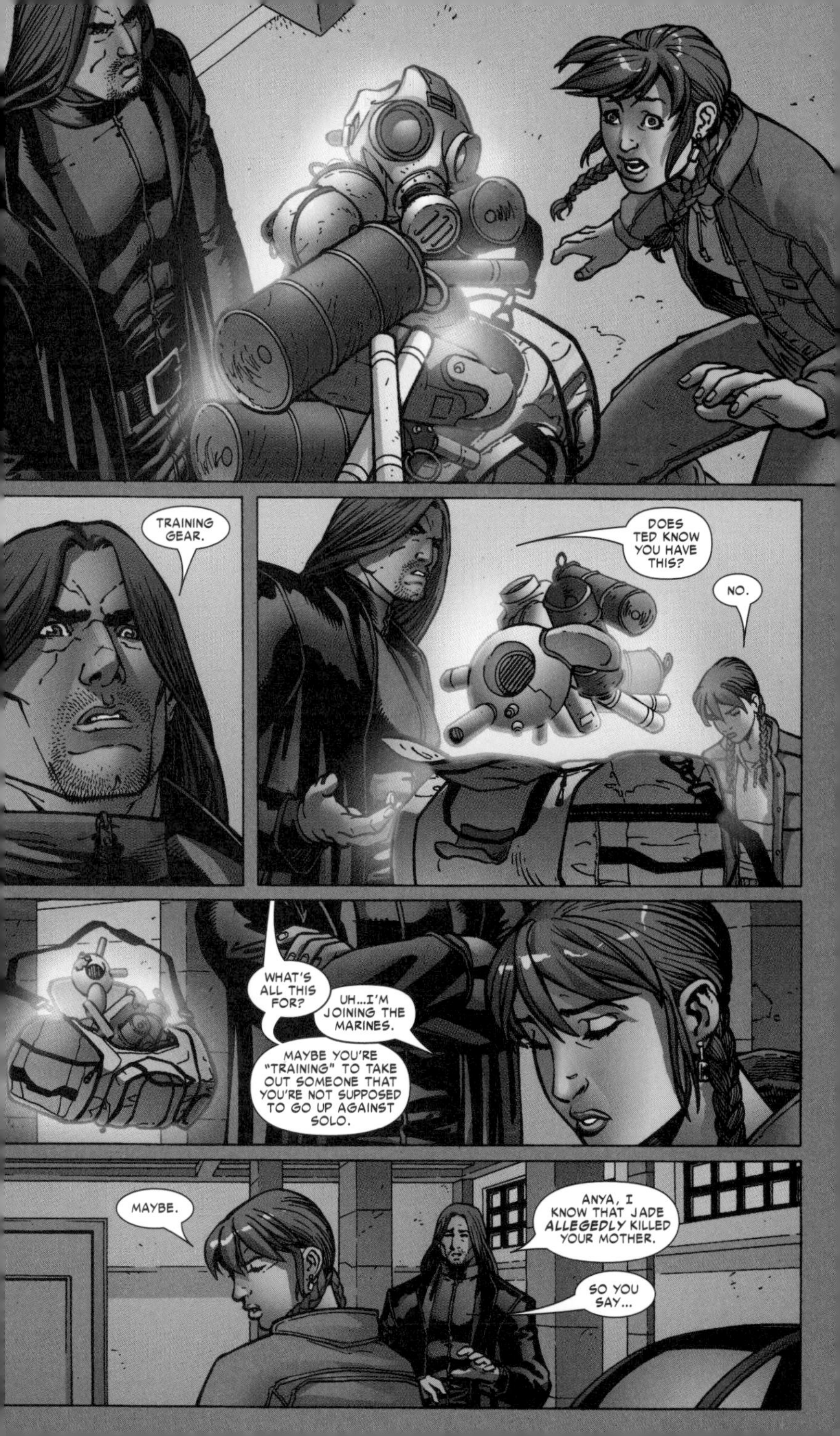
TRAINING GEAR.
DOES TED KNOW YOU HAVE THIS?
NO.
WHAT'S ALL THIS FOR?
UH...I'M JOINING THE MARINES.
MAYBE YOU'RE "TRAINING" TO TAKE OUT SOMEONE THAT YOU'RE NOT SUPPOSED TO GO UP AGAINST SOLO.
MAYBE.
ANYA, I KNOW THAT JADE *ALLEGEDLY* KILLED YOUR MOTHER.
SO YOU SAY...

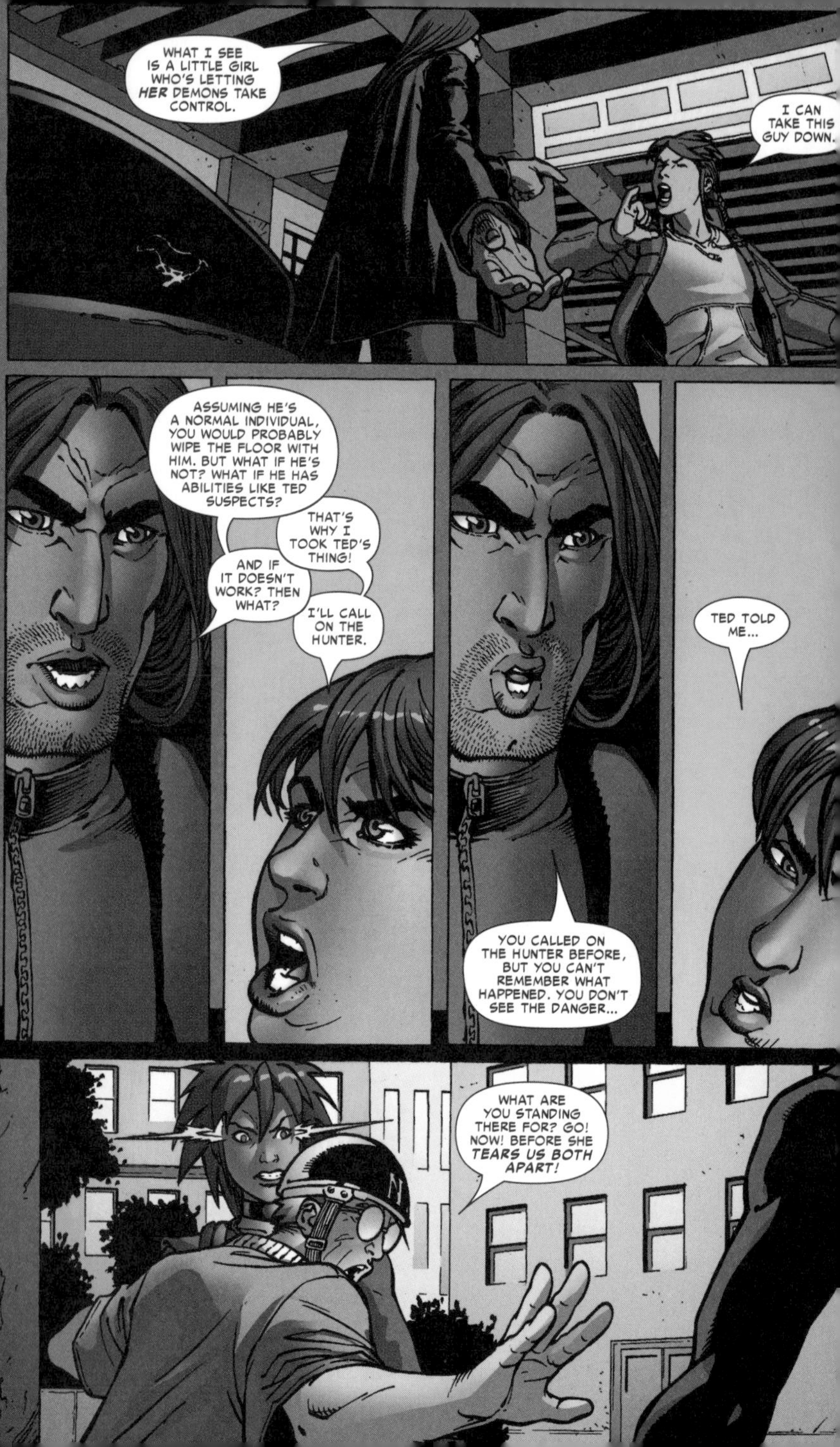
WHAT I SEE IS A LITTLE GIRL WHO'S LETTING *HER* DEMONS TAKE CONTROL.
I CAN TAKE THIS GUY DOWN.
ASSUMING HE'S A NORMAL INDIVIDUAL, YOU WOULD PROBABLY WIPE THE FLOOR WITH HIM. BUT WHAT IF HE'S NOT? WHAT IF HE HAS ABILITIES LIKE TED SUSPECTS?
THAT'S WHY I TOOK TED'S THING!
AND IF IT DOESN'T WORK? THEN WHAT?
I'LL CALL ON THE HUNTER.
YOU CALLED ON THE HUNTER BEFORE, BUT YOU CAN'T REMEMBER WHAT HAPPENED. YOU DON'T SEE THE DANGER...
TED TOLD ME...
WHAT ARE YOU STANDING THERE FOR? GO! NOW! BEFORE SHE *TEARS US BOTH APART!*

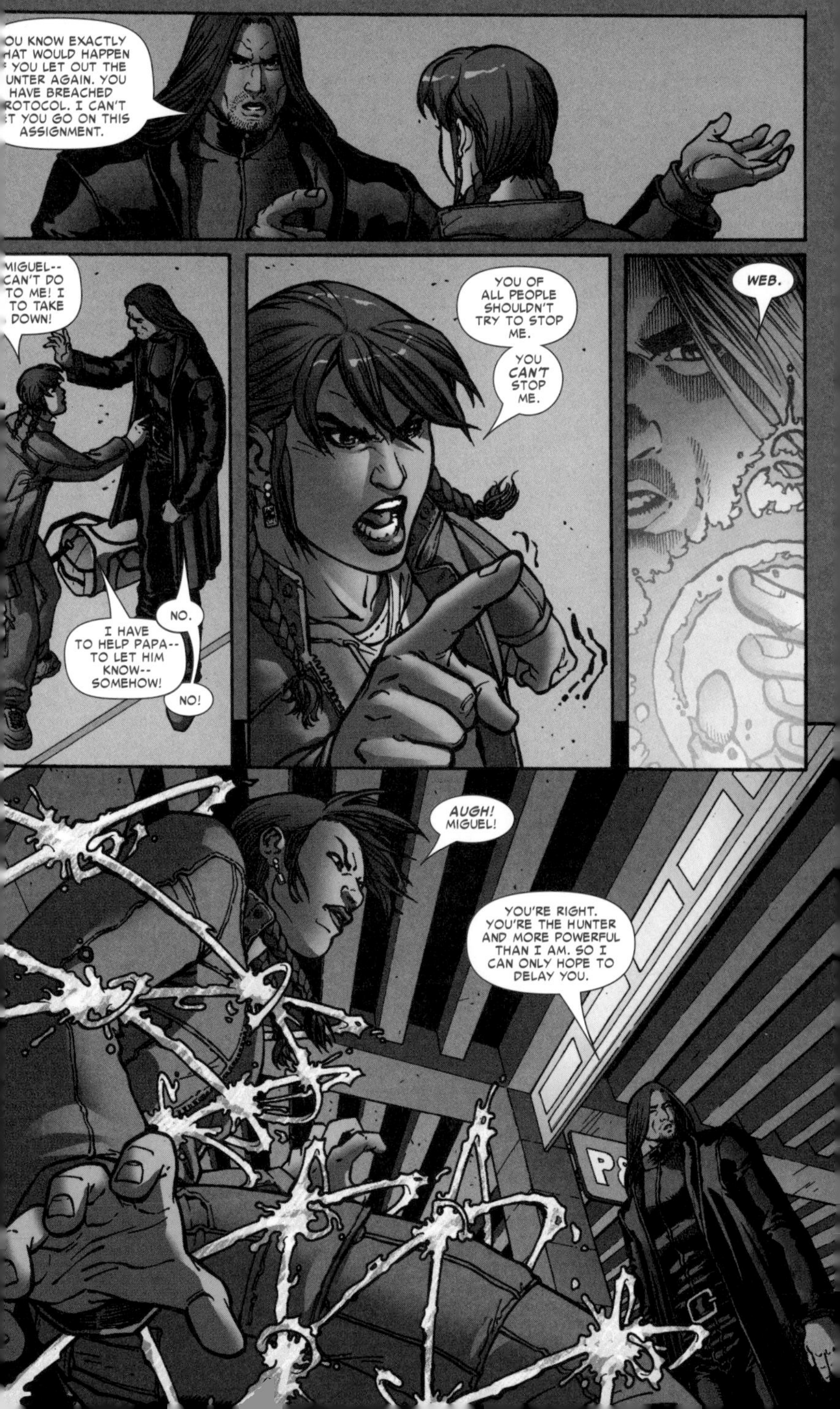
OU KNOW EXACTLY HAT WOULD HAPPEN F YOU LET OUT THE UNTER AGAIN. YOU HAVE BREACHED ROTOCOL. I CAN'T T YOU GO ON THIS ASSIGNMENT.
MIGUEL-- CAN'T DO TO ME! I TO TAKE DOWN!
NO.
I HAVE TO HELP PAPA-- TO LET HIM KNOW-- SOMEHOW!
NO!
YOU OF ALL PEOPLE SHOULDN'T TRY TO STOP ME.
YOU *CAN'T* STOP ME.
WEB.
AUGH! MIGUEL!
YOU'RE RIGHT. YOU'RE THE HUNTER AND MORE POWERFUL THAN I AM. SO I CAN ONLY HOPE TO DELAY YOU.

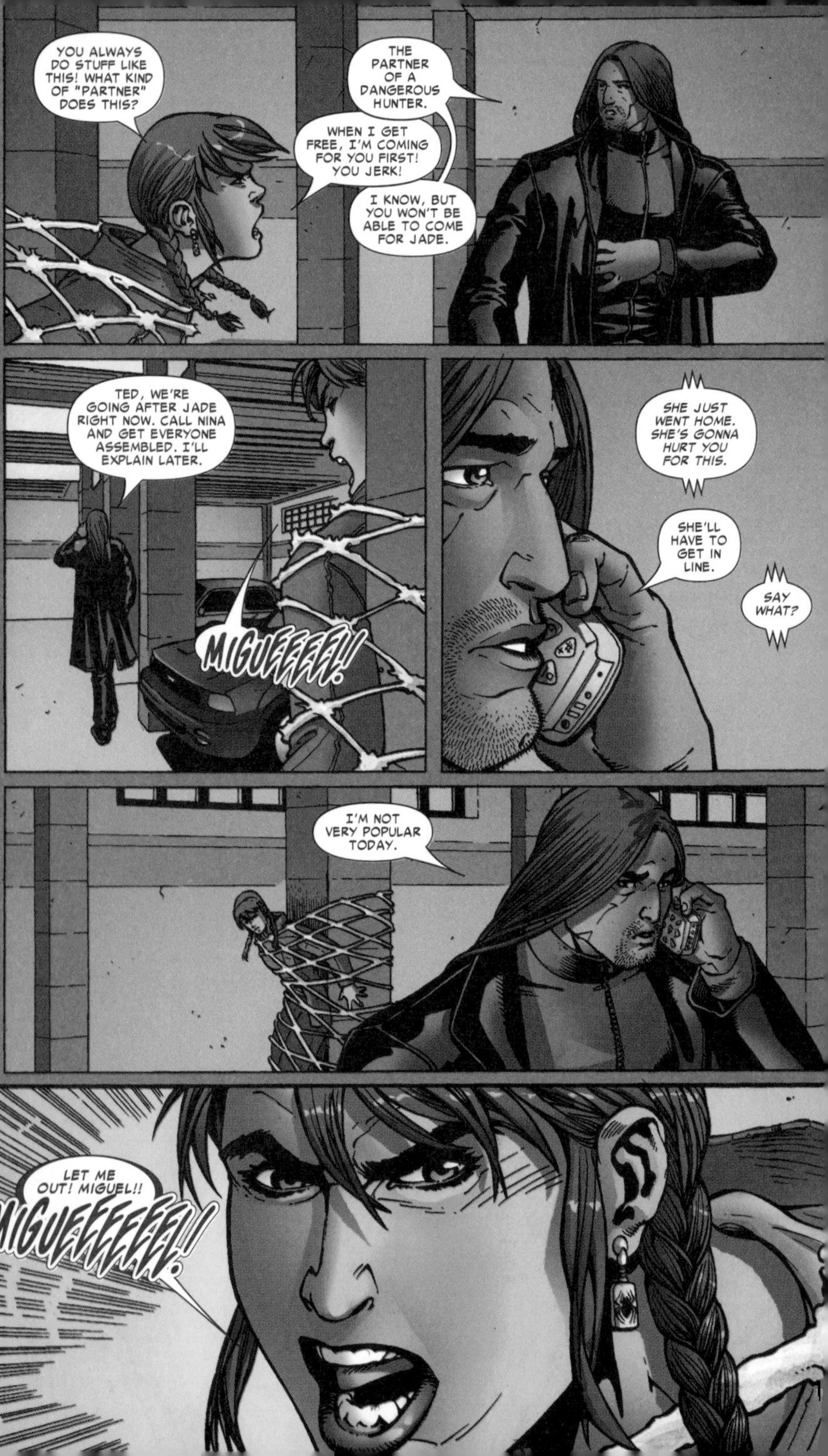
YOU ALWAYS DO STUFF LIKE THIS! WHAT KIND OF "PARTNER" DOES THIS?
THE PARTNER OF A DANGEROUS HUNTER.
WHEN I GET FREE, I'M COMING FOR YOU FIRST! YOU JERK!
I KNOW, BUT YOU WON'T BE ABLE TO COME FOR JADE.
TED, WE'RE GOING AFTER JADE RIGHT NOW. CALL NINA AND GET EVERYONE ASSEMBLED. I'LL EXPLAIN LATER.
MIGUEEEEEL!!
SHE JUST WENT HOME. SHE'S GONNA HURT YOU FOR THIS.
SHE'LL HAVE TO GET IN LINE.
SAY WHAT?
I'M NOT VERY POPULAR TODAY.
LET ME OUT! MIGUEL!!
MIGUEEEEEEL!!

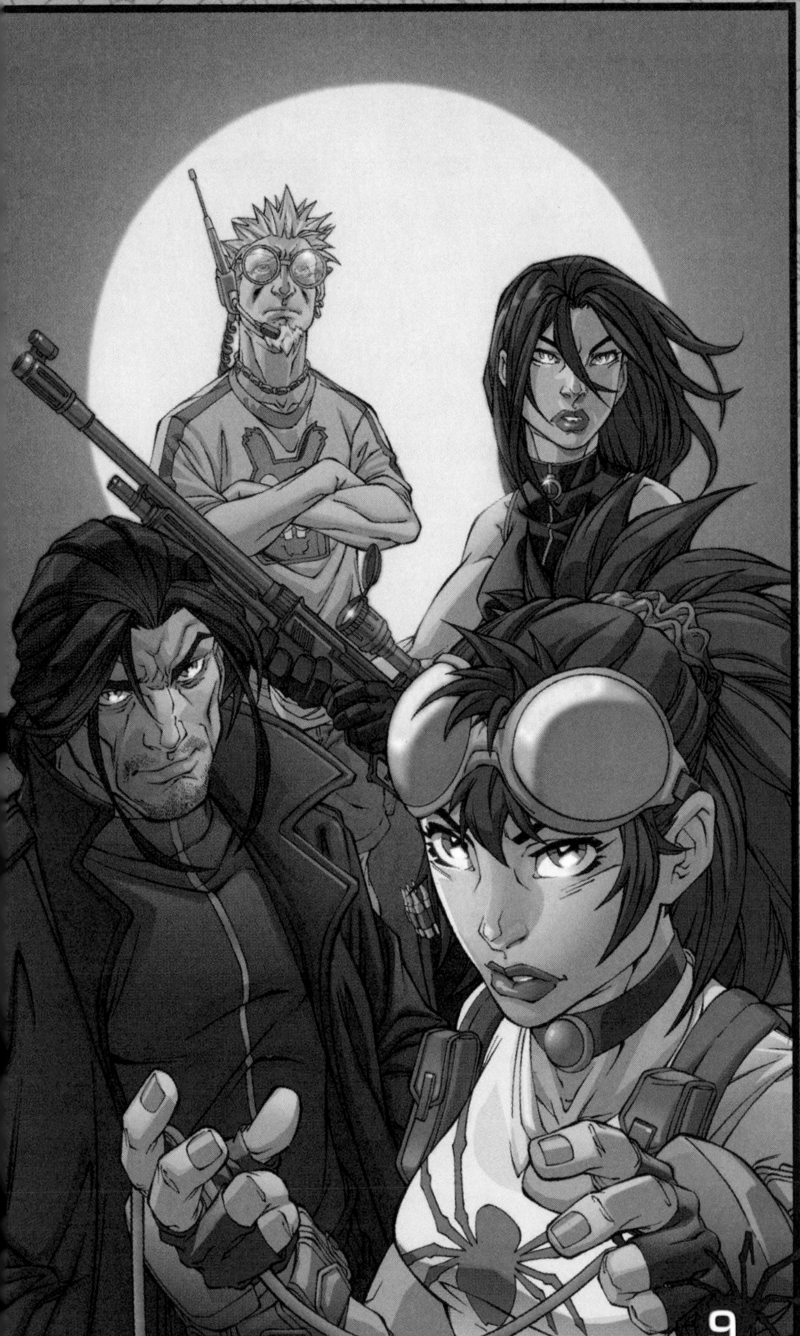

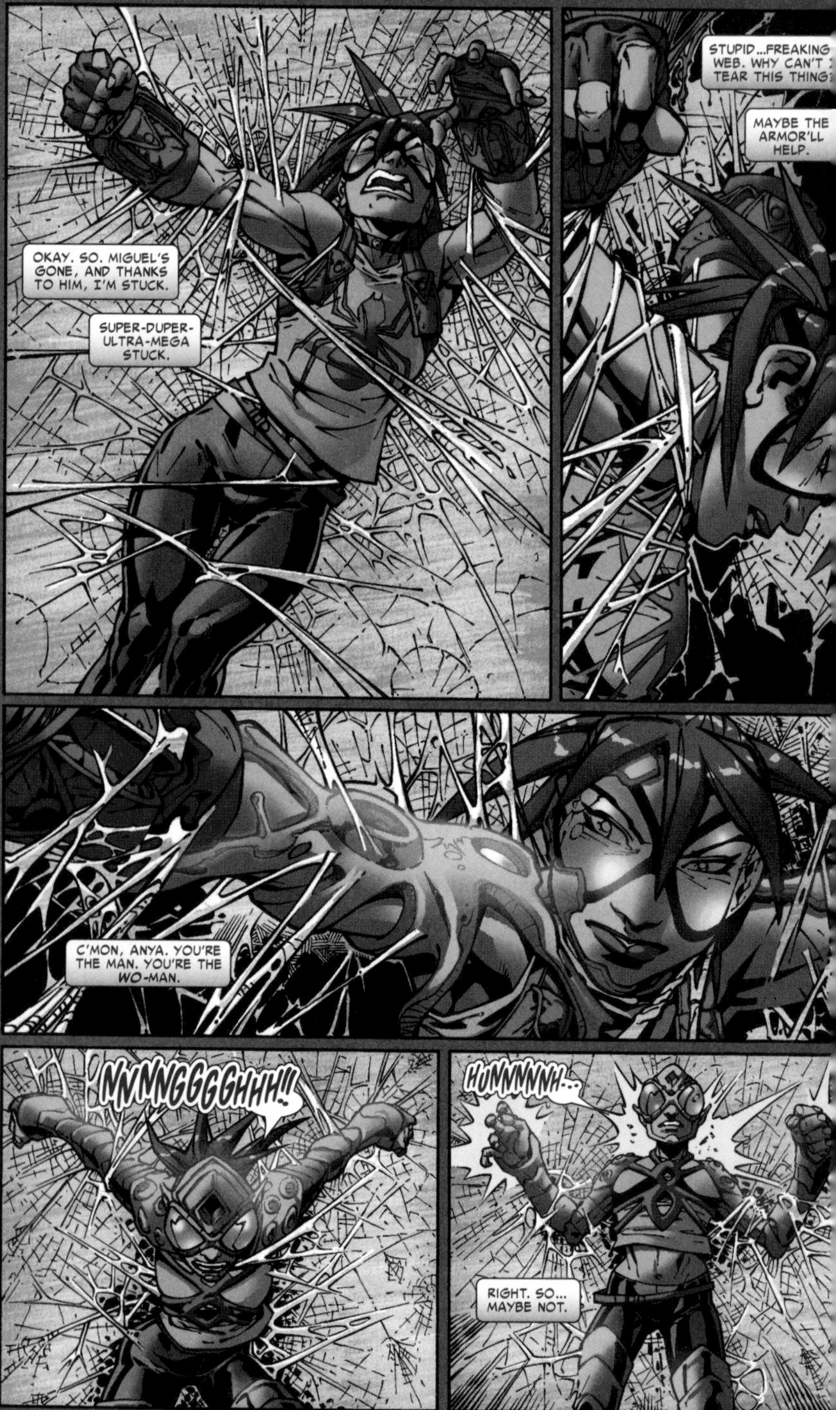
OKAY. SO. MIGUEL'S GONE, AND THANKS TO HIM, I'M STUCK.
SUPER-DUPER-ULTRA-MEGA STUCK.
STUPID...FREAKING WEB. WHY CAN'T I TEAR THIS THING?
MAYBE THE ARMOR'LL HELP.
C'MON, ANYA. YOU'RE THE MAN. YOU'RE THE WO-MAN.
NNNNGGGGHHH!!
HUNNNNNH...
RIGHT. SO... MAYBE NOT.

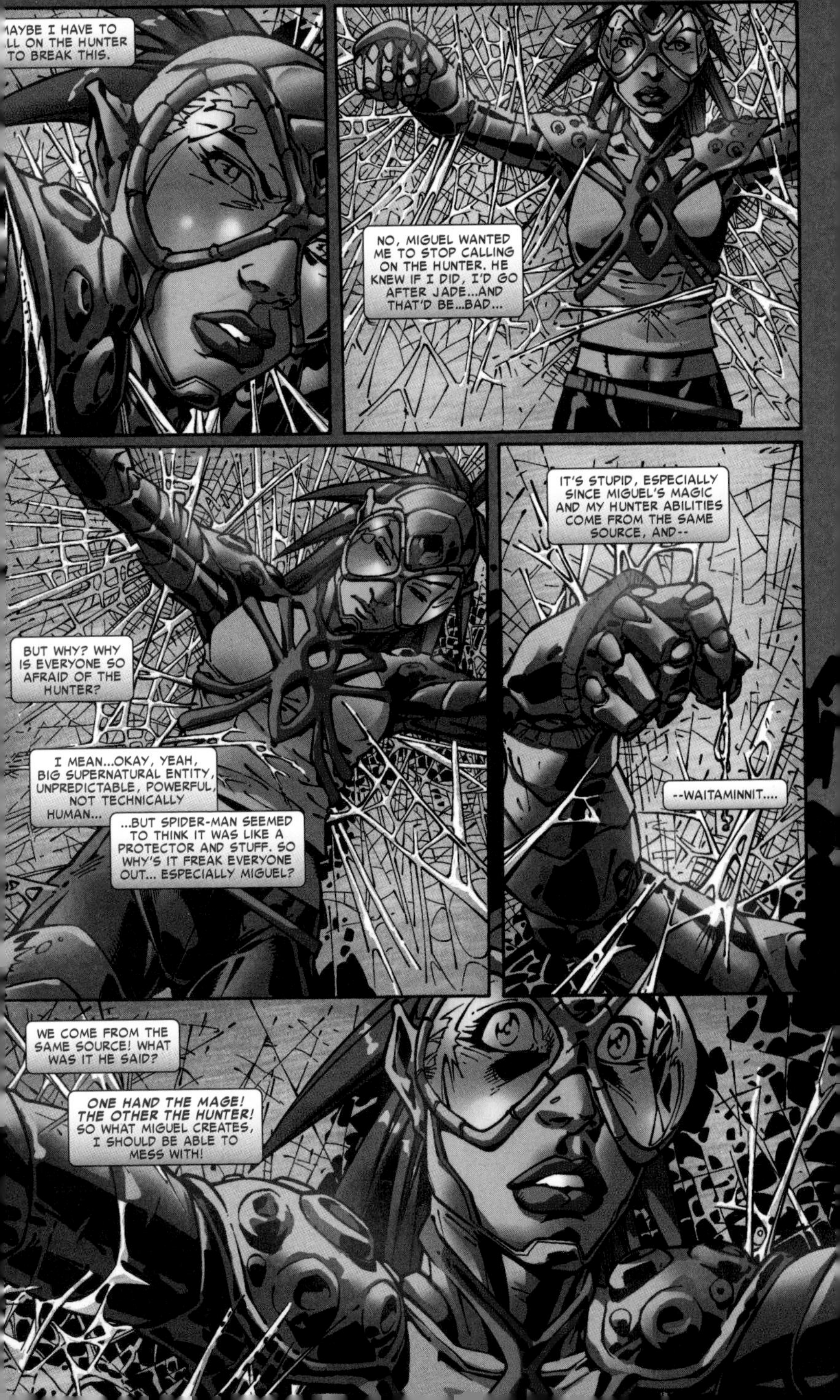

MAYBE I HAVE TO CALL ON THE HUNTER TO BREAK THIS.
NO, MIGUEL WANTED ME TO STOP CALLING ON THE HUNTER. HE KNEW IF I DID, I'D GO AFTER JADE...AND THAT'D BE...BAD...
BUT WHY? WHY IS EVERYONE SO AFRAID OF THE HUNTER?
I MEAN...OKAY, YEAH, BIG SUPERNATURAL ENTITY, UNPREDICTABLE, POWERFUL, NOT TECHNICALLY HUMAN...
...BUT SPIDER-MAN SEEMED TO THINK IT WAS LIKE A PROTECTOR AND STUFF. SO WHY'S IT FREAK EVERYONE OUT... ESPECIALLY MIGUEL?
IT'S STUPID, ESPECIALLY SINCE MIGUEL'S MAGIC AND MY HUNTER ABILITIES COME FROM THE SAME SOURCE, AND--
--WAITAMINNIT....
WE COME FROM THE SAME SOURCE! WHAT WAS IT HE SAID?
ONE HAND THE MAGE! THE OTHER THE HUNTER! SO WHAT MIGUEL CREATES, I SHOULD BE ABLE TO MESS WITH!

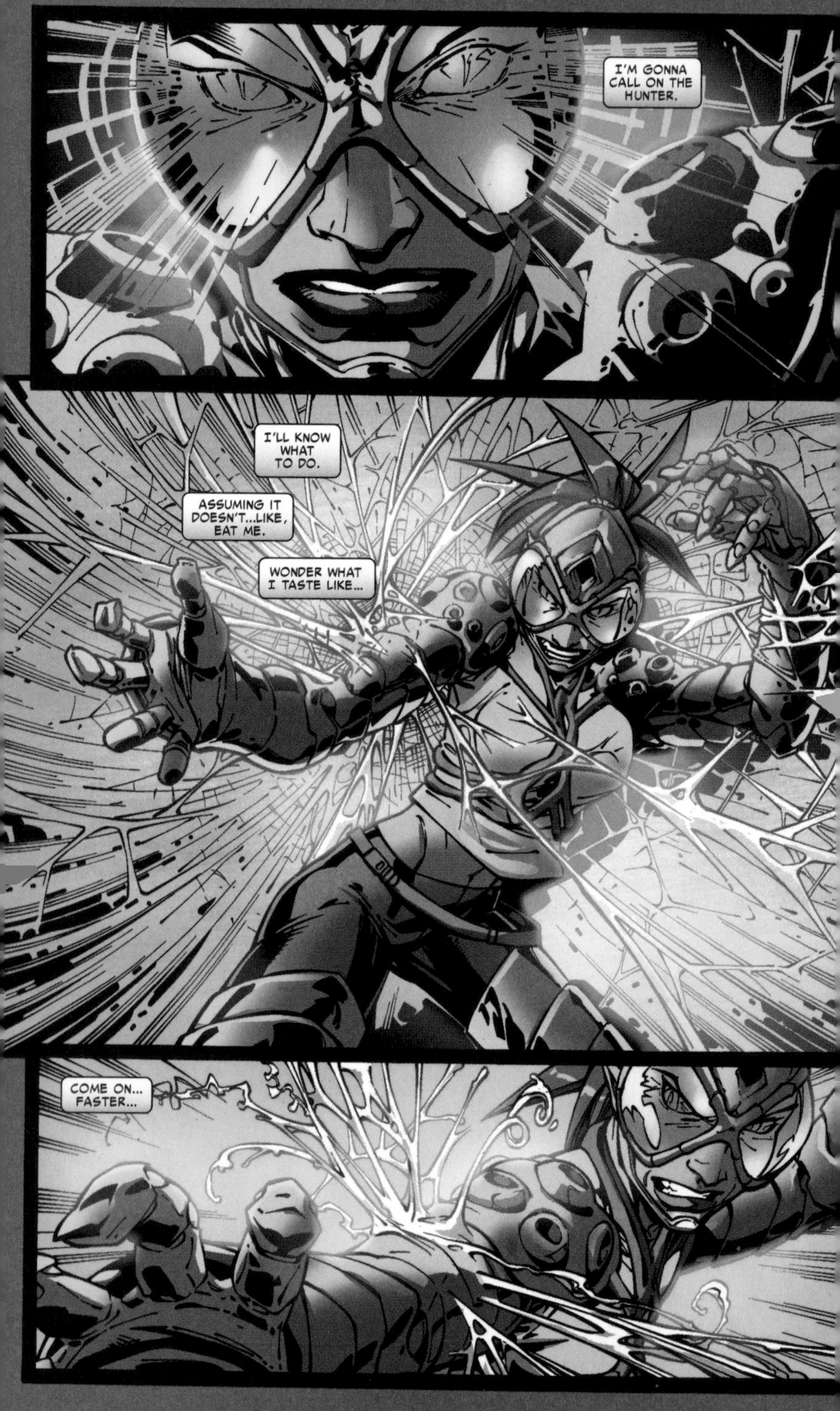
I'M GONNA CALL ON THE HUNTER.
I'LL KNOW WHAT TO DO.
ASSUMING IT DOESN'T...LIKE, EAT ME.
WONDER WHAT I TASTE LIKE...
COME ON... FASTER...

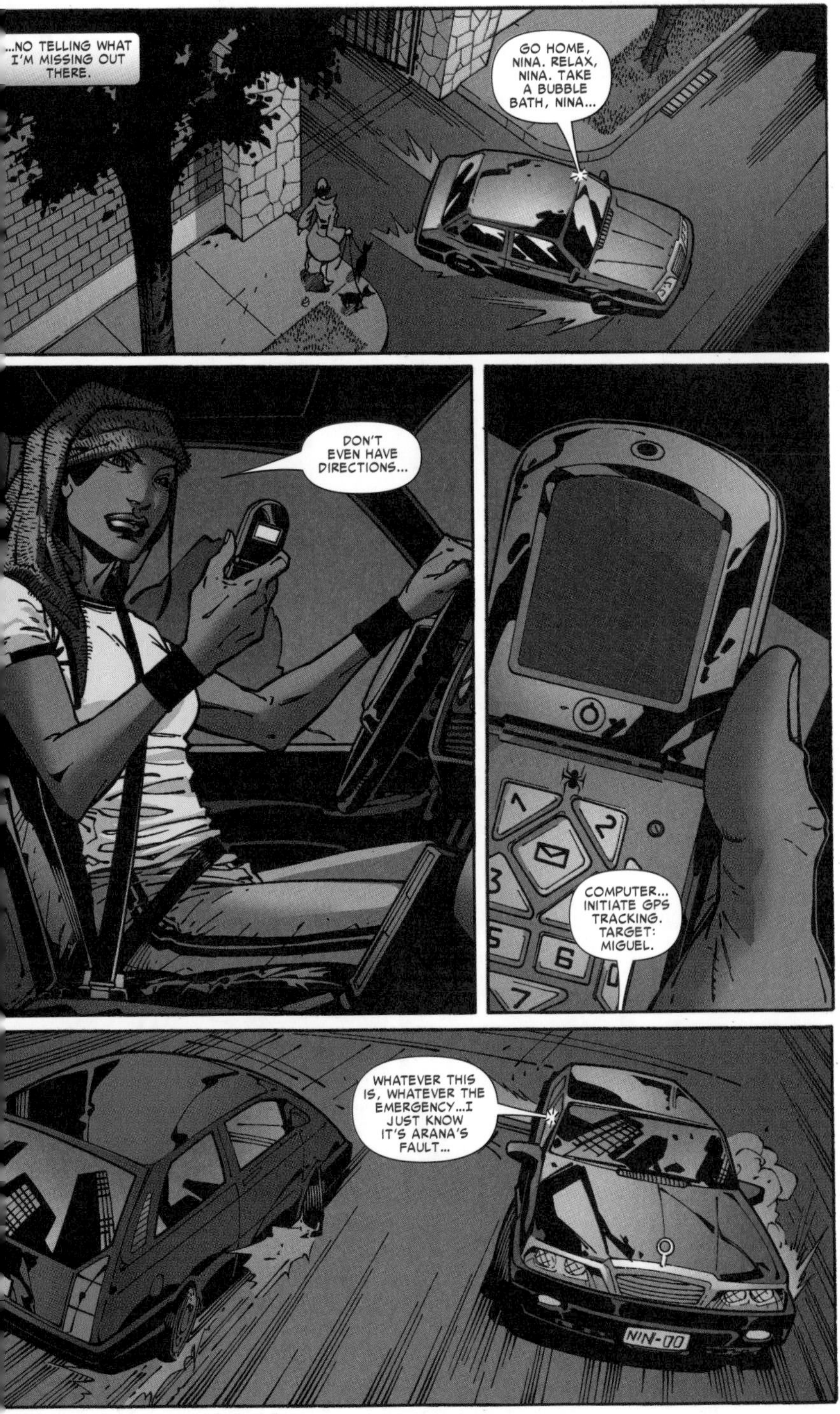

...NO TELLING WHAT I'M MISSING OUT THERE.
GO HOME, NINA. RELAX, NINA. TAKE A BUBBLE BATH, NINA...
DON'T EVEN HAVE DIRECTIONS...
COMPUTER... INITIATE GPS TRACKING. TARGET: MIGUEL.
WHATEVER THIS IS, WHATEVER THE EMERGENCY...I JUST KNOW IT'S ARANA'S FAULT...
NIN-70

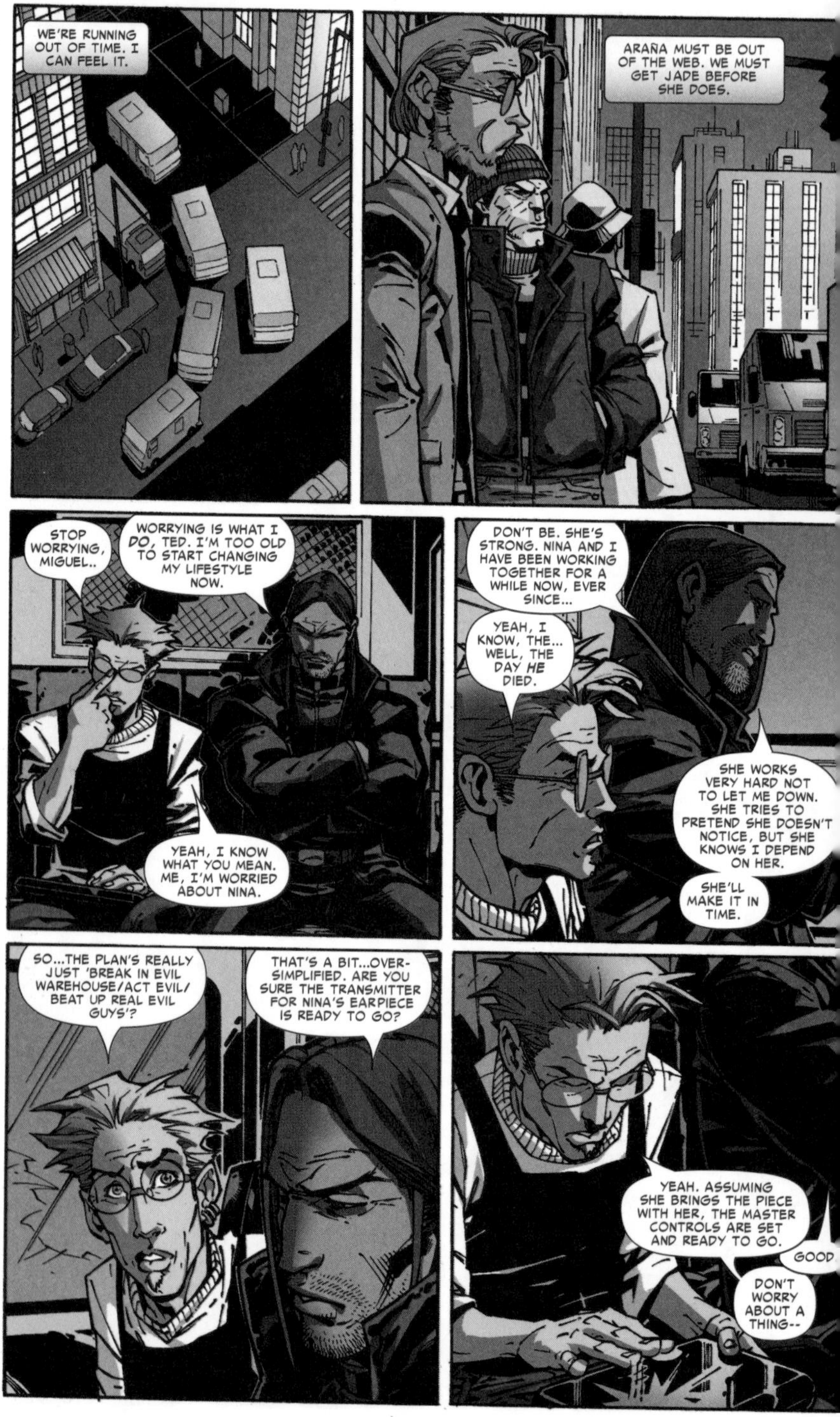
WE'RE RUNNING OUT OF TIME. I CAN FEEL IT.
ARAÑA MUST BE OUT OF THE WEB. WE MUST GET JADE BEFORE SHE DOES.
STOP WORRYING, MIGUEL..
WORRYING IS WHAT I DO, TED. I'M TOO OLD TO START CHANGING MY LIFESTYLE NOW.
YEAH, I KNOW WHAT YOU MEAN. ME, I'M WORRIED ABOUT NINA.
DON'T BE. SHE'S STRONG. NINA AND I HAVE BEEN WORKING TOGETHER FOR A WHILE NOW, EVER SINCE...
YEAH, I KNOW, THE... WELL, THE DAY HE DIED.
SHE WORKS VERY HARD NOT TO LET ME DOWN. SHE TRIES TO PRETEND SHE DOESN'T NOTICE, BUT SHE KNOWS I DEPEND ON HER.
SHE'LL MAKE IT IN TIME.
SO...THE PLAN'S REALLY JUST 'BREAK IN EVIL WAREHOUSE/ACT EVIL/ BEAT UP REAL EVIL GUYS'?
THAT'S A BIT...OVER-SIMPLIFIED. ARE YOU SURE THE TRANSMITTER FOR NINA'S EARPIECE IS READY TO GO?
YEAH. ASSUMING SHE BRINGS THE PIECE WITH HER, THE MASTER CONTROLS ARE SET AND READY TO GO.
GOOD
DON'T WORRY ABOUT A THING--

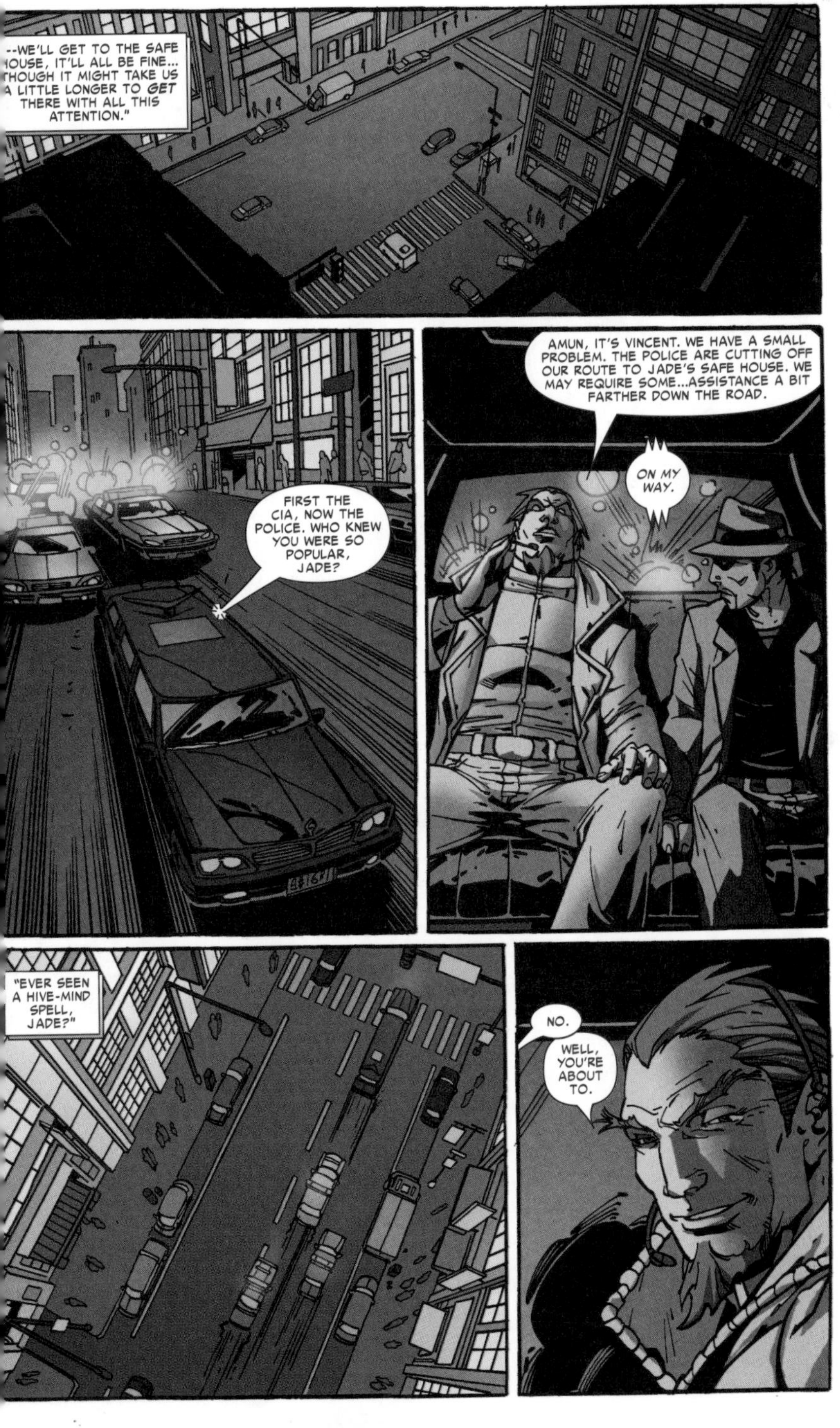

--WE'LL GET TO THE SAFE HOUSE, IT'LL ALL BE FINE... THOUGH IT MIGHT TAKE US A LITTLE LONGER TO GET THERE WITH ALL THIS ATTENTION."
FIRST THE CIA, NOW THE POLICE. WHO KNEW YOU WERE SO POPULAR, JADE?
AMUN, IT'S VINCENT. WE HAVE A SMALL PROBLEM. THE POLICE ARE CUTTING OFF OUR ROUTE TO JADE'S SAFE HOUSE. WE MAY REQUIRE SOME...ASSISTANCE A BIT FARTHER DOWN THE ROAD.
ON MY WAY.
"EVER SEEN A HIVE-MIND SPELL, JADE?"
NO.
WELL, YOU'RE ABOUT TO.

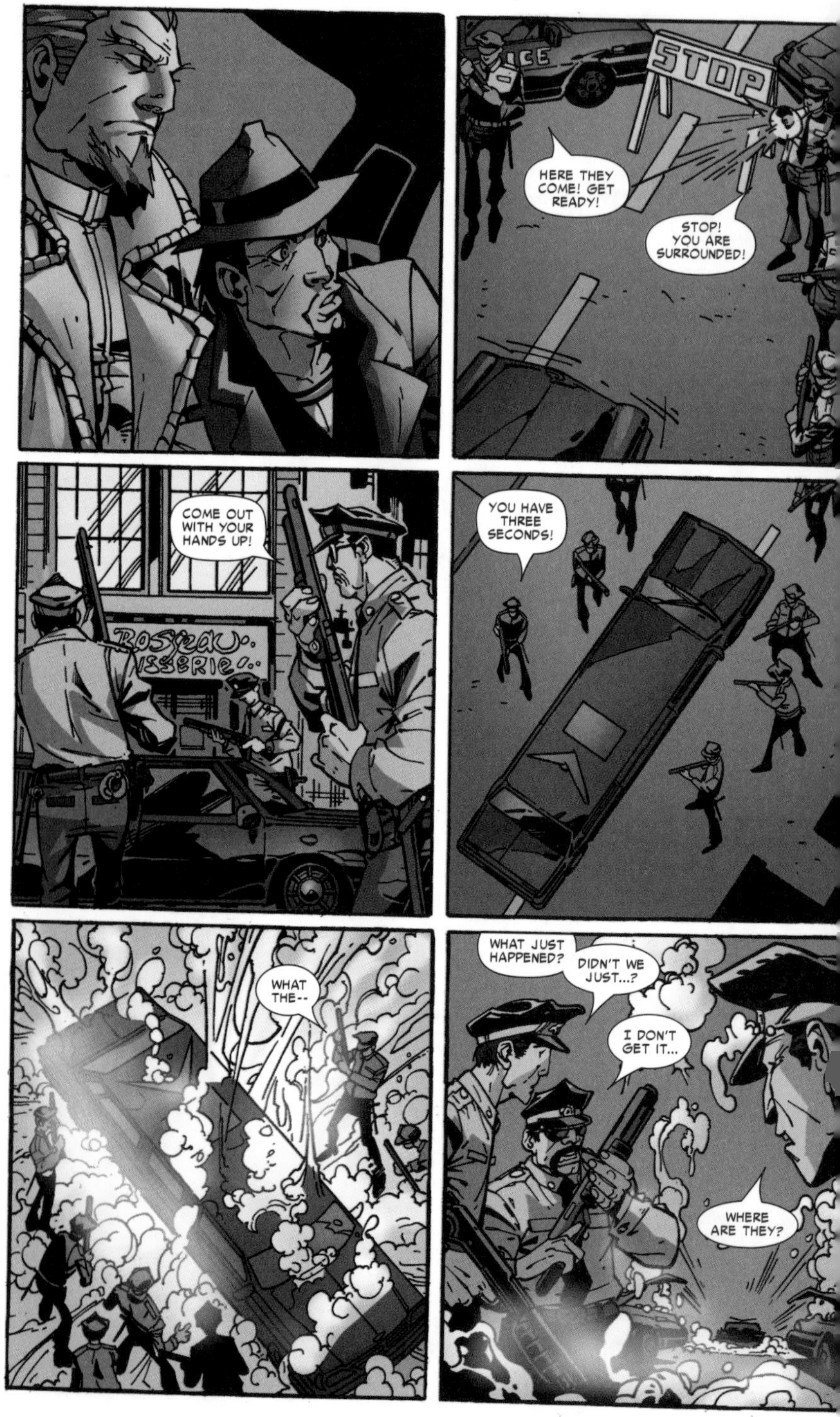
HERE THEY COME! GET READY!
STOP! YOU ARE SURROUNDED!
COME OUT WITH YOUR HANDS UP!
YOU HAVE THREE SECONDS!
WHAT THE--
WHAT JUST HAPPENED?
DIDN'T WE JUST...?
I DON'T GET IT...
WHERE ARE THEY?

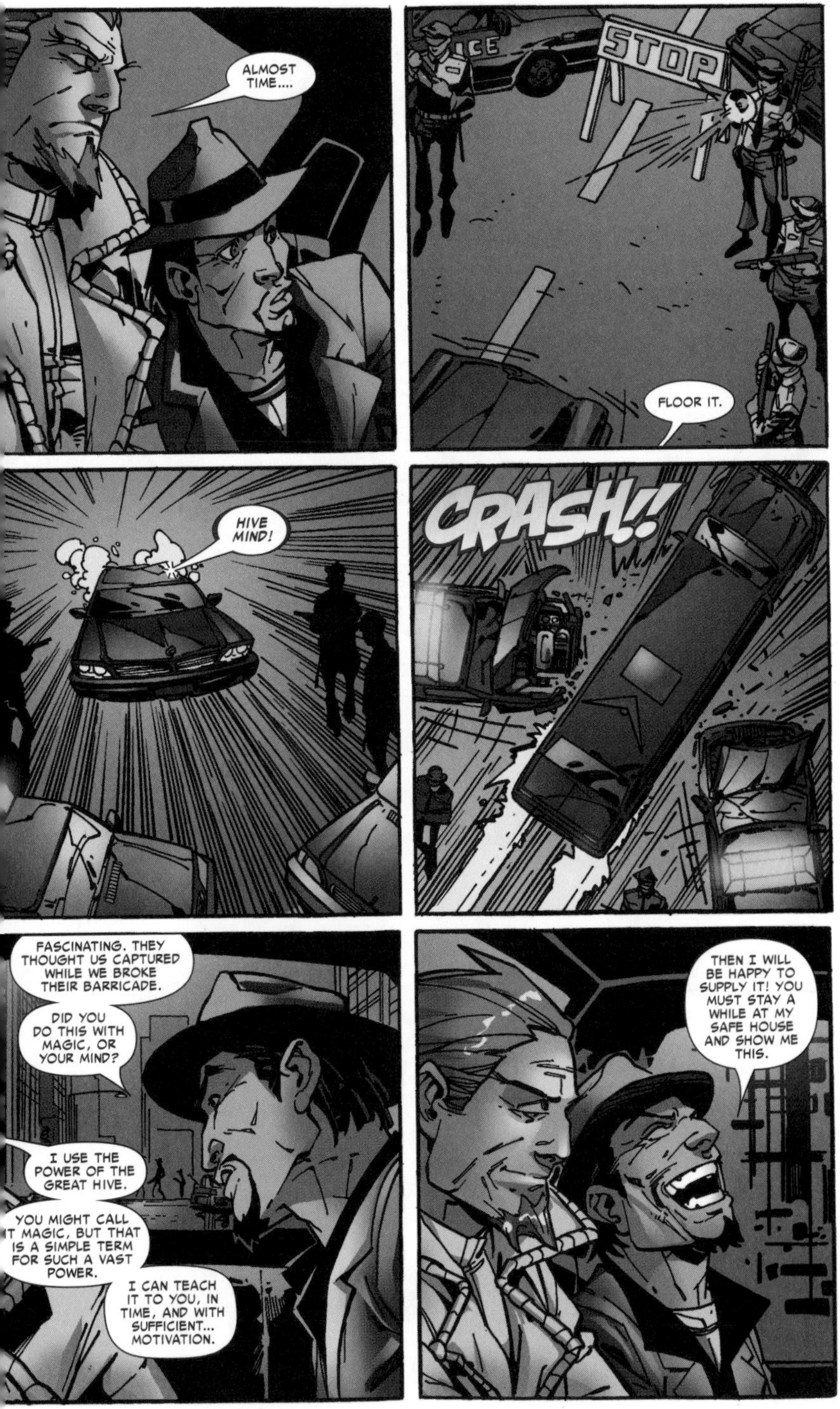
ALMOST TIME....
FLOOR IT.
HIVE MIND!
CRASH!!
FASCINATING. THEY THOUGHT US CAPTURED WHILE WE BROKE THEIR BARRICADE.
DID YOU DO THIS WITH MAGIC, OR YOUR MIND?
I USE THE POWER OF THE GREAT HIVE.
YOU MIGHT CALL IT MAGIC, BUT THAT IS A SIMPLE TERM FOR SUCH A VAST POWER.
I CAN TEACH IT TO YOU, IN TIME, AND WITH SUFFICIENT... MOTIVATION.
THEN I WILL BE HAPPY TO SUPPLY IT! YOU MUST STAY A WHILE AT MY SAFE HOUSE AND SHOW ME THIS.

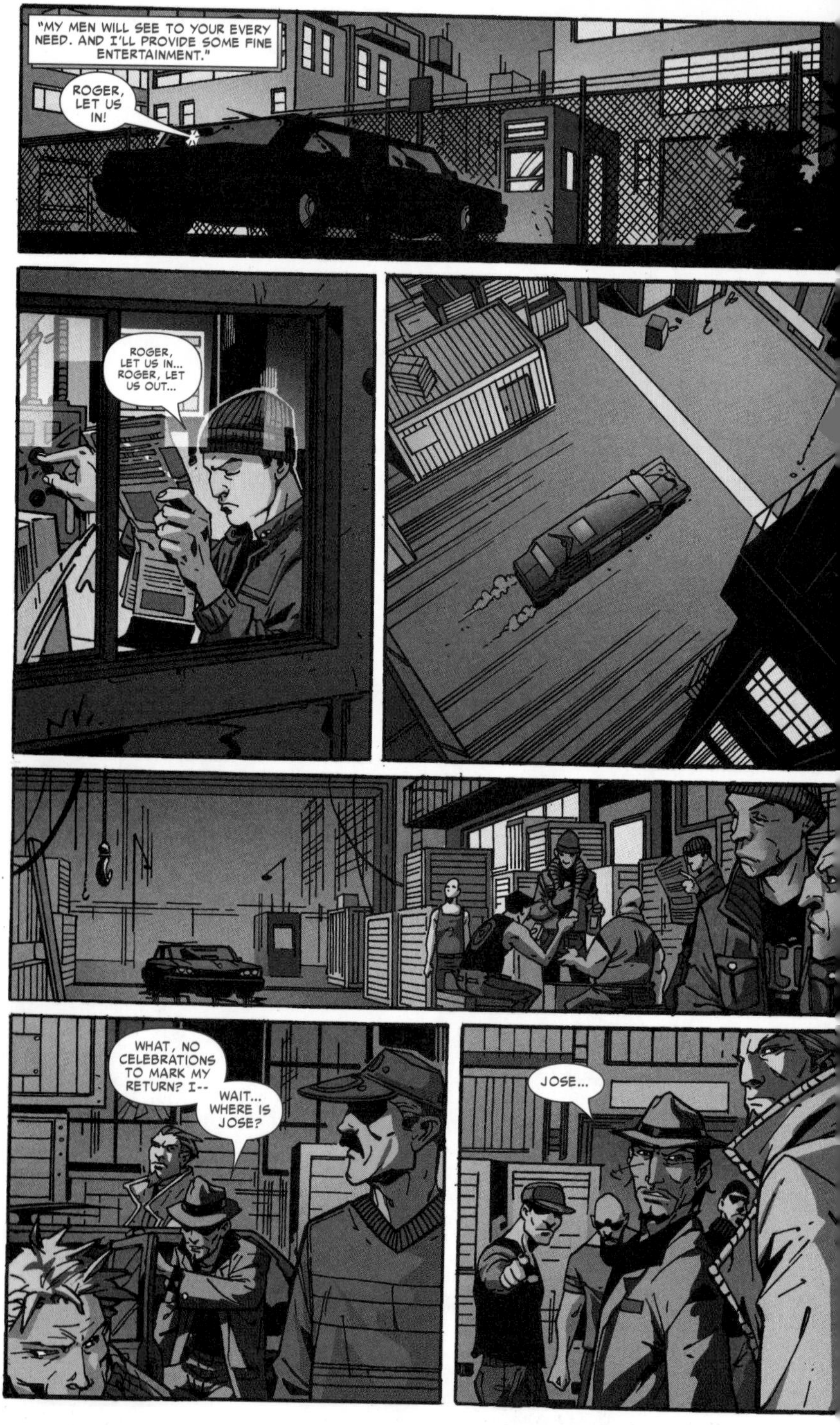
"MY MEN WILL SEE TO YOUR EVERY NEED. AND I'LL PROVIDE SOME FINE ENTERTAINMENT."
ROGER, LET US IN!
ROGER, LET US IN... ROGER, LET US OUT...
WHAT, NO CELEBRATIONS TO MARK MY RETURN? I--
WAIT... WHERE IS JOSE?
JOSE...

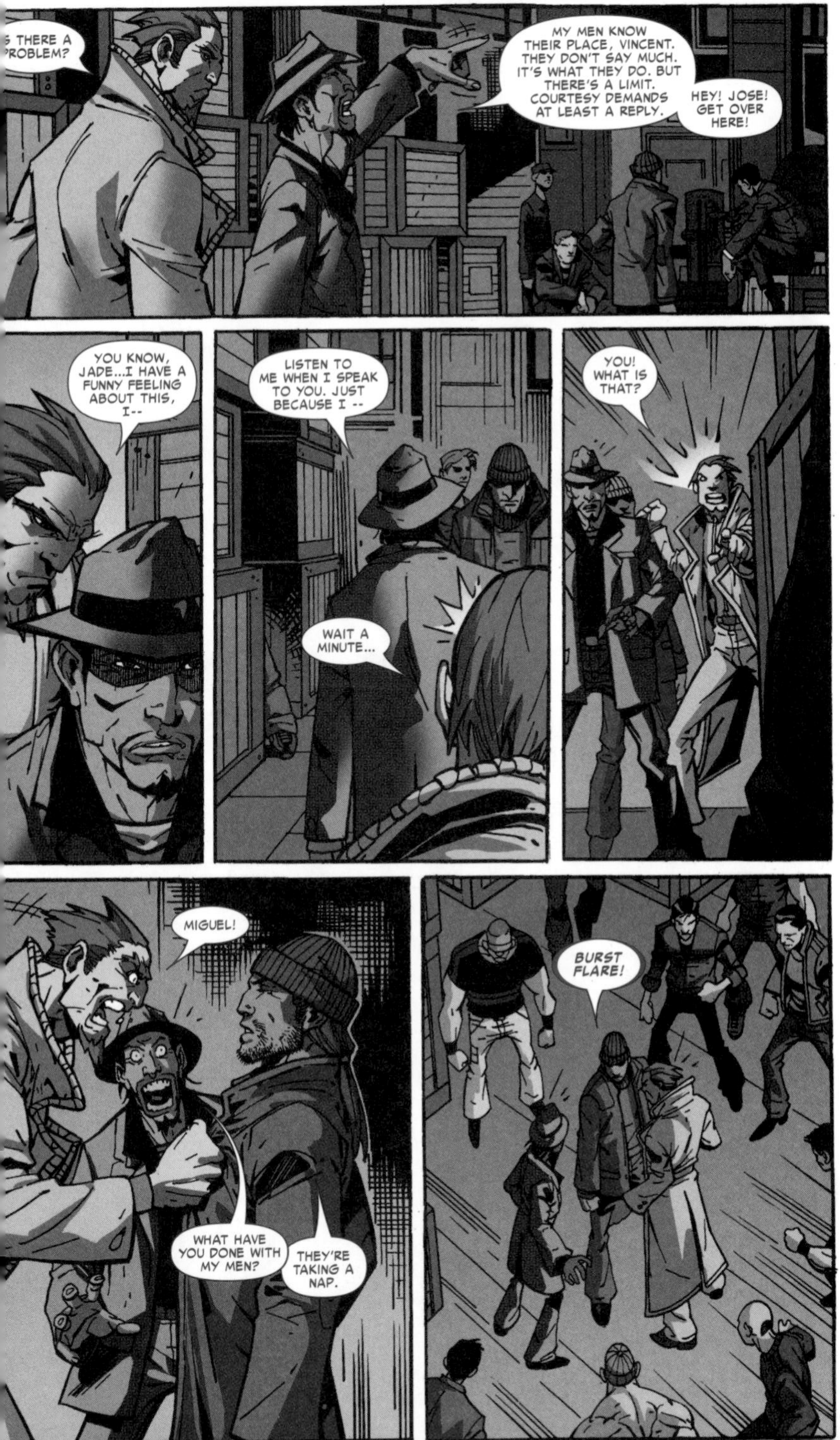
S THERE A PROBLEM?
MY MEN KNOW THEIR PLACE, VINCENT. THEY DON'T SAY MUCH. IT'S WHAT THEY DO. BUT THERE'S A LIMIT. COURTESY DEMANDS AT LEAST A REPLY.
HEY! JOSE! GET OVER HERE!
YOU KNOW, JADE...I HAVE A FUNNY FEELING ABOUT THIS, I--
LISTEN TO ME WHEN I SPEAK TO YOU. JUST BECAUSE I --
WAIT A MINUTE...
YOU! WHAT IS THAT?
MIGUEL!
WHAT HAVE YOU DONE WITH MY MEN?
THEY'RE TAKING A NAP.
BURST FLARE!

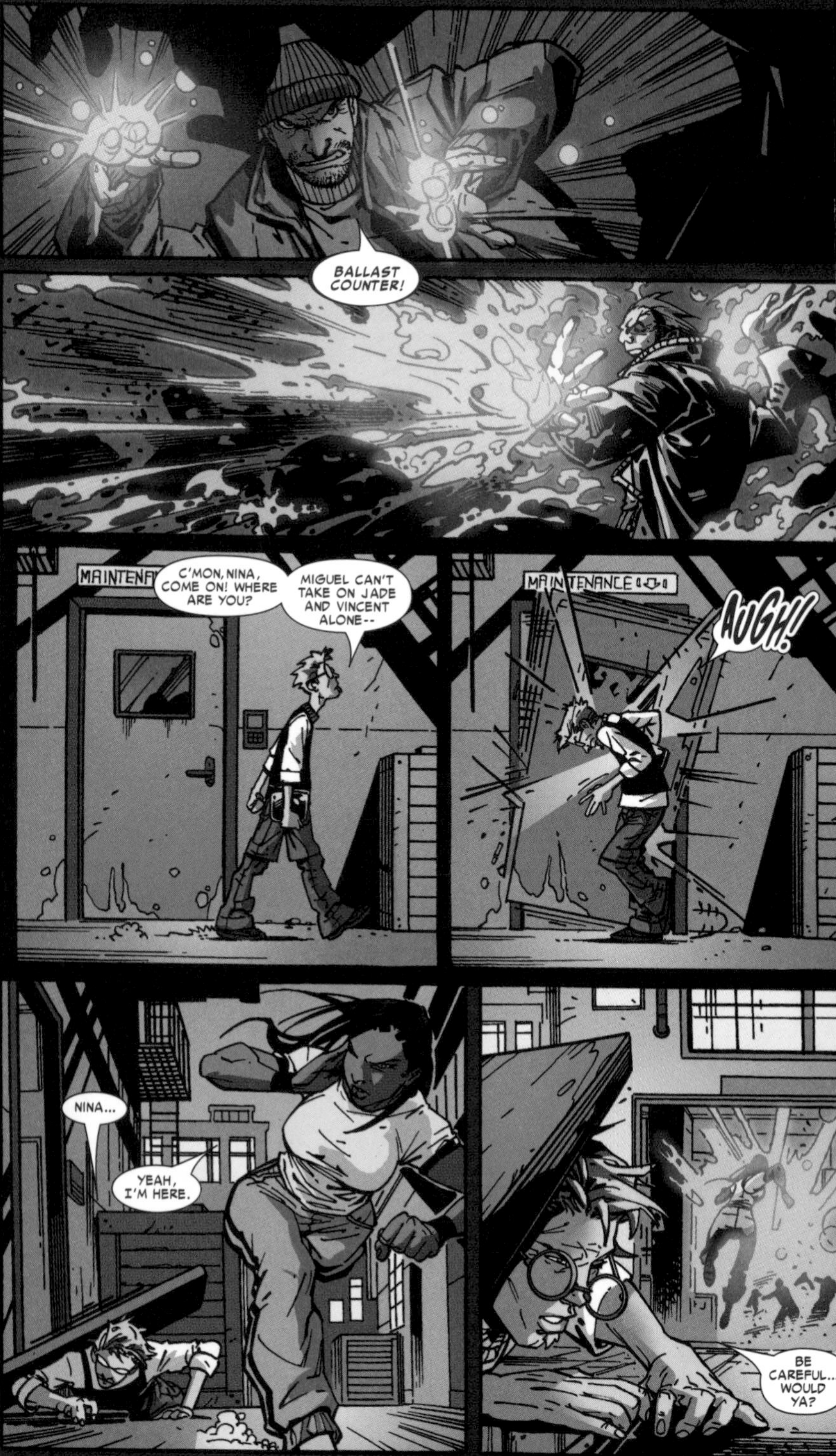
BALLAST COUNTER!
MAINTENANCE
C'MON, NINA, COME ON! WHERE ARE YOU?
MIGUEL CAN'T TAKE ON JADE AND VINCENT ALONE--
MAINTENANCE
AUGH!
NINA...
YEAH, I'M HERE.
BE CAREFUL... WOULD YA?

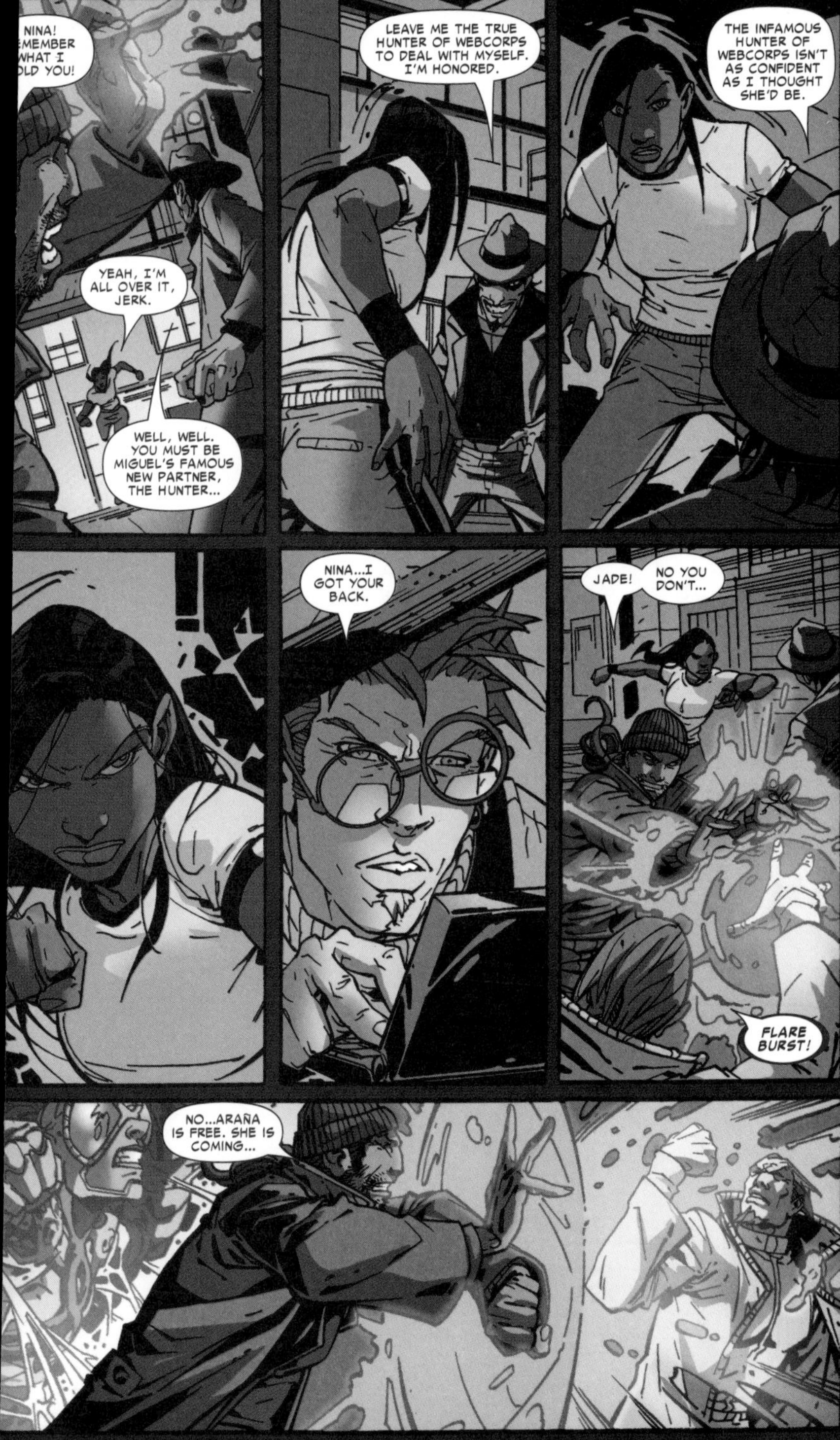
NINA! REMEMBER WHAT I TOLD YOU!
YEAH, I'M ALL OVER IT, JERK.
WELL, WELL. YOU MUST BE MIGUEL'S FAMOUS NEW PARTNER, THE HUNTER...
LEAVE ME THE TRUE HUNTER OF WEBCORPS TO DEAL WITH MYSELF. I'M HONORED.
THE INFAMOUS HUNTER OF WEBCORPS ISN'T AS CONFIDENT AS I THOUGHT SHE'D BE.
NINA...I GOT YOUR BACK.
JADE!
NO YOU DON'T...
FLARE BURST!
NO...ARAÑA IS FREE. SHE IS COMING...

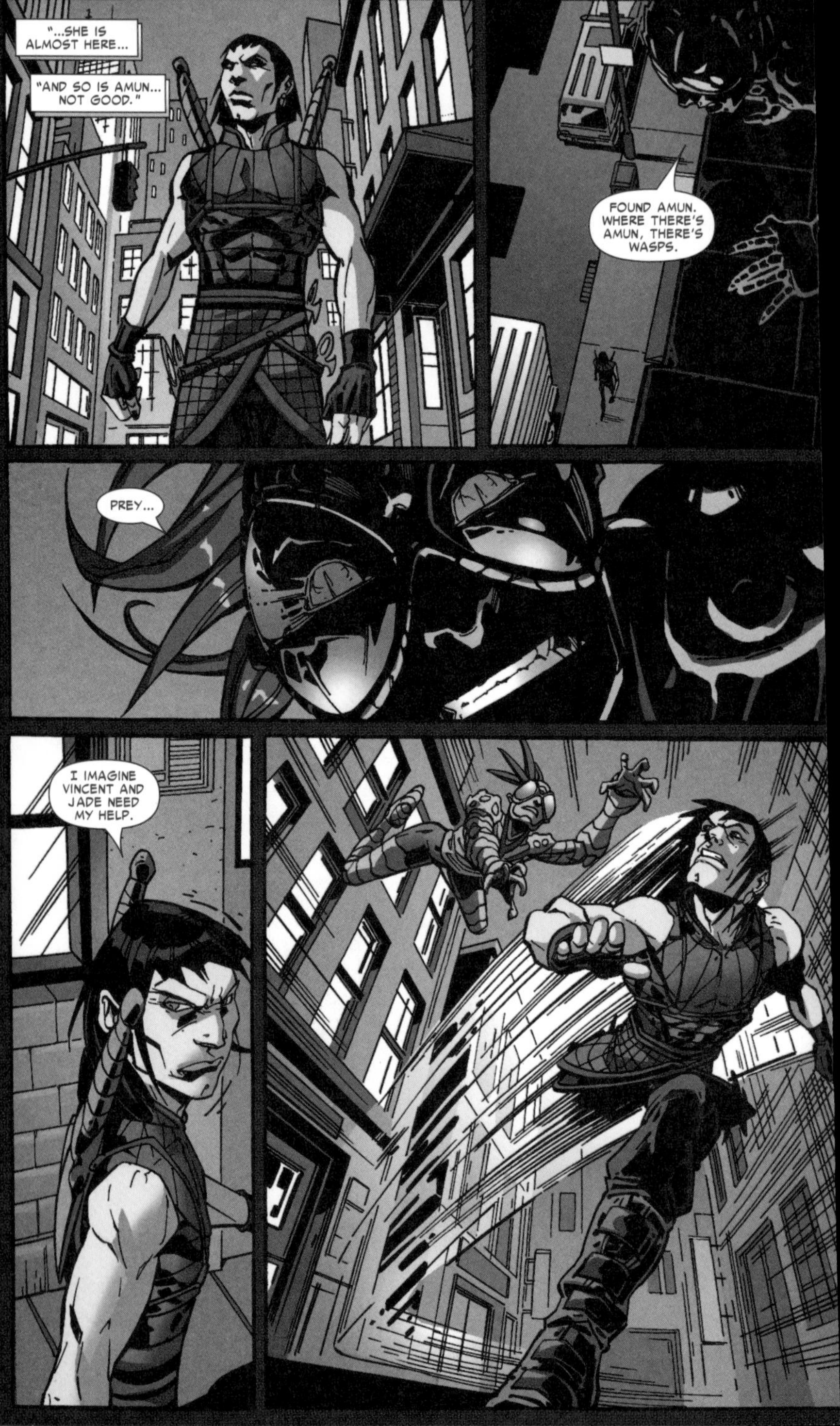
"...SHE IS ALMOST HERE...
"AND SO IS AMUN... NOT GOOD."
FOUND AMUN. WHERE THERE'S AMUN, THERE'S WASPS.
PREY...
I IMAGINE VINCENT AND JADE NEED MY HELP.

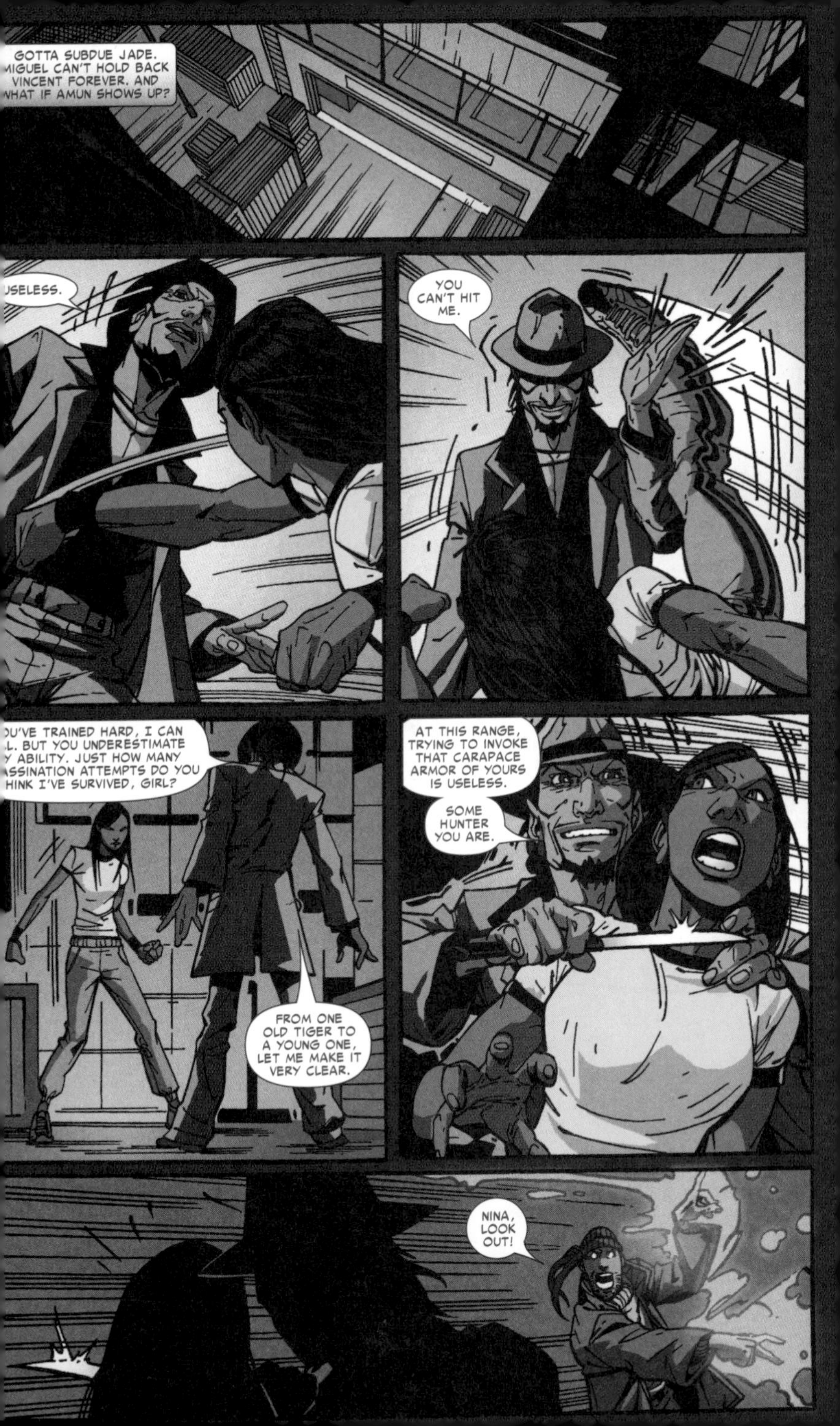
GOTTA SUBDUE JADE. MIGUEL CAN'T HOLD BACK VINCENT FOREVER. AND WHAT IF AMUN SHOWS UP?
USELESS.
YOU CAN'T HIT ME.
OU'VE TRAINED HARD, I CAN L. BUT YOU UNDERESTIMATE Y ABILITY. JUST HOW MANY SSINATION ATTEMPTS DO YOU HINK I'VE SURVIVED, GIRL?
FROM ONE OLD TIGER TO A YOUNG ONE, LET ME MAKE IT VERY CLEAR.
AT THIS RANGE, TRYING TO INVOKE THAT CARAPACE ARMOR OF YOURS IS USELESS.
SOME HUNTER YOU ARE.
NINA, LOOK OUT!

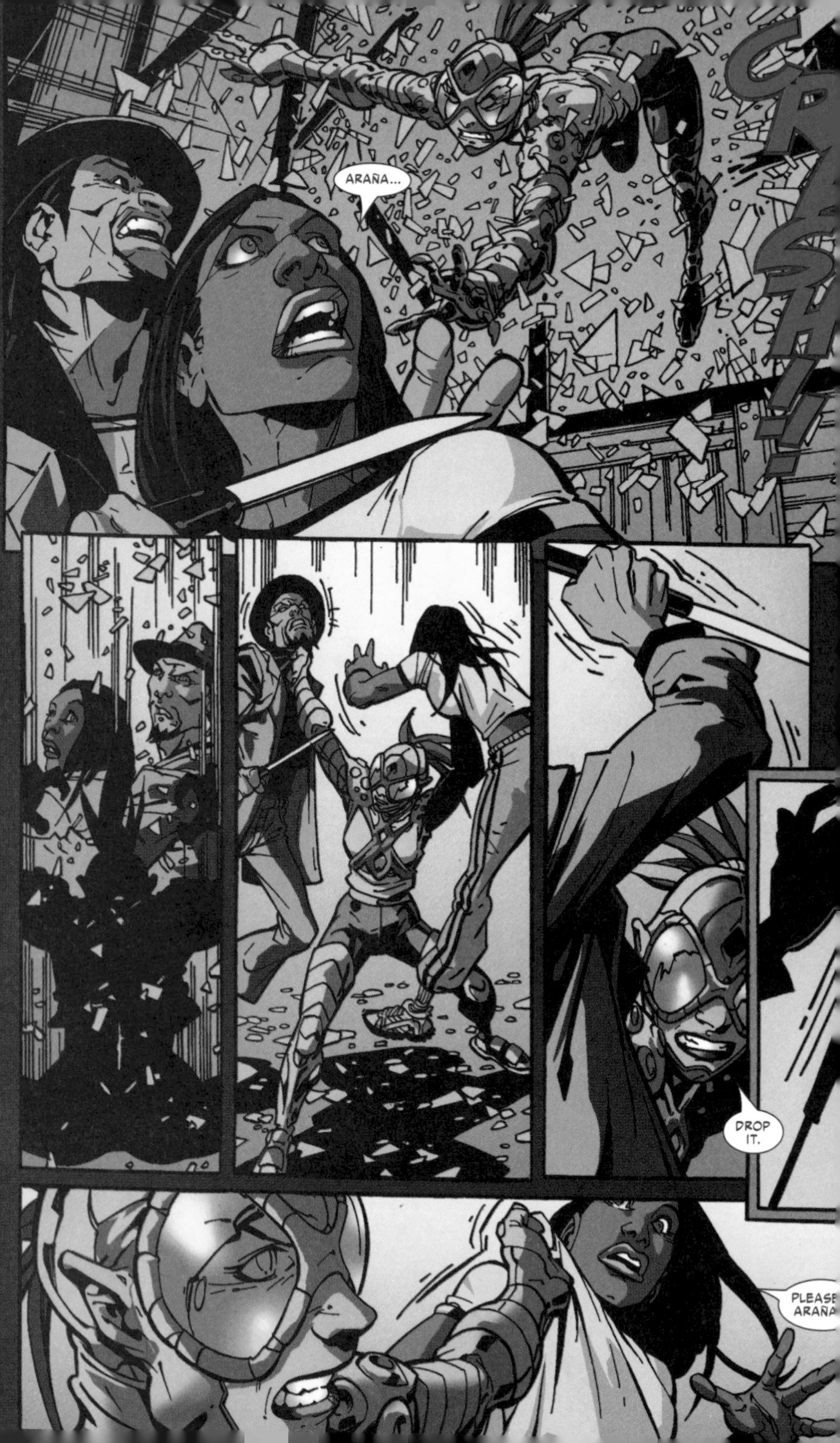

CRASH!!
ARAÑA...
DROP IT.
PLEASE ARAÑA

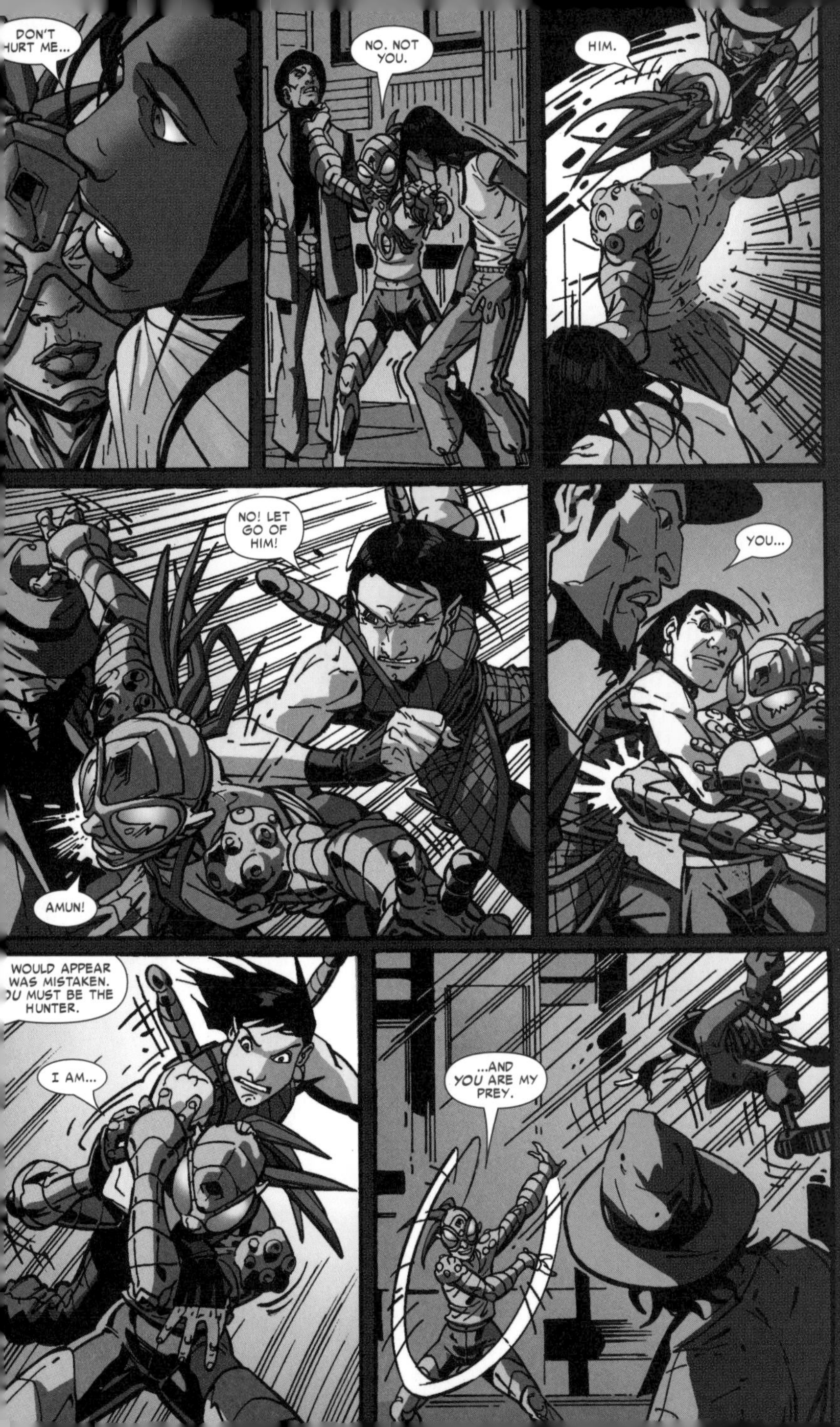
DON'T
HURT ME...
NO. NOT
YOU.
HIM.
NO! LET
GO OF
HIM!
AMUN!
YOU...
WOULD APPEAR
WAS MISTAKEN.
OU MUST BE THE
HUNTER.
I AM...
...AND
YOU ARE MY
PREY.

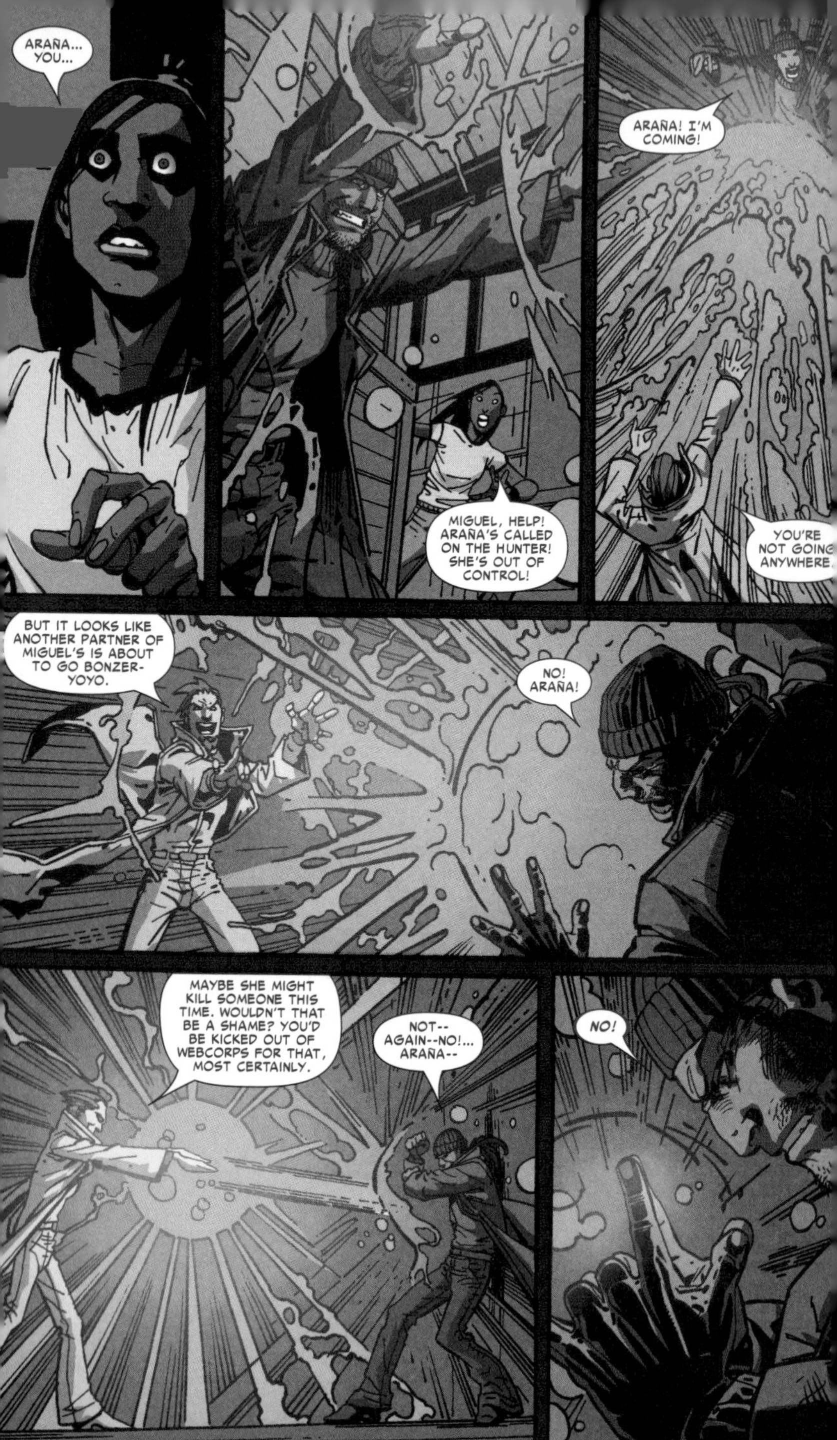
ARAÑA... YOU...
MIGUEL, HELP! ARAÑA'S CALLED ON THE HUNTER! SHE'S OUT OF CONTROL!
ARAÑA! I'M COMING!
YOU'RE NOT GOING ANYWHERE.
BUT IT LOOKS LIKE ANOTHER PARTNER OF MIGUEL'S IS ABOUT TO GO BONZER-YOYO.
NO! ARAÑA!
MAYBE SHE MIGHT KILL SOMEONE THIS TIME. WOULDN'T THAT BE A SHAME? YOU'D BE KICKED OUT OF WEBCORPS FOR THAT, MOST CERTAINLY.
NOT-- AGAIN--NO!... ARAÑA--
NO!

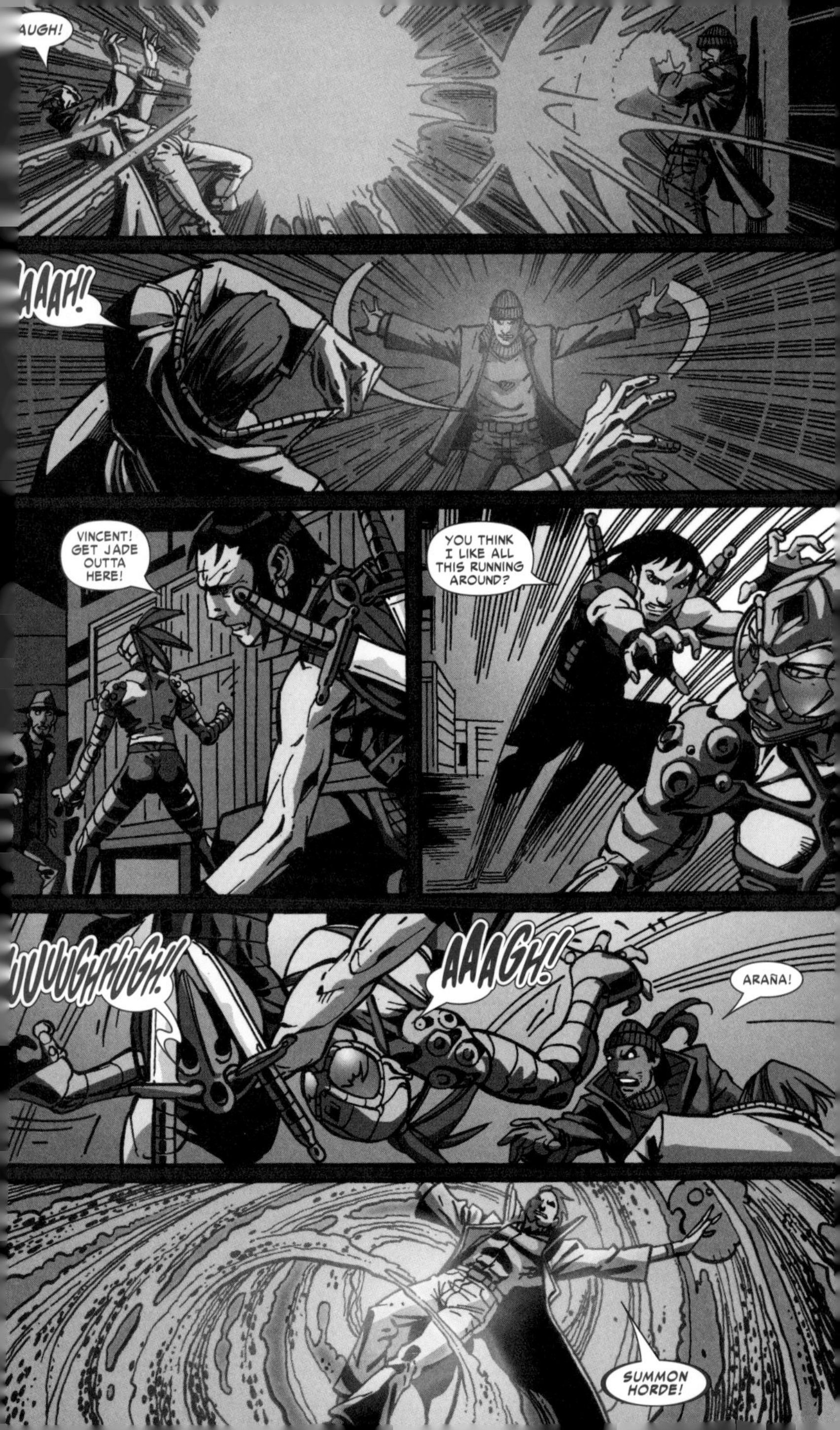
AUGH!
AAAH!
VINCENT! GET JADE OUTTA HERE!
YOU THINK I LIKE ALL THIS RUNNING AROUND?
AAAGH!
ARAÑA!
SUMMON HORDE!

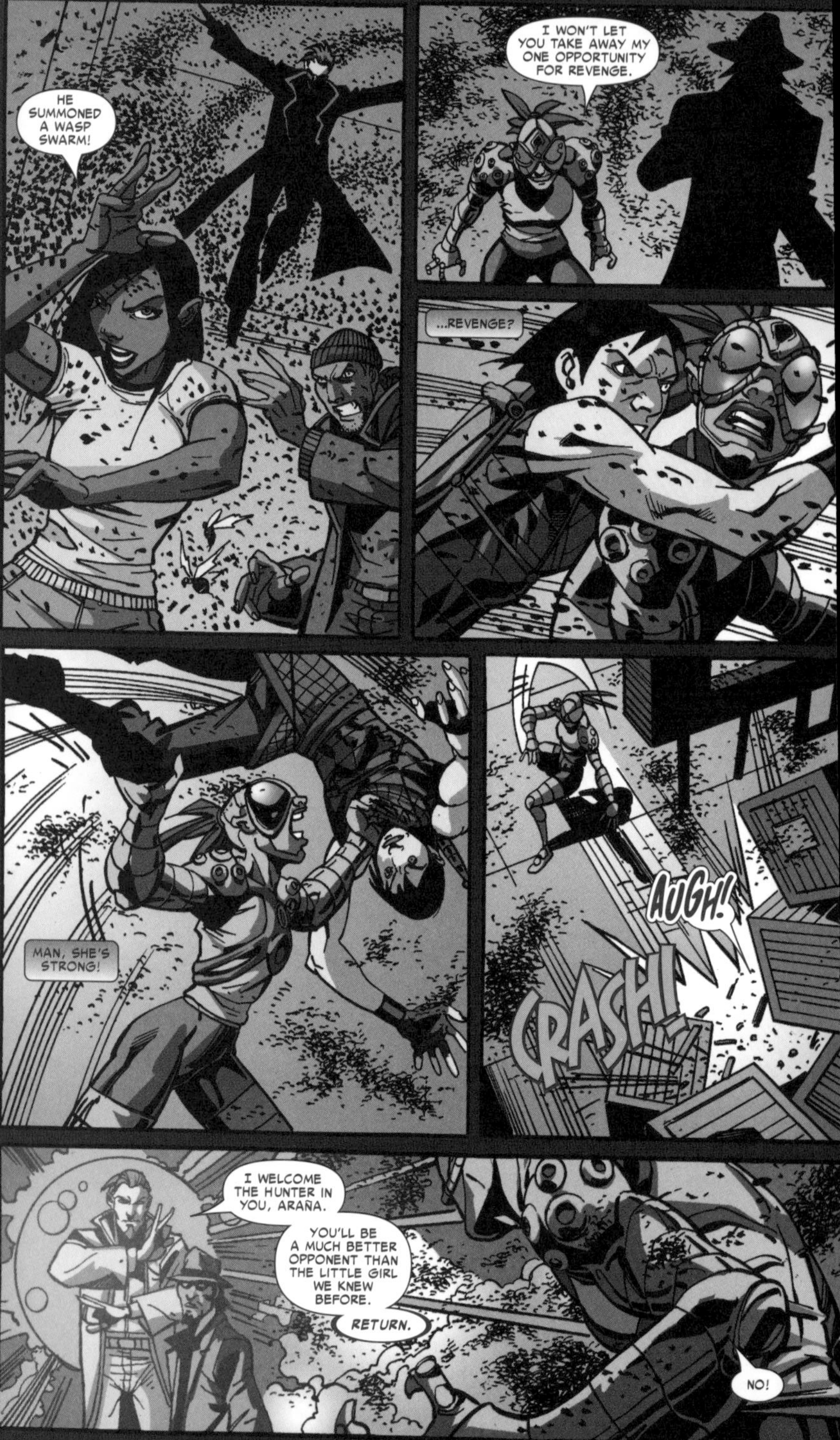
HE SUMMONED A WASP SWARM!
I WON'T LET YOU TAKE AWAY MY ONE OPPORTUNITY FOR REVENGE.
...REVENGE?
MAN, SHE'S STRONG!
AUGH!
CRASH!
I WELCOME THE HUNTER IN YOU, ARAÑA.
YOU'LL BE A MUCH BETTER OPPONENT THAN THE LITTLE GIRL WE KNEW BEFORE.
RETURN.
NO!

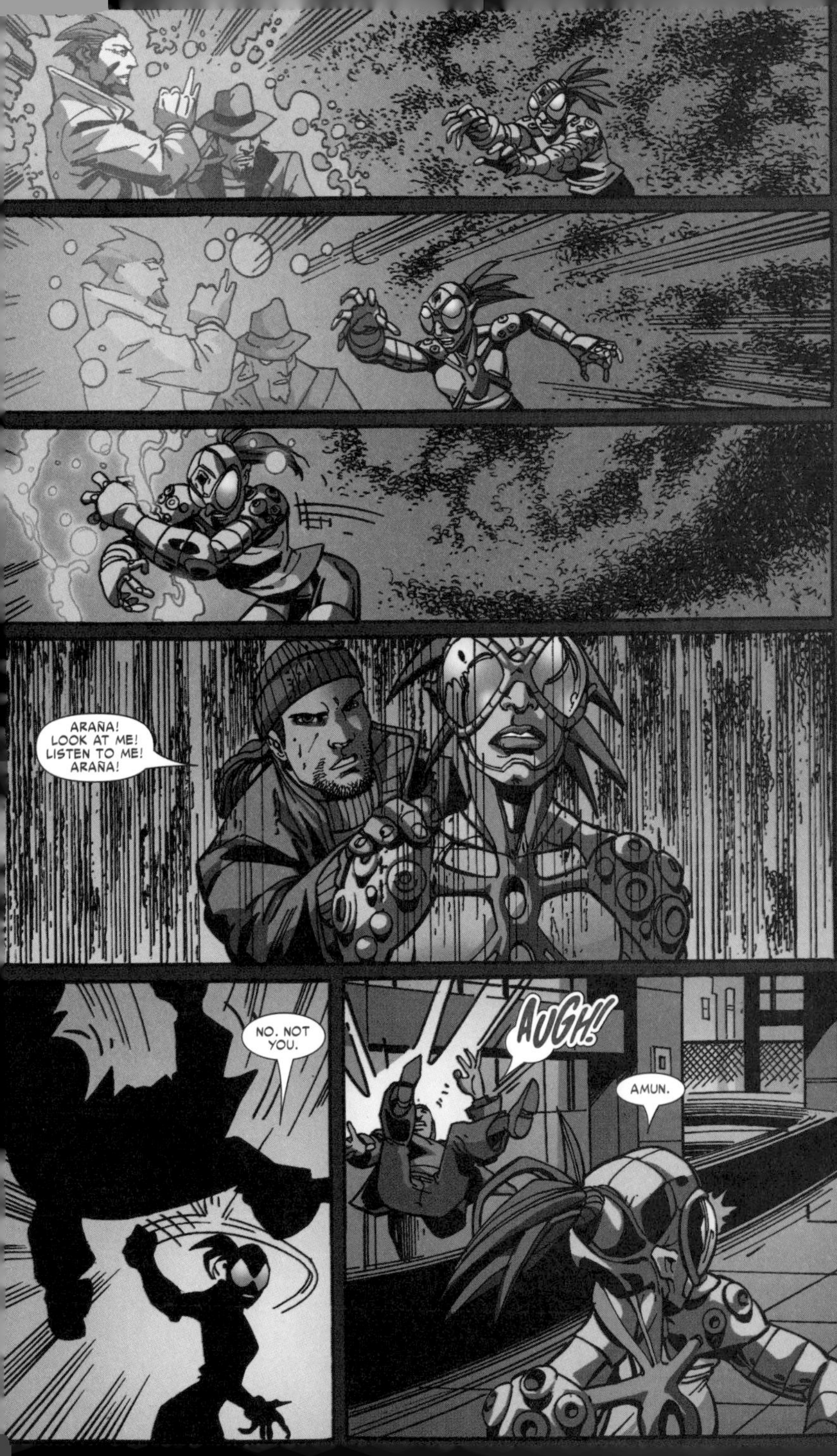
ARAÑA! LOOK AT ME! LISTEN TO ME! ARAÑA!
NO. NOT YOU.
AUGH!
AMUN.

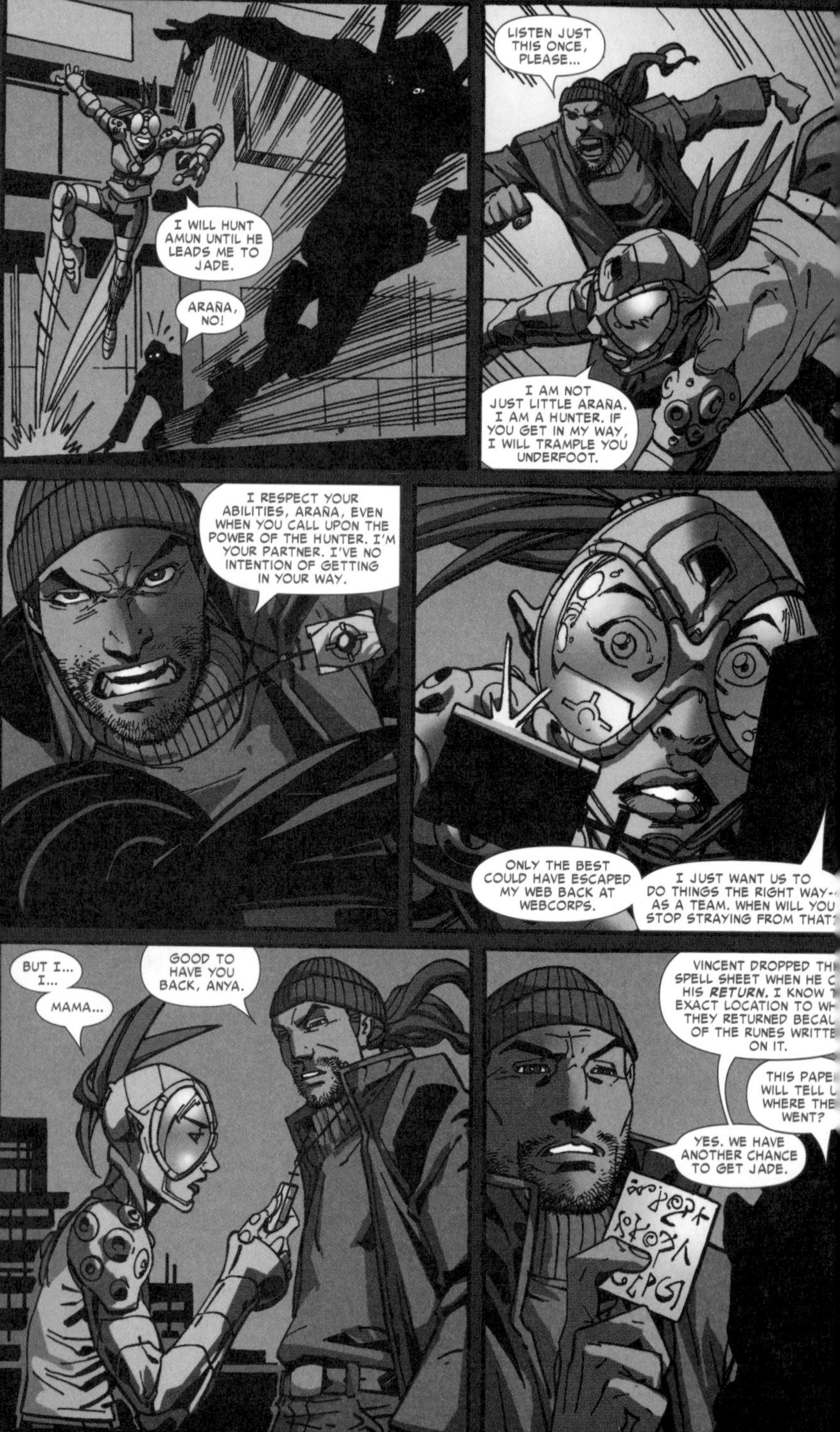
I WILL HUNT AMUN UNTIL HE LEADS ME TO JADE.
ARAÑA, NO!
LISTEN JUST THIS ONCE, PLEASE...
I AM NOT JUST LITTLE ARAÑA. I AM A HUNTER. IF YOU GET IN MY WAY, I WILL TRAMPLE YOU UNDERFOOT.
I RESPECT YOUR ABILITIES, ARAÑA, EVEN WHEN YOU CALL UPON THE POWER OF THE HUNTER. I'M YOUR PARTNER. I'VE NO INTENTION OF GETTING IN YOUR WAY.
ONLY THE BEST COULD HAVE ESCAPED MY WEB BACK AT WEBCORPS.
I JUST WANT US TO DO THINGS THE RIGHT WAY-- AS A TEAM. WHEN WILL YOU STOP STRAYING FROM THAT?
BUT I... I...
GOOD TO HAVE YOU BACK, ANYA.
MAMA...
VINCENT DROPPED TH SPELL SHEET WHEN HE C HIS *RETURN.* I KNOW T EXACT LOCATION TO WH THEY RETURNED BECAU OF THE RUNES WRITTE ON IT.
THIS PAPE WILL TELL U WHERE THE WENT?
YES. WE HAVE ANOTHER CHANCE TO GET JADE.

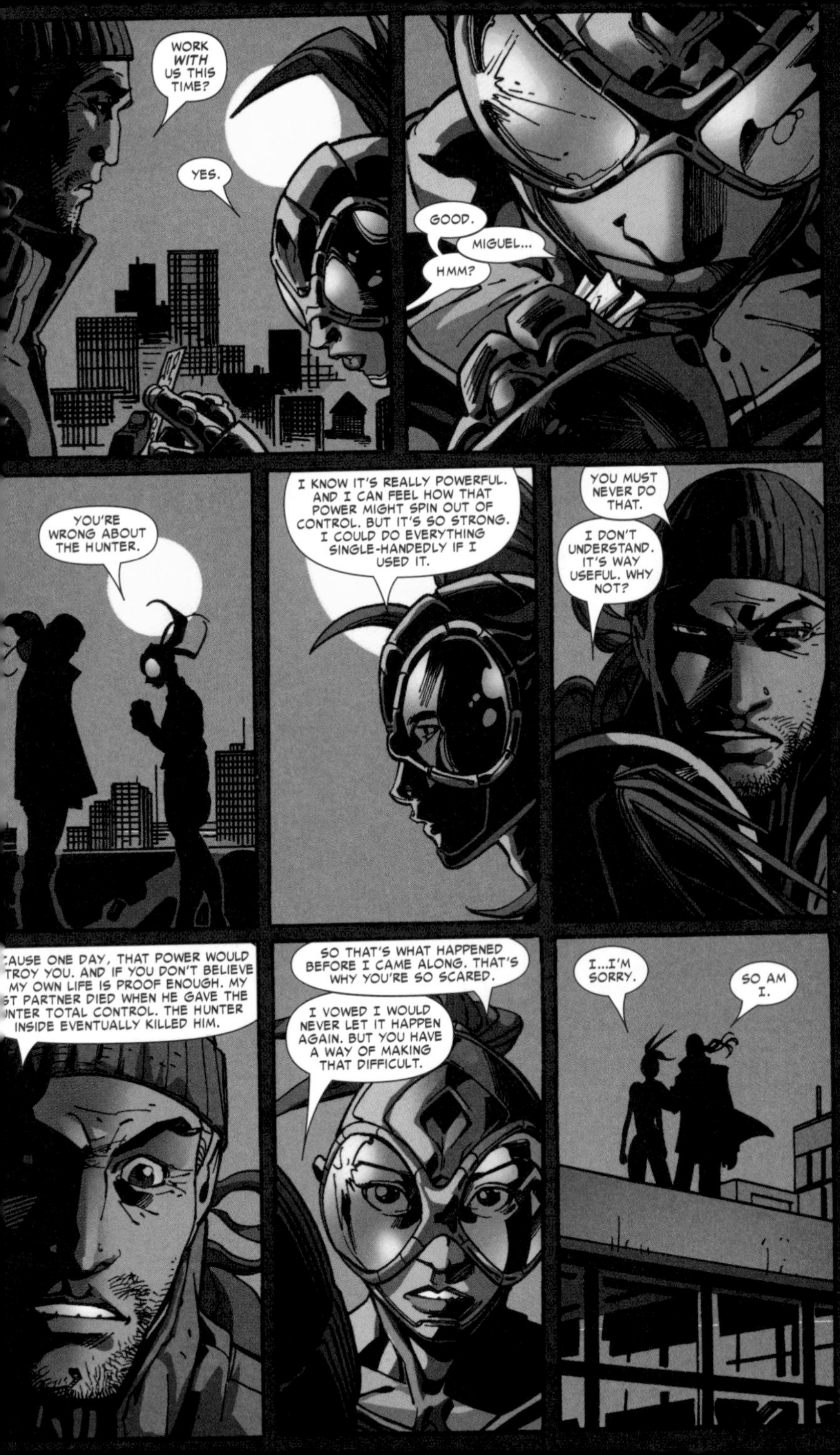

WORK WITH US THIS TIME?
YES.
GOOD.
MIGUEL...
HMM?
YOU'RE WRONG ABOUT THE HUNTER.
I KNOW IT'S REALLY POWERFUL. AND I CAN FEEL HOW THAT POWER MIGHT SPIN OUT OF CONTROL. BUT IT'S SO STRONG. I COULD DO EVERYTHING SINGLE-HANDEDLY IF I USED IT.
YOU MUST NEVER DO THAT.
I DON'T UNDERSTAND. IT'S WAY USEFUL. WHY NOT?
CAUSE ONE DAY, THAT POWER WOULD TROY YOU. AND IF YOU DON'T BELIEVE MY OWN LIFE IS PROOF ENOUGH. MY ST PARTNER DIED WHEN HE GAVE THE UNTER TOTAL CONTROL. THE HUNTER INSIDE EVENTUALLY KILLED HIM.
SO THAT'S WHAT HAPPENED BEFORE I CAME ALONG. THAT'S WHY YOU'RE SO SCARED.
I VOWED I WOULD NEVER LET IT HAPPEN AGAIN. BUT YOU HAVE A WAY OF MAKING THAT DIFFICULT.
I...I'M SORRY.
SO AM I.

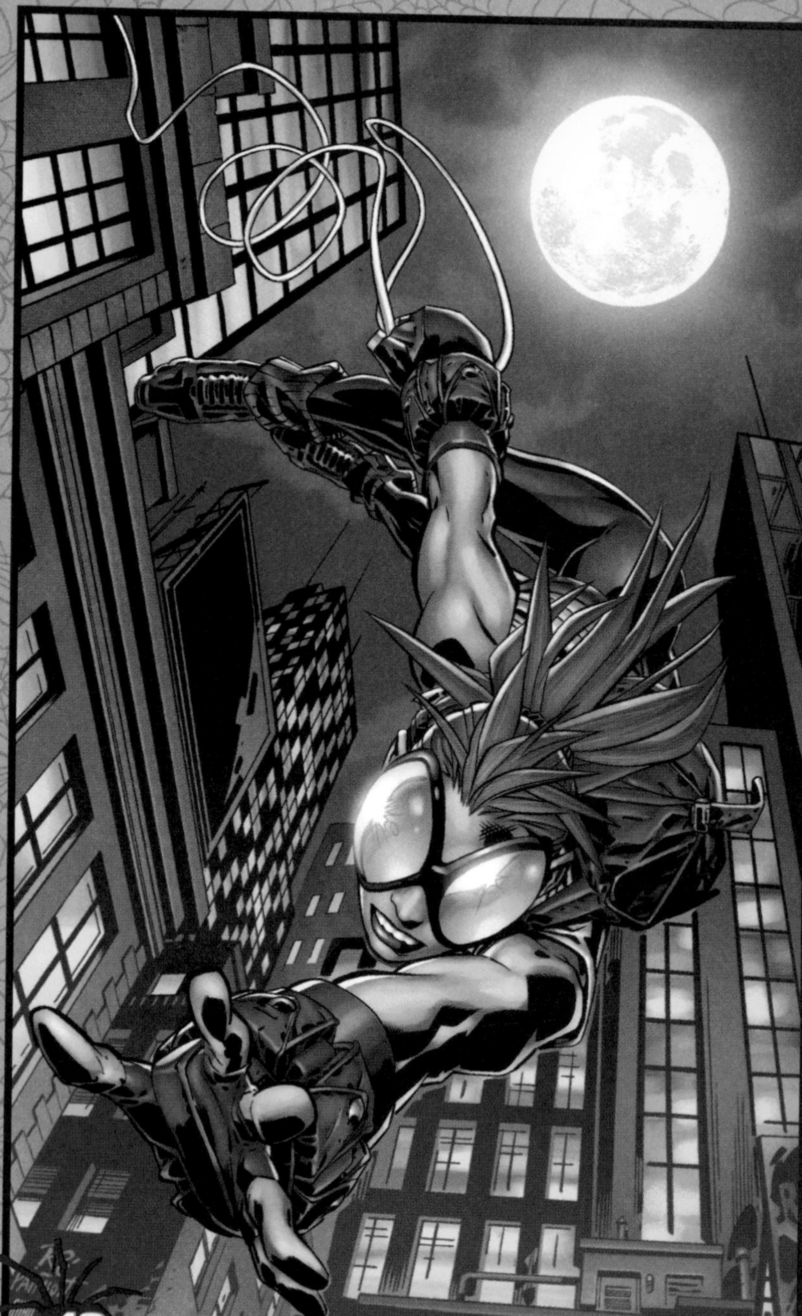

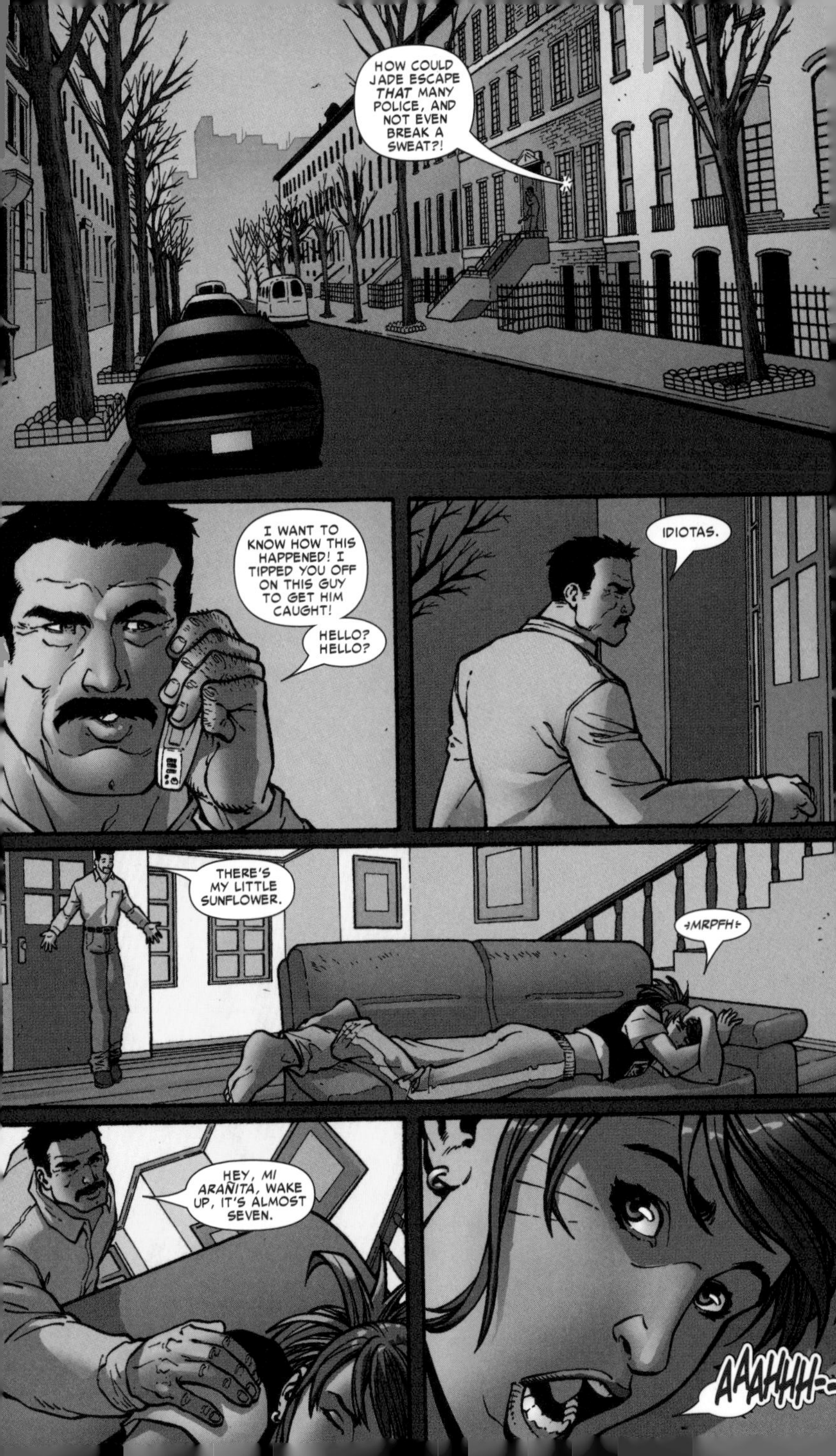
HOW COULD JADE ESCAPE THAT MANY POLICE, AND NOT EVEN BREAK A SWEAT?!
I WANT TO KNOW HOW THIS HAPPENED! I TIPPED YOU OFF ON THIS GUY TO GET HIM CAUGHT!
HELLO? HELLO?
IDIOTAS.
THERE'S MY LITTLE SUNFLOWER.
MRPFH
HEY, MI ARAÑITA, WAKE UP, IT'S ALMOST SEVEN.
AAAHHH-

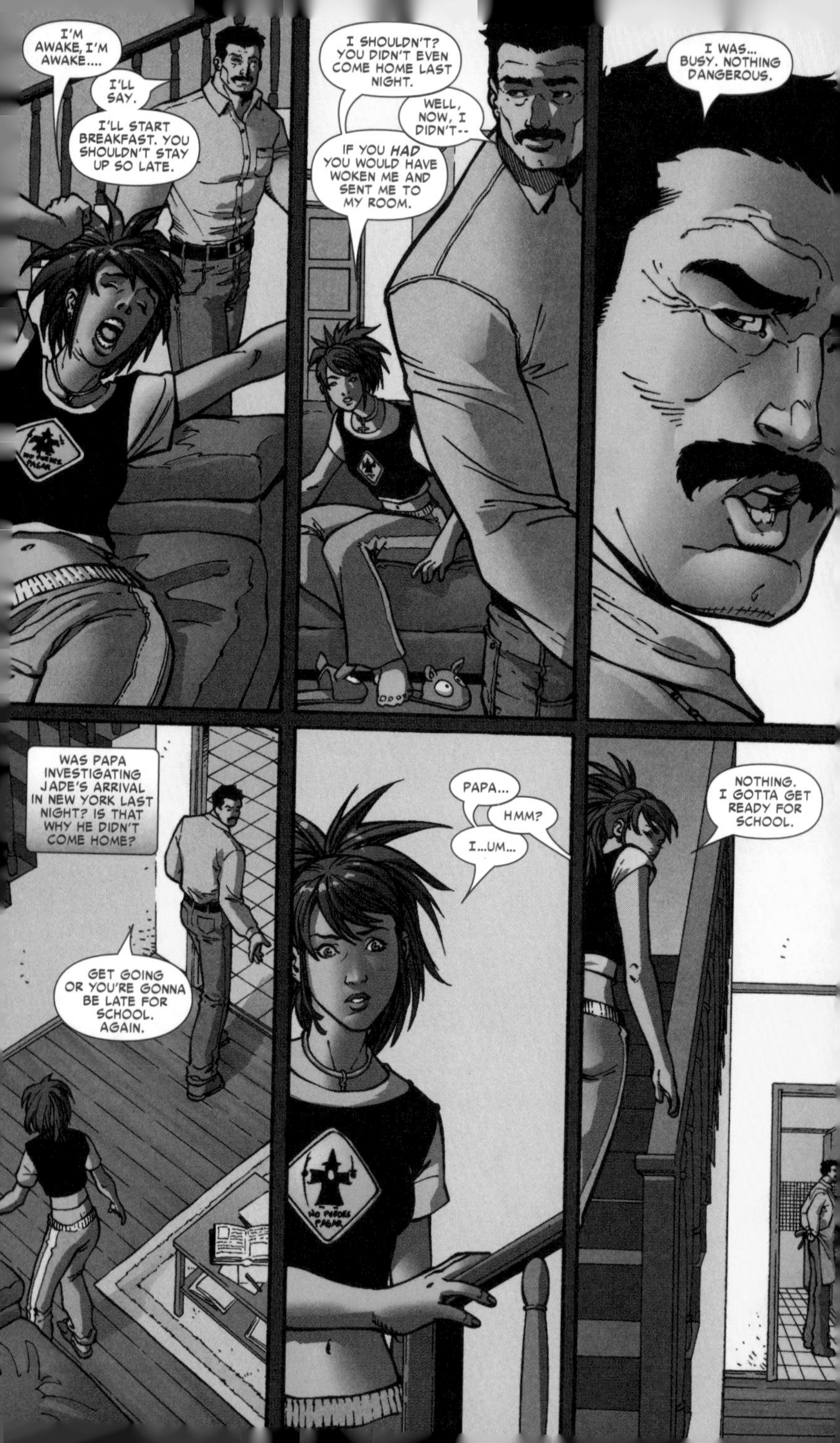
I'M AWAKE, I'M AWAKE....
I'LL SAY.
I'LL START BREAKFAST. YOU SHOULDN'T STAY UP SO LATE.
I SHOULDN'T? YOU DIDN'T EVEN COME HOME LAST NIGHT.
WELL, NOW, I DIDN'T--
IF YOU HAD YOU WOULD HAVE WOKEN ME AND SENT ME TO MY ROOM.
I WAS... BUSY. NOTHING DANGEROUS.
WAS PAPA INVESTIGATING JADE'S ARRIVAL IN NEW YORK LAST NIGHT? IS THAT WHY HE DIDN'T COME HOME?
GET GOING OR YOU'RE GONNA BE LATE FOR SCHOOL. AGAIN.
PAPA...
HMM?
I...UM...
NOTHING. I GOTTA GET READY FOR SCHOOL.

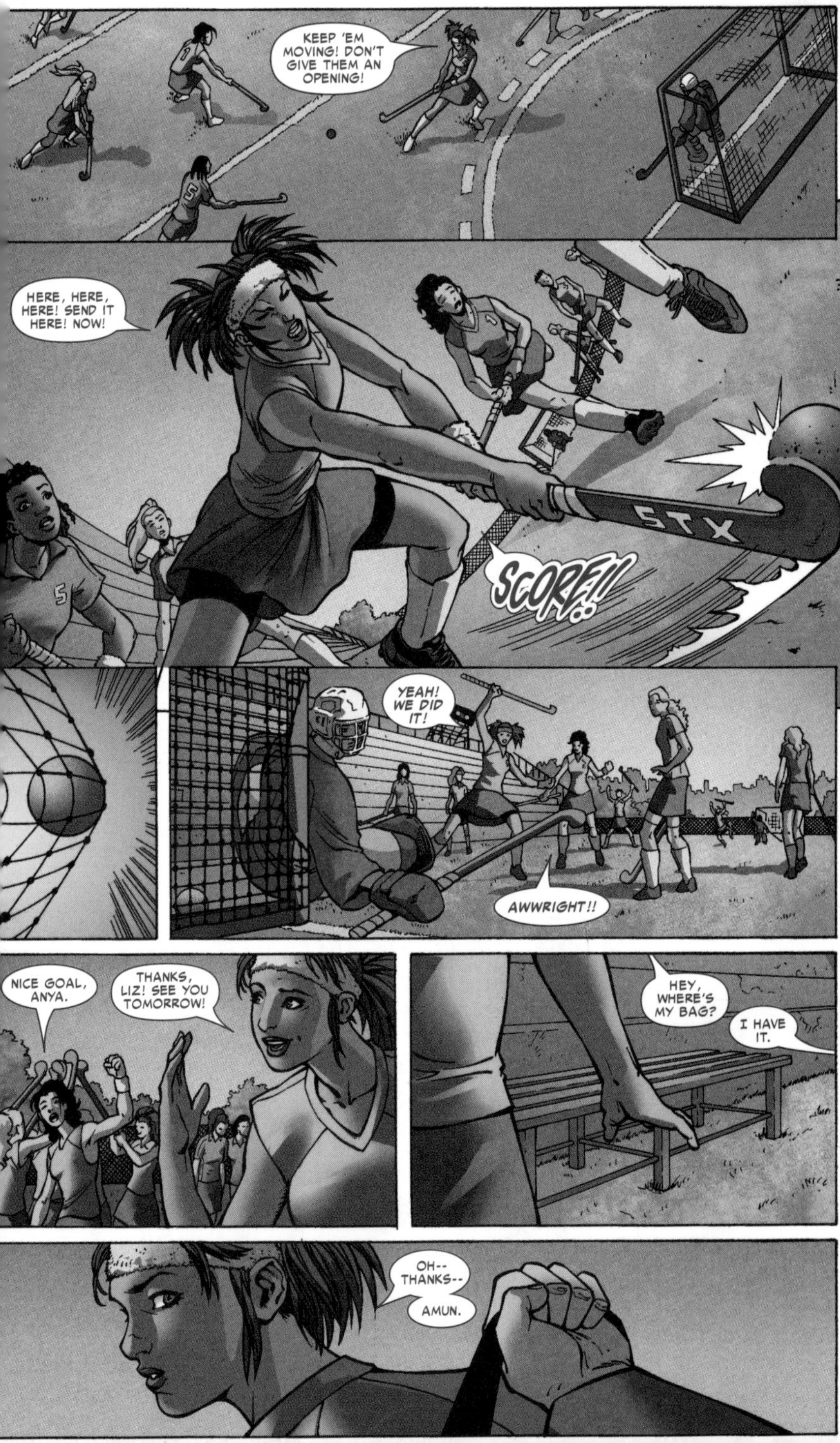
KEEP 'EM MOVING! DON'T GIVE THEM AN OPENING!
HERE, HERE, HERE! SEND IT HERE! NOW!
STX
SCORE!!
YEAH! WE DID IT!
AWWRIGHT!!
NICE GOAL, ANYA.
THANKS, LIZ! SEE YOU TOMORROW!
HEY, WHERE'S MY BAG?
I HAVE IT.
OH-- THANKS--
AMUN.

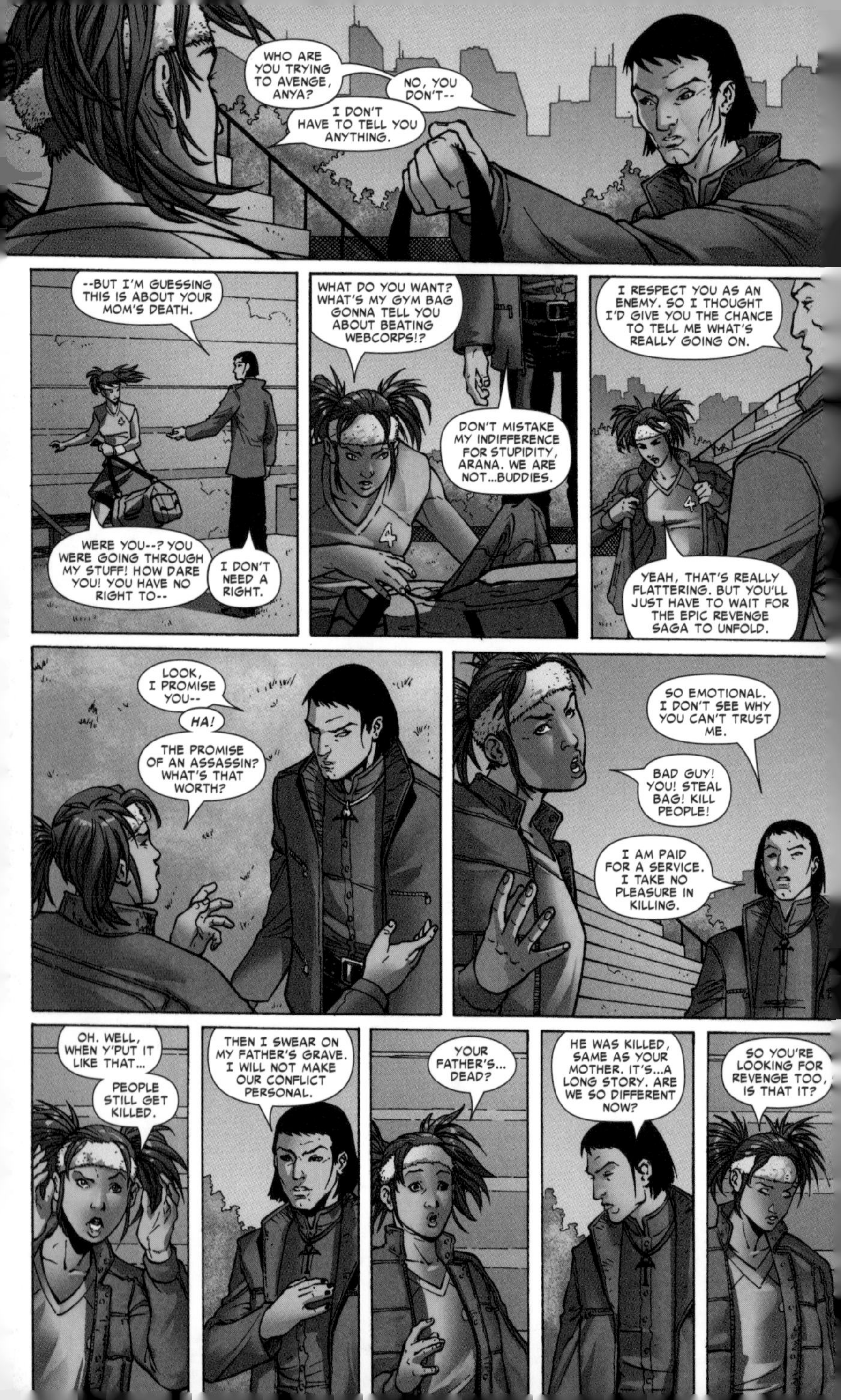
WHO ARE YOU TRYING TO AVENGE, ANYA?
NO, YOU DON'T--
I DON'T HAVE TO TELL YOU ANYTHING.
--BUT I'M GUESSING THIS IS ABOUT YOUR MOM'S DEATH.
WERE YOU--? YOU WERE GOING THROUGH MY STUFF! HOW DARE YOU! YOU HAVE NO RIGHT TO--
I DON'T NEED A RIGHT.
WHAT DO YOU WANT? WHAT'S MY GYM BAG GONNA TELL YOU ABOUT BEATING WEBCORPS!?
DON'T MISTAKE MY INDIFFERENCE FOR STUPIDITY, ARANA. WE ARE NOT...BUDDIES.
I RESPECT YOU AS AN ENEMY. SO I THOUGHT I'D GIVE YOU THE CHANCE TO TELL ME WHAT'S REALLY GOING ON.
YEAH, THAT'S REALLY FLATTERING. BUT YOU'LL JUST HAVE TO WAIT FOR THE EPIC REVENGE SAGA TO UNFOLD.
LOOK, I PROMISE YOU--
HA!
THE PROMISE OF AN ASSASSIN? WHAT'S THAT WORTH?
SO EMOTIONAL. I DON'T SEE WHY YOU CAN'T TRUST ME.
BAD GUY! YOU! STEAL BAG! KILL PEOPLE!
I AM PAID FOR A SERVICE. I TAKE NO PLEASURE IN KILLING.
OH. WELL, WHEN Y'PUT IT LIKE THAT...
PEOPLE STILL GET KILLED.
THEN I SWEAR ON MY FATHER'S GRAVE. I WILL NOT MAKE OUR CONFLICT PERSONAL.
YOUR FATHER'S... DEAD?
HE WAS KILLED, SAME AS YOUR MOTHER. IT'S...A LONG STORY. ARE WE SO DIFFERENT NOW?
SO YOU'RE LOOKING FOR REVENGE TOO, IS THAT IT?

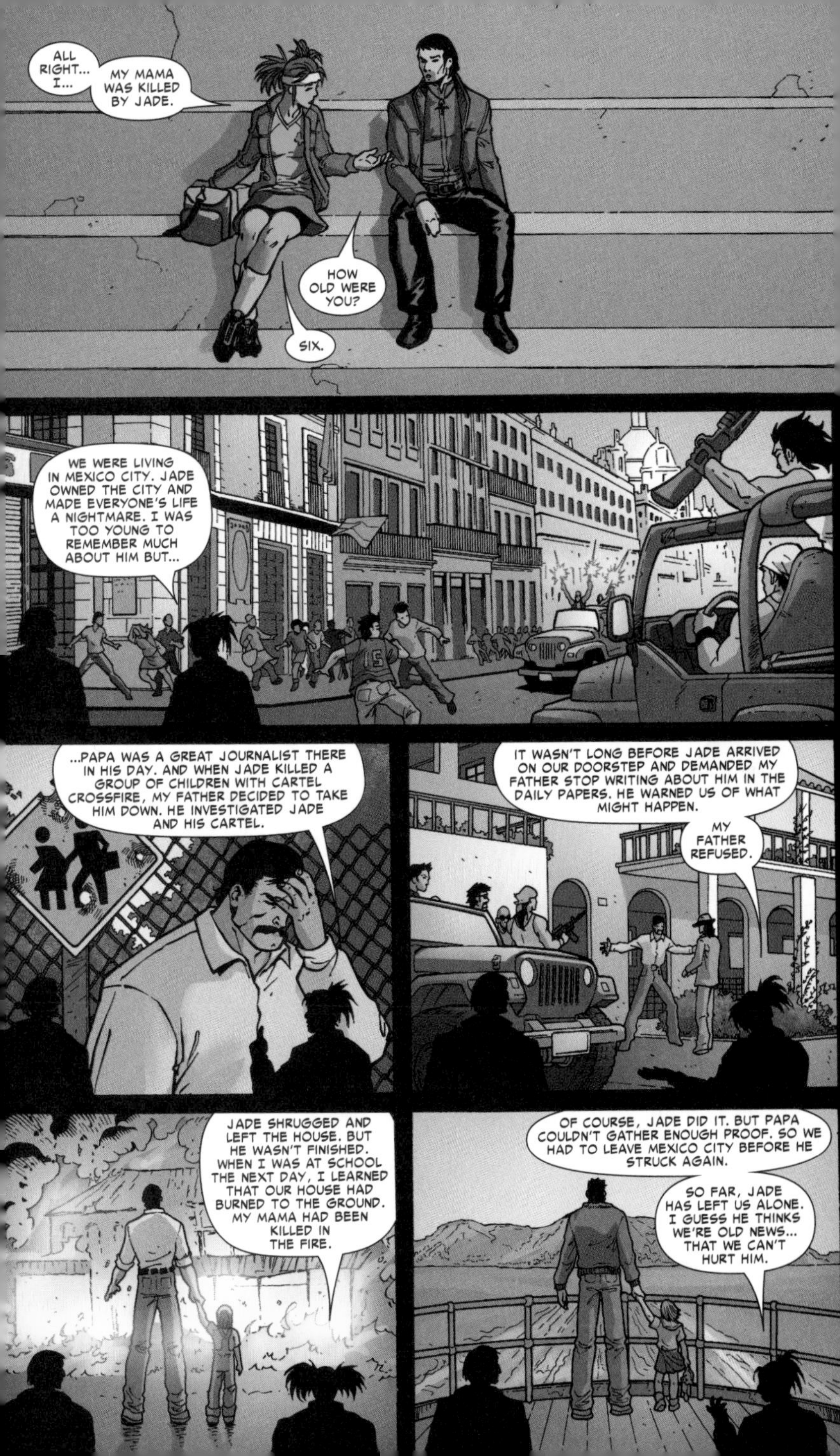

ALL RIGHT... I...
MY MAMA WAS KILLED BY JADE.
HOW OLD WERE YOU?
SIX.
WE WERE LIVING IN MEXICO CITY. JADE OWNED THE CITY AND MADE EVERYONE'S LIFE A NIGHTMARE. I WAS TOO YOUNG TO REMEMBER MUCH ABOUT HIM BUT...
...PAPA WAS A GREAT JOURNALIST THERE IN HIS DAY. AND WHEN JADE KILLED A GROUP OF CHILDREN WITH CARTEL CROSSFIRE, MY FATHER DECIDED TO TAKE HIM DOWN. HE INVESTIGATED JADE AND HIS CARTEL.
IT WASN'T LONG BEFORE JADE ARRIVED ON OUR DOORSTEP AND DEMANDED MY FATHER STOP WRITING ABOUT HIM IN THE DAILY PAPERS. HE WARNED US OF WHAT MIGHT HAPPEN.
MY FATHER REFUSED.
JADE SHRUGGED AND LEFT THE HOUSE. BUT HE WASN'T FINISHED. WHEN I WAS AT SCHOOL THE NEXT DAY, I LEARNED THAT OUR HOUSE HAD BURNED TO THE GROUND. MY MAMA HAD BEEN KILLED IN THE FIRE.
OF COURSE, JADE DID IT. BUT PAPA COULDN'T GATHER ENOUGH PROOF. SO WE HAD TO LEAVE MEXICO CITY BEFORE HE STRUCK AGAIN.
SO FAR, JADE HAS LEFT US ALONE. I GUESS HE THINKS WE'RE OLD NEWS... THAT WE CAN'T HURT HIM.

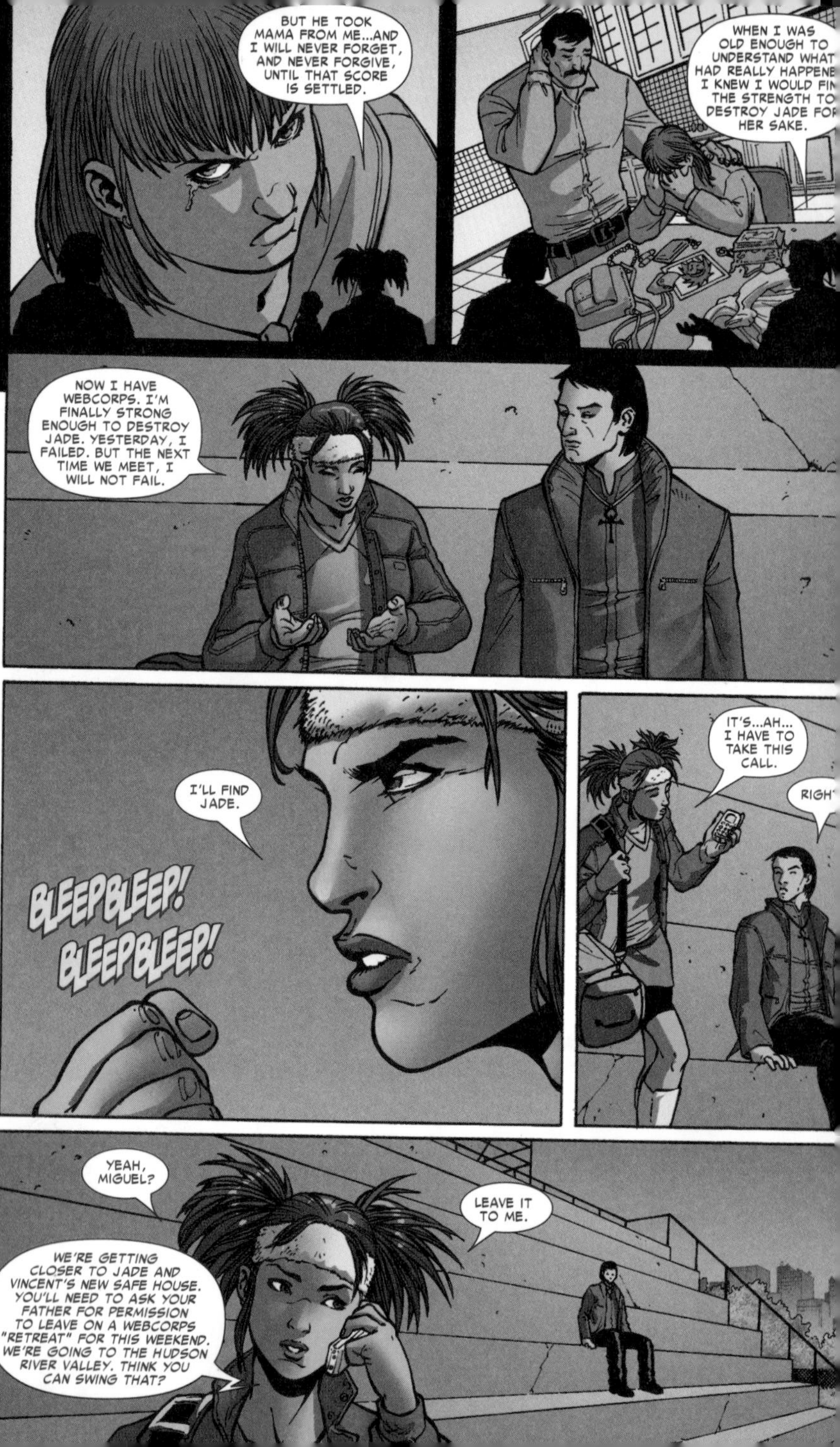

BUT HE TOOK MAMA FROM ME...AND I WILL NEVER FORGET, AND NEVER FORGIVE, UNTIL THAT SCORE IS SETTLED.
WHEN I WAS OLD ENOUGH TO UNDERSTAND WHAT HAD REALLY HAPPENE I KNEW I WOULD FIN THE STRENGTH TO DESTROY JADE FO HER SAKE.
NOW I HAVE WEBCORPS. I'M FINALLY STRONG ENOUGH TO DESTROY JADE. YESTERDAY, I FAILED. BUT THE NEXT TIME WE MEET, I WILL NOT FAIL.
I'LL FIND JADE.
BLEEPBLEEP! BLEEPBLEEP!
IT'S...AH... I HAVE TO TAKE THIS CALL.
RIGH
YEAH, MIGUEL?
WE'RE GETTING CLOSER TO JADE AND VINCENT'S NEW SAFE HOUSE. YOU'LL NEED TO ASK YOUR FATHER FOR PERMISSION TO LEAVE ON A WEBCORPS "RETREAT" FOR THIS WEEKEND. WE'RE GOING TO THE HUDSON RIVER VALLEY. THINK YOU CAN SWING THAT?
LEAVE IT TO ME.

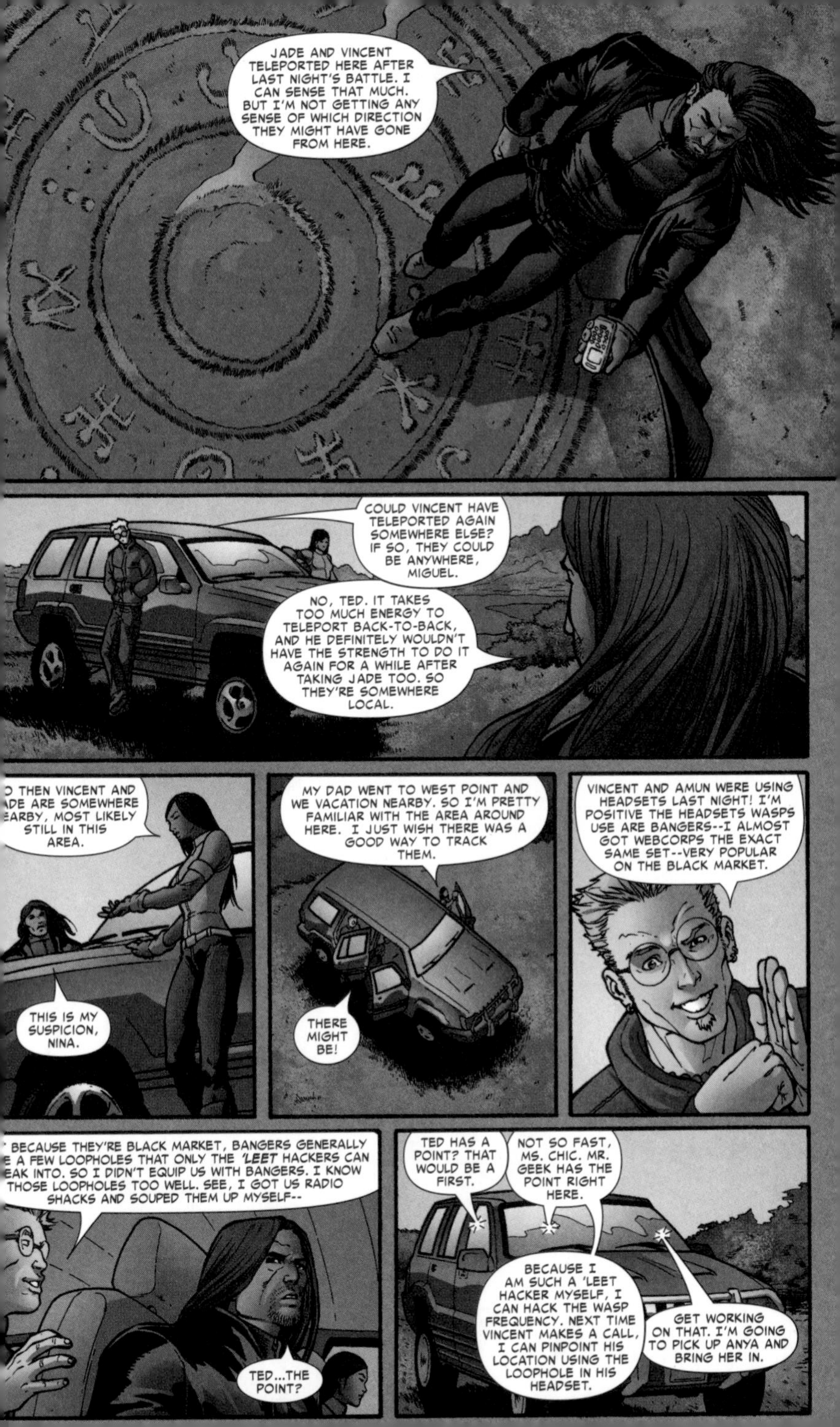
JADE AND VINCENT TELEPORTED HERE AFTER LAST NIGHT'S BATTLE. I CAN SENSE THAT MUCH. BUT I'M NOT GETTING ANY SENSE OF WHICH DIRECTION THEY MIGHT HAVE GONE FROM HERE.
COULD VINCENT HAVE TELEPORTED AGAIN SOMEWHERE ELSE? IF SO, THEY COULD BE ANYWHERE, MIGUEL.
NO, TED. IT TAKES TOO MUCH ENERGY TO TELEPORT BACK-TO-BACK, AND HE DEFINITELY WOULDN'T HAVE THE STRENGTH TO DO IT AGAIN FOR A WHILE AFTER TAKING JADE TOO. SO THEY'RE SOMEWHERE LOCAL.
VINCENT AND ADE ARE SOMEWHERE EARBY, MOST LIKELY STILL IN THIS AREA.
THIS IS MY SUSPICION, NINA.
MY DAD WENT TO WEST POINT AND WE VACATION NEARBY. SO I'M PRETTY FAMILIAR WITH THE AREA AROUND HERE. I JUST WISH THERE WAS A GOOD WAY TO TRACK THEM.
THERE MIGHT BE!
VINCENT AND AMUN WERE USING HEADSETS LAST NIGHT! I'M POSITIVE THE HEADSETS WASPS USE ARE BANGERS--I ALMOST GOT WEBCORPS THE EXACT SAME SET--VERY POPULAR ON THE BLACK MARKET.
BECAUSE THEY'RE BLACK MARKET, BANGERS GENERALLY A FEW LOOPHOLES THAT ONLY THE 'LEET HACKERS CAN EAK INTO. SO I DIDN'T EQUIP US WITH BANGERS. I KNOW THOSE LOOPHOLES TOO WELL. SEE, I GOT US RADIO SHACKS AND SOUPED THEM UP MYSELF--
TED...THE POINT?
TED HAS A POINT? THAT WOULD BE A FIRST.
NOT SO FAST, MS. CHIC. MR. GEEK HAS THE POINT RIGHT HERE.
BECAUSE I AM SUCH A 'LEET HACKER MYSELF, I CAN HACK THE WASP FREQUENCY. NEXT TIME VINCENT MAKES A CALL, I CAN PINPOINT HIS LOCATION USING THE LOOPHOLE IN HIS HEADSET.
GET WORKING ON THAT. I'M GOING TO PICK UP ANYA AND BRING HER IN.

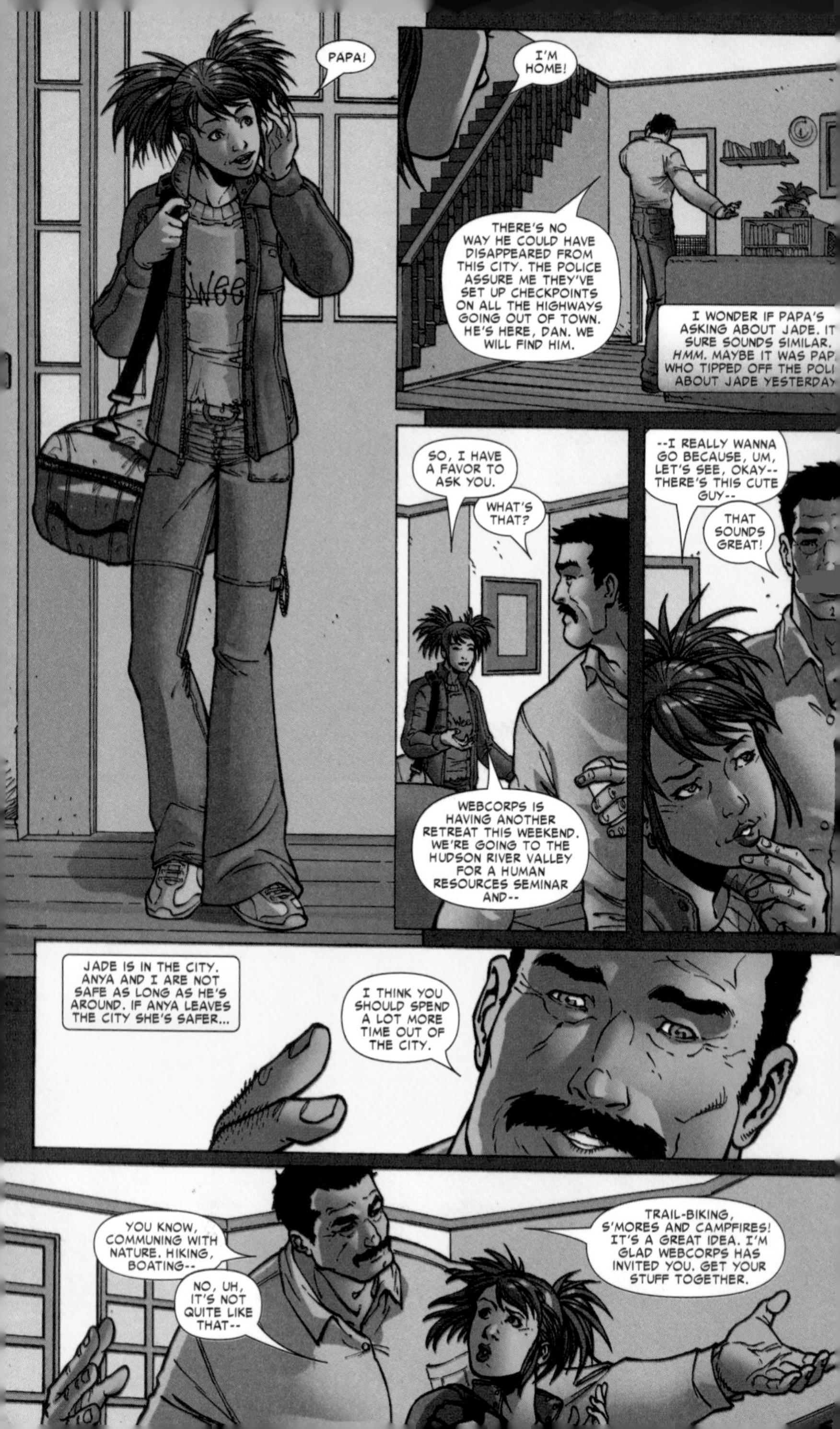
PAPA!
I'M HOME!
THERE'S NO WAY HE COULD HAVE DISAPPEARED FROM THIS CITY. THE POLICE ASSURE ME THEY'VE SET UP CHECKPOINTS ON ALL THE HIGHWAYS GOING OUT OF TOWN. HE'S HERE, DAN. WE WILL FIND HIM.
I WONDER IF PAPA'S ASKING ABOUT JADE. IT SURE SOUNDS SIMILAR. HMM. MAYBE IT WAS PAPA WHO TIPPED OFF THE POLI ABOUT JADE YESTERDAY
SO, I HAVE A FAVOR TO ASK YOU.
WHAT'S THAT?
WEBCORPS IS HAVING ANOTHER RETREAT THIS WEEKEND. WE'RE GOING TO THE HUDSON RIVER VALLEY FOR A HUMAN RESOURCES SEMINAR AND--
--I REALLY WANNA GO BECAUSE, UM, LET'S SEE, OKAY-- THERE'S THIS CUTE GUY--
THAT SOUNDS GREAT!
JADE IS IN THE CITY. ANYA AND I ARE NOT SAFE AS LONG AS HE'S AROUND. IF ANYA LEAVES THE CITY SHE'S SAFER...
I THINK YOU SHOULD SPEND A LOT MORE TIME OUT OF THE CITY.
YOU KNOW, COMMUNING WITH NATURE. HIKING, BOATING--
NO, UH, IT'S NOT QUITE LIKE THAT--
TRAIL-BIKING, S'MORES AND CAMPFIRES! IT'S A GREAT IDEA. I'M GLAD WEBCORPS HAS INVITED YOU. GET YOUR STUFF TOGETHER.

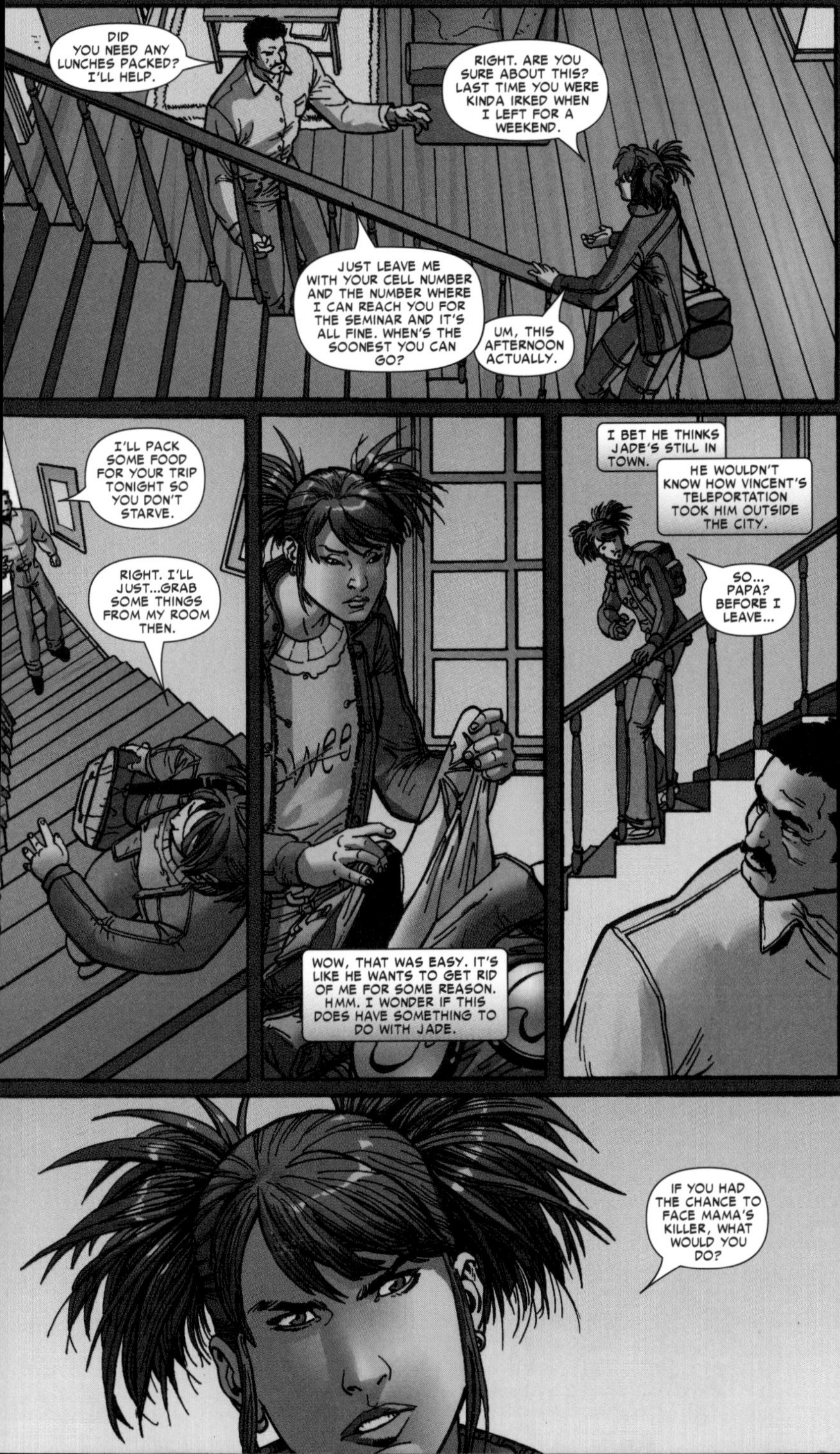

DID YOU NEED ANY LUNCHES PACKED? I'LL HELP.
RIGHT. ARE YOU SURE ABOUT THIS? LAST TIME YOU WERE KINDA IRKED WHEN I LEFT FOR A WEEKEND.
JUST LEAVE ME WITH YOUR CELL NUMBER AND THE NUMBER WHERE I CAN REACH YOU FOR THE SEMINAR AND IT'S ALL FINE. WHEN'S THE SOONEST YOU CAN GO?
UM, THIS AFTERNOON ACTUALLY.
I'LL PACK SOME FOOD FOR YOUR TRIP TONIGHT SO YOU DON'T STARVE.
RIGHT. I'LL JUST...GRAB SOME THINGS FROM MY ROOM THEN.
WOW, THAT WAS EASY. IT'S LIKE HE WANTS TO GET RID OF ME FOR SOME REASON. HMM. I WONDER IF THIS DOES HAVE SOMETHING TO DO WITH JADE.
I BET HE THINKS JADE'S STILL IN TOWN.
HE WOULDN'T KNOW HOW VINCENT'S TELEPORTATION TOOK HIM OUTSIDE THE CITY.
SO... PAPA? BEFORE I LEAVE...
IF YOU HAD THE CHANCE TO FACE MAMA'S KILLER, WHAT WOULD YOU DO?

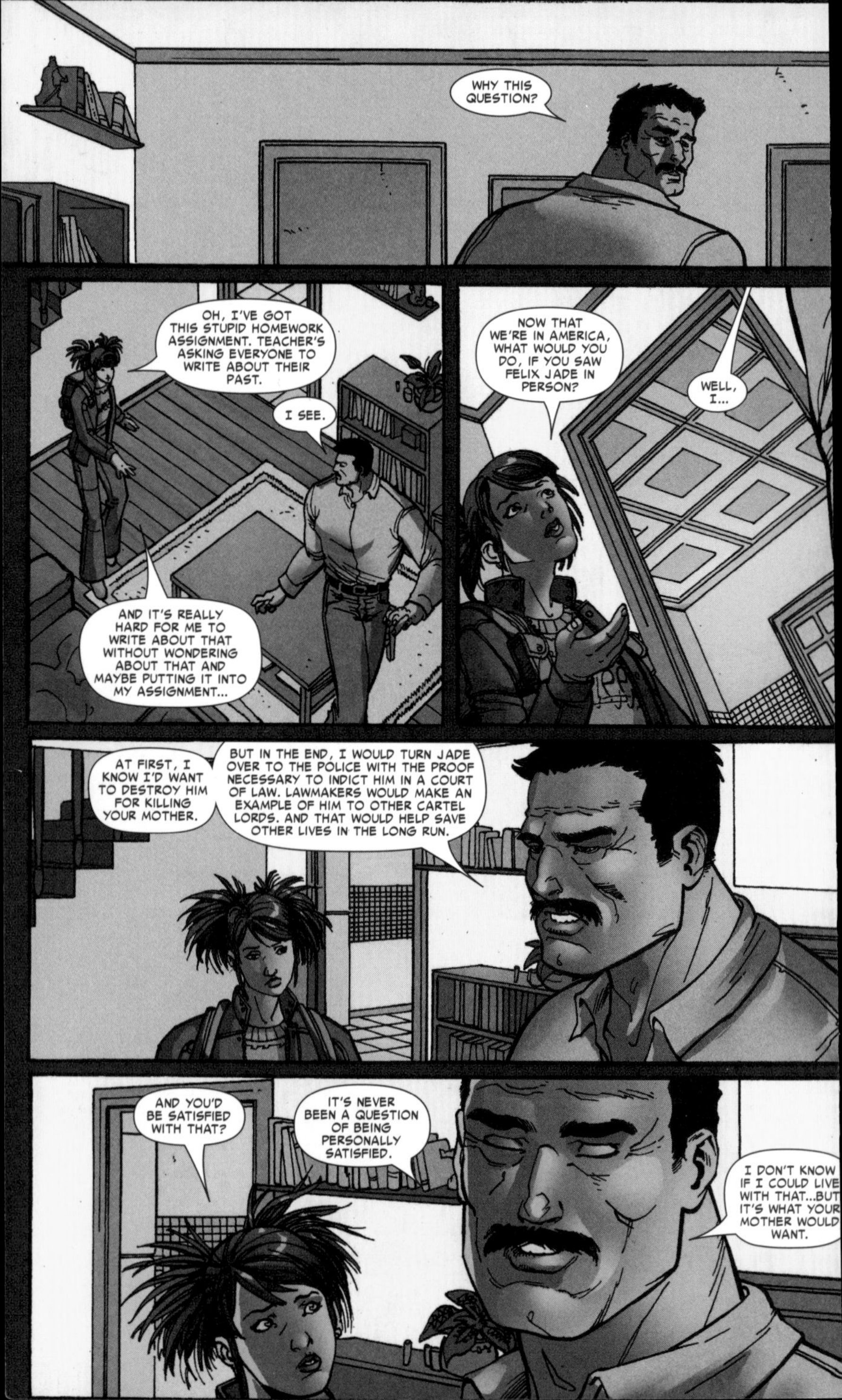
WHY THIS QUESTION?
OH, I'VE GOT THIS STUPID HOMEWORK ASSIGNMENT. TEACHER'S ASKING EVERYONE TO WRITE ABOUT THEIR PAST.
I SEE.
AND IT'S REALLY HARD FOR ME TO WRITE ABOUT THAT WITHOUT WONDERING ABOUT THAT AND MAYBE PUTTING IT INTO MY ASSIGNMENT...
NOW THAT WE'RE IN AMERICA, WHAT WOULD YOU DO, IF YOU SAW FELIX JADE IN PERSON?
WELL, I...
AT FIRST, I KNOW I'D WANT TO DESTROY HIM FOR KILLING YOUR MOTHER.
BUT IN THE END, I WOULD TURN JADE OVER TO THE POLICE WITH THE PROOF NECESSARY TO INDICT HIM IN A COURT OF LAW. LAWMAKERS WOULD MAKE AN EXAMPLE OF HIM TO OTHER CARTEL LORDS. AND THAT WOULD HELP SAVE OTHER LIVES IN THE LONG RUN.
AND YOU'D BE SATISFIED WITH THAT?
IT'S NEVER BEEN A QUESTION OF BEING PERSONALLY SATISFIED.
I DON'T KNOW IF I COULD LIVE WITH THAT...BUT IT'S WHAT YOUR MOTHER WOULD WANT.

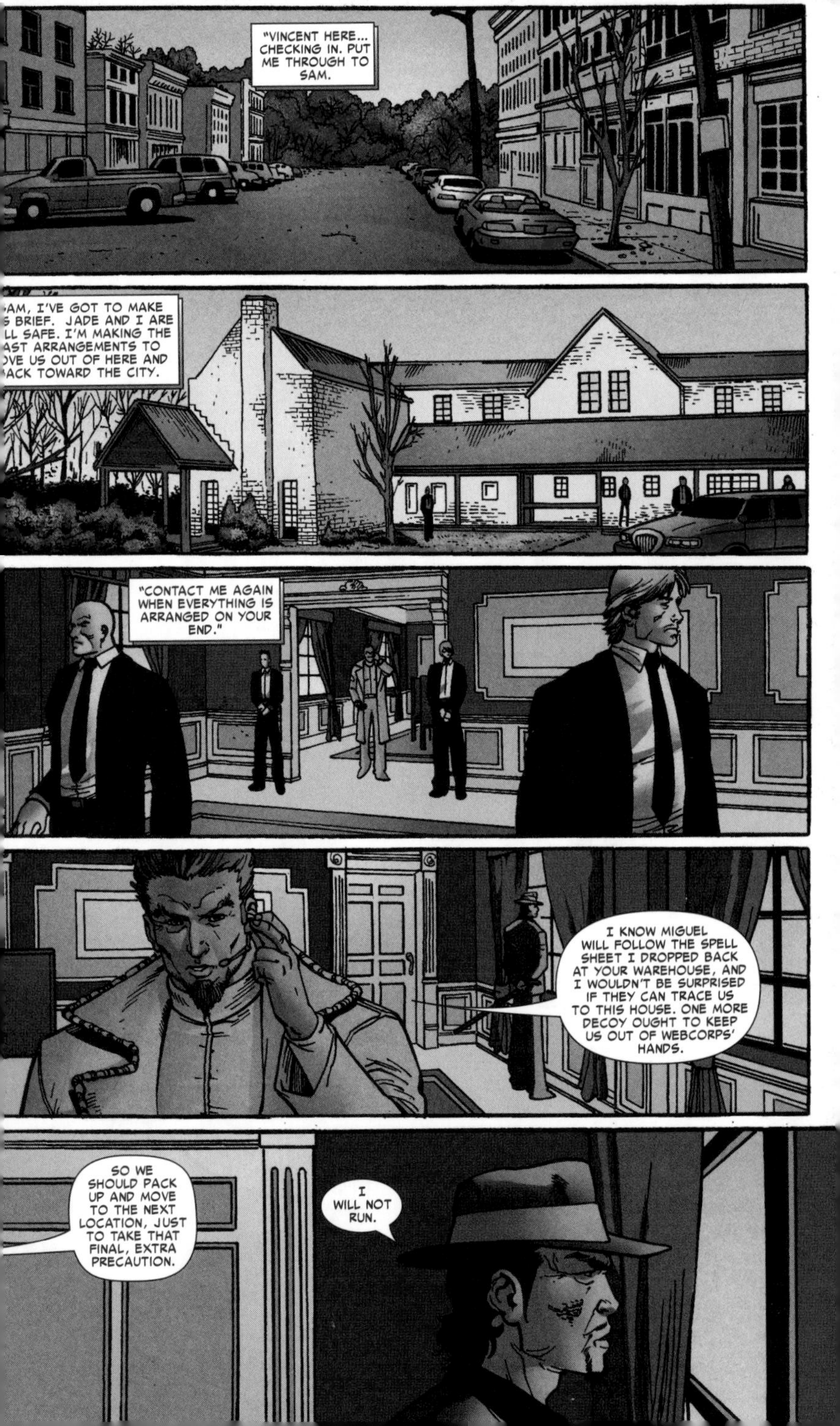
"VINCENT HERE... CHECKING IN. PUT ME THROUGH TO SAM.
AM, I'VE GOT TO MAKE S BRIEF. JADE AND I ARE LL SAFE. I'M MAKING THE AST ARRANGEMENTS TO OVE US OUT OF HERE AND ACK TOWARD THE CITY.
"CONTACT ME AGAIN WHEN EVERYTHING IS ARRANGED ON YOUR END."
I KNOW MIGUEL WILL FOLLOW THE SPELL SHEET I DROPPED BACK AT YOUR WAREHOUSE, AND I WOULDN'T BE SURPRISED IF THEY CAN TRACE US TO THIS HOUSE. ONE MORE DECOY OUGHT TO KEEP US OUT OF WEBCORPS' HANDS.
SO WE SHOULD PACK UP AND MOVE TO THE NEXT LOCATION, JUST TO TAKE THAT FINAL, EXTRA PRECAUTION.
I WILL NOT RUN.

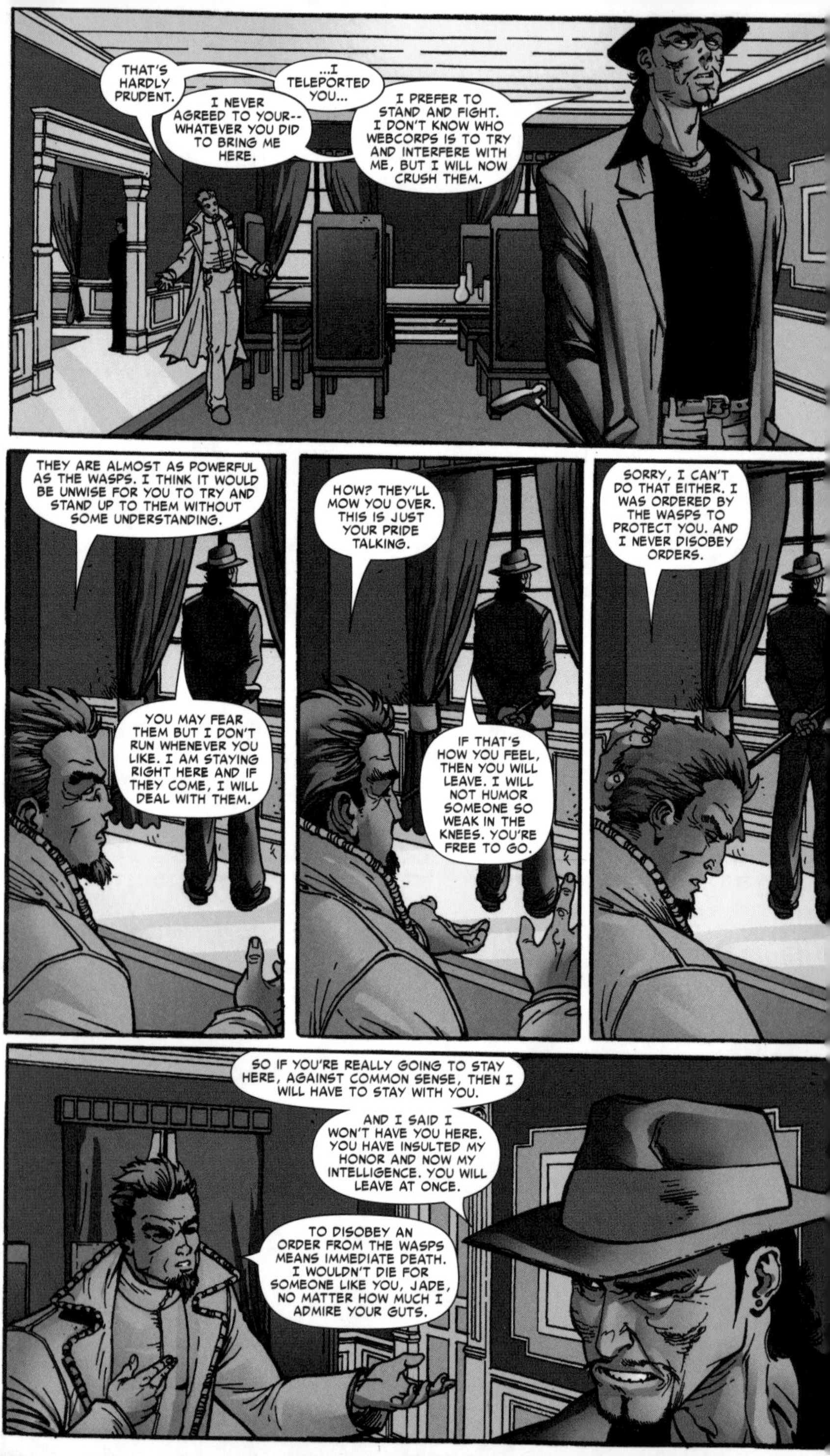

THAT'S HARDLY PRUDENT.
...I TELEPORTED YOU...
I NEVER AGREED TO YOUR-- WHATEVER YOU DID TO BRING ME HERE.
I PREFER TO STAND AND FIGHT. I DON'T KNOW WHO WEBCORPS IS TO TRY AND INTERFERE WITH ME, BUT I WILL NOW CRUSH THEM.
THEY ARE ALMOST AS POWERFUL AS THE WASPS. I THINK IT WOULD BE UNWISE FOR YOU TO TRY AND STAND UP TO THEM WITHOUT SOME UNDERSTANDING.
YOU MAY FEAR THEM BUT I DON'T RUN WHENEVER YOU LIKE. I AM STAYING RIGHT HERE AND IF THEY COME, I WILL DEAL WITH THEM.
HOW? THEY'LL MOW YOU OVER. THIS IS JUST YOUR PRIDE TALKING.
IF THAT'S HOW YOU FEEL, THEN YOU WILL LEAVE. I WILL NOT HUMOR SOMEONE SO WEAK IN THE KNEES. YOU'RE FREE TO GO.
SORRY, I CAN'T DO THAT EITHER. I WAS ORDERED BY THE WASPS TO PROTECT YOU. AND I NEVER DISOBEY ORDERS.
SO IF YOU'RE REALLY GOING TO STAY HERE, AGAINST COMMON SENSE, THEN I WILL HAVE TO STAY WITH YOU.
AND I SAID I WON'T HAVE YOU HERE. YOU HAVE INSULTED MY HONOR AND NOW MY INTELLIGENCE. YOU WILL LEAVE AT ONCE.
TO DISOBEY AN ORDER FROM THE WASPS MEANS IMMEDIATE DEATH. I WOULDN'T DIE FOR SOMEONE LIKE YOU, JADE, NO MATTER HOW MUCH I ADMIRE YOUR GUTS.

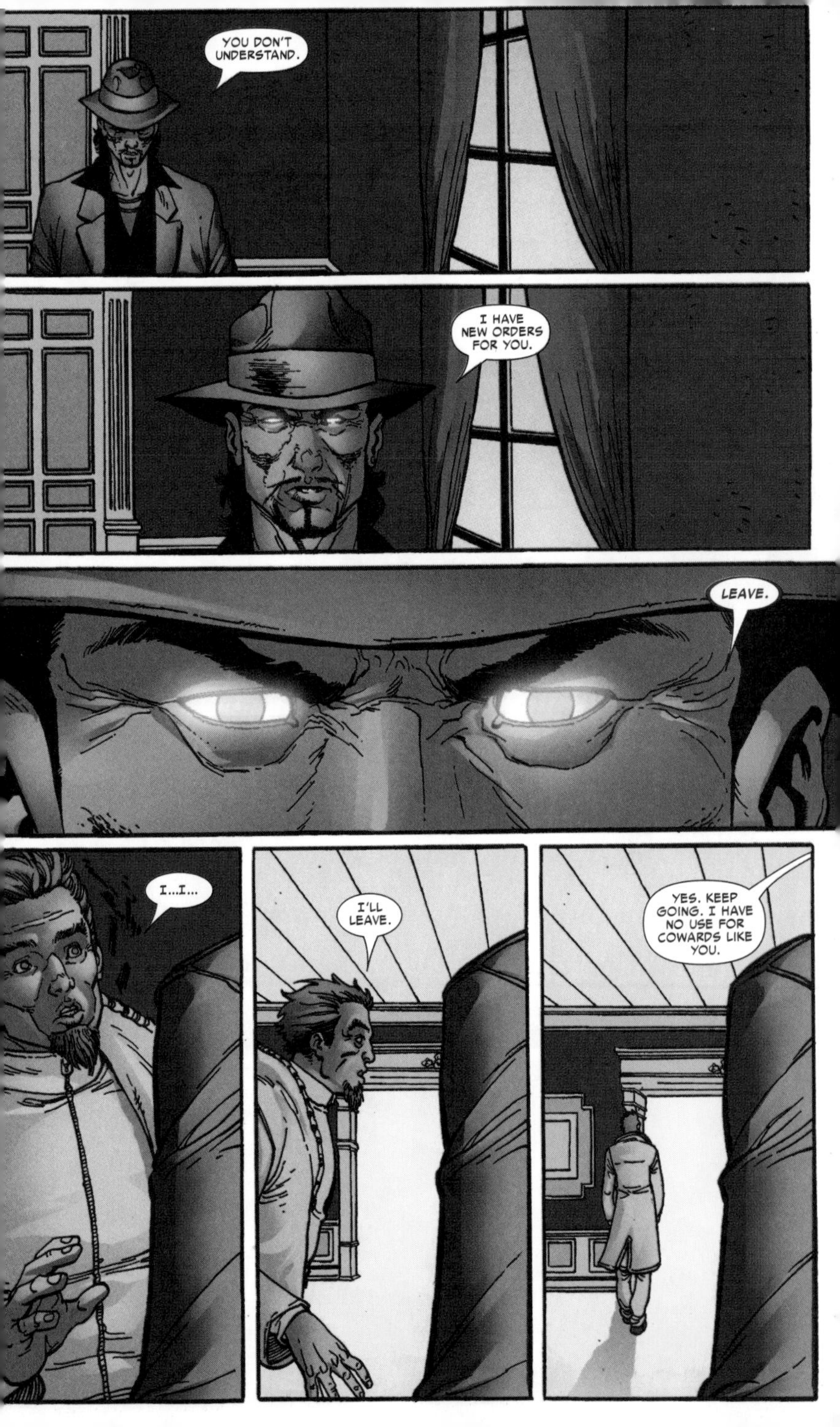
YOU DON'T UNDERSTAND.
I HAVE NEW ORDERS FOR YOU.
LEAVE.
I...I...
I'LL LEAVE.
YES. KEEP GOING. I HAVE NO USE FOR COWARDS LIKE YOU.

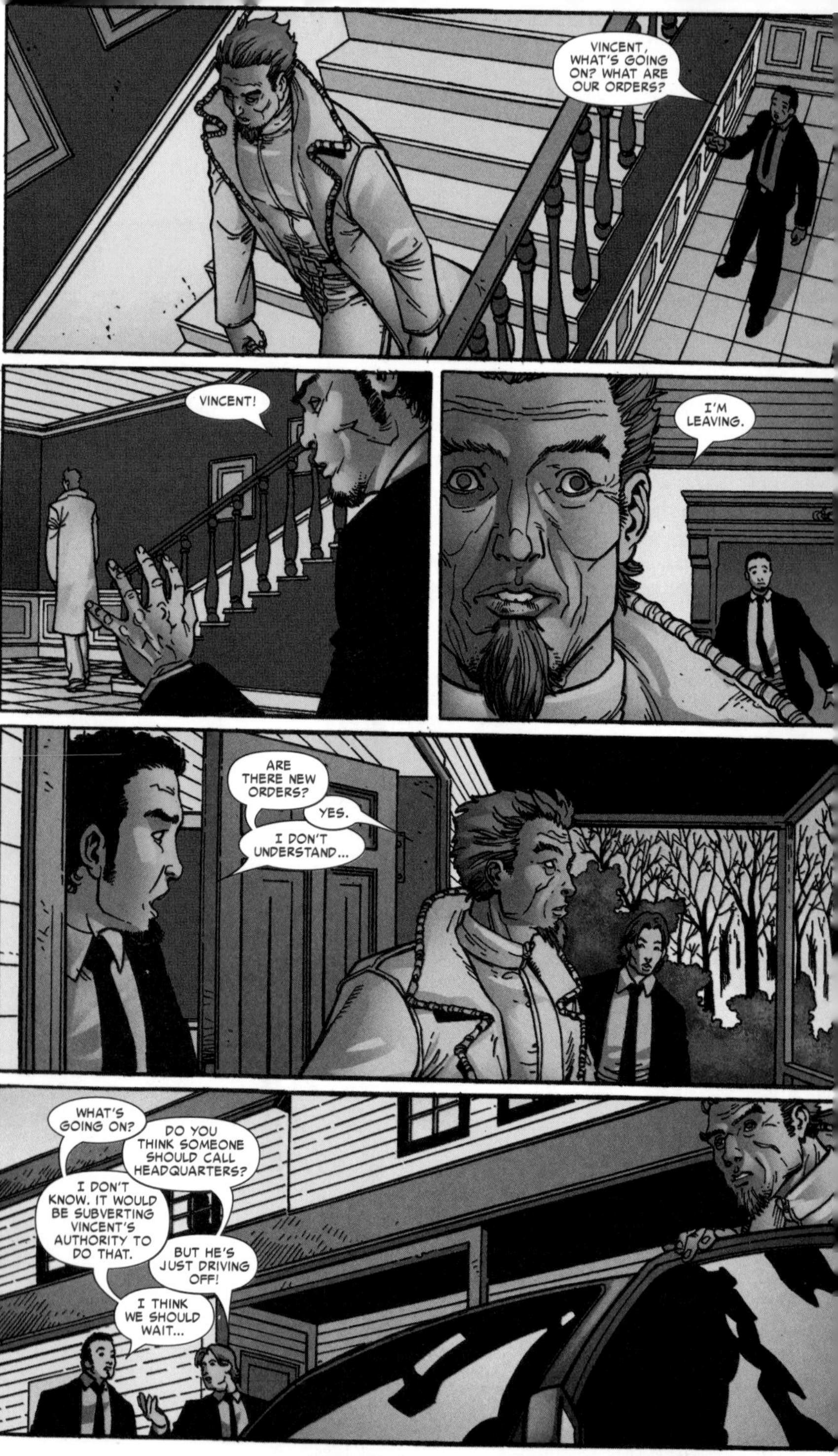
VINCENT, WHAT'S GOING ON? WHAT ARE OUR ORDERS?
VINCENT!
I'M LEAVING.
ARE THERE NEW ORDERS?
YES.
I DON'T UNDERSTAND...
WHAT'S GOING ON?
DO YOU THINK SOMEONE SHOULD CALL HEADQUARTERS?
I DON'T KNOW. IT WOULD BE SUBVERTING VINCENT'S AUTHORITY TO DO THAT.
BUT HE'S JUST DRIVING OFF!
I THINK WE SHOULD WAIT...

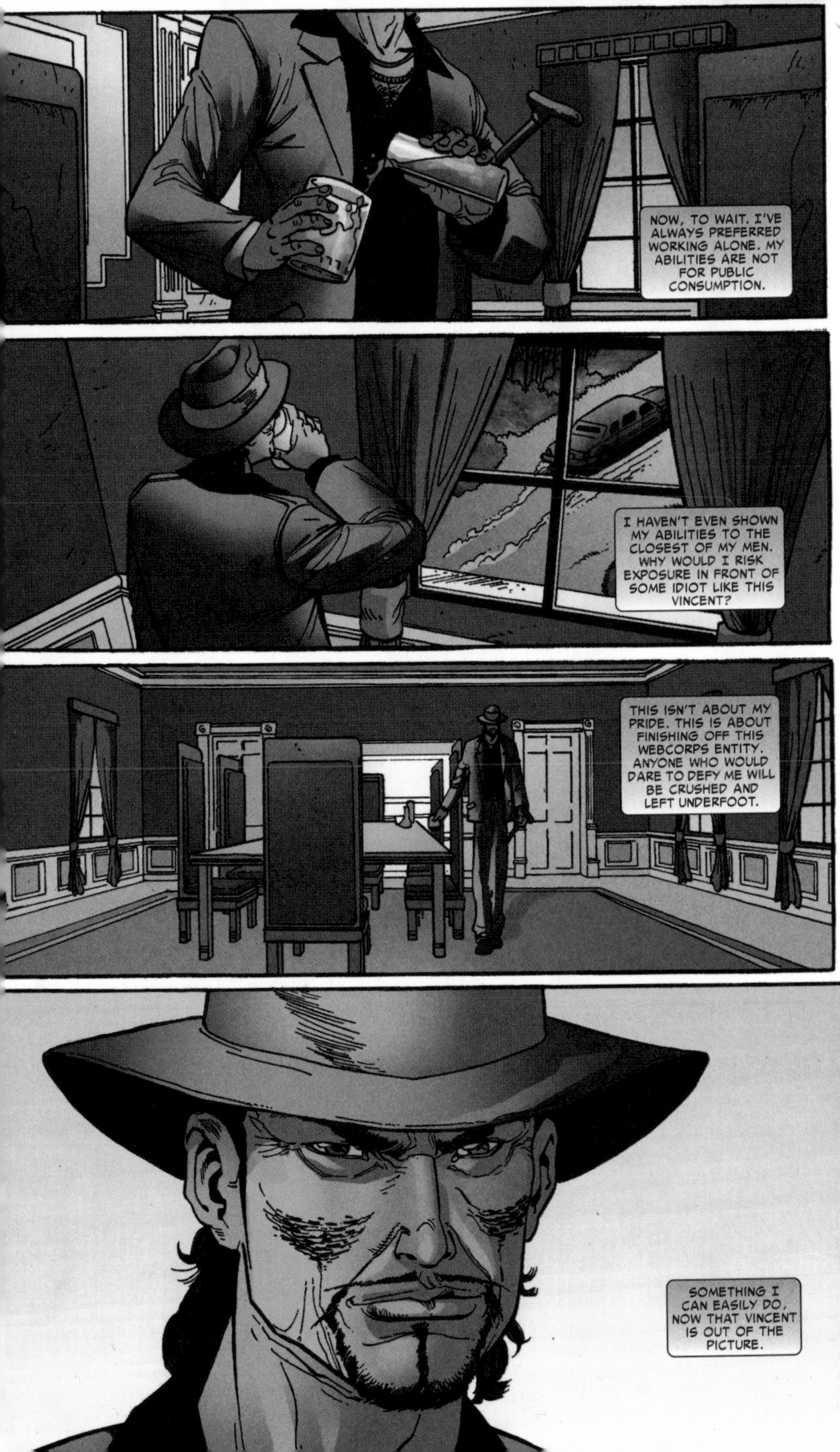
NOW, TO WAIT. I'VE ALWAYS PREFERRED WORKING ALONE. MY ABILITIES ARE NOT FOR PUBLIC CONSUMPTION.
I HAVEN'T EVEN SHOWN MY ABILITIES TO THE CLOSEST OF MY MEN. WHY WOULD I RISK EXPOSURE IN FRONT OF SOME IDIOT LIKE THIS VINCENT?
THIS ISN'T ABOUT MY PRIDE. THIS IS ABOUT FINISHING OFF THIS WEBCORPS ENTITY. ANYONE WHO WOULD DARE TO DEFY ME WILL BE CRUSHED AND LEFT UNDERFOOT.
SOMETHING I CAN EASILY DO, NOW THAT VINCENT IS OUT OF THE PICTURE.

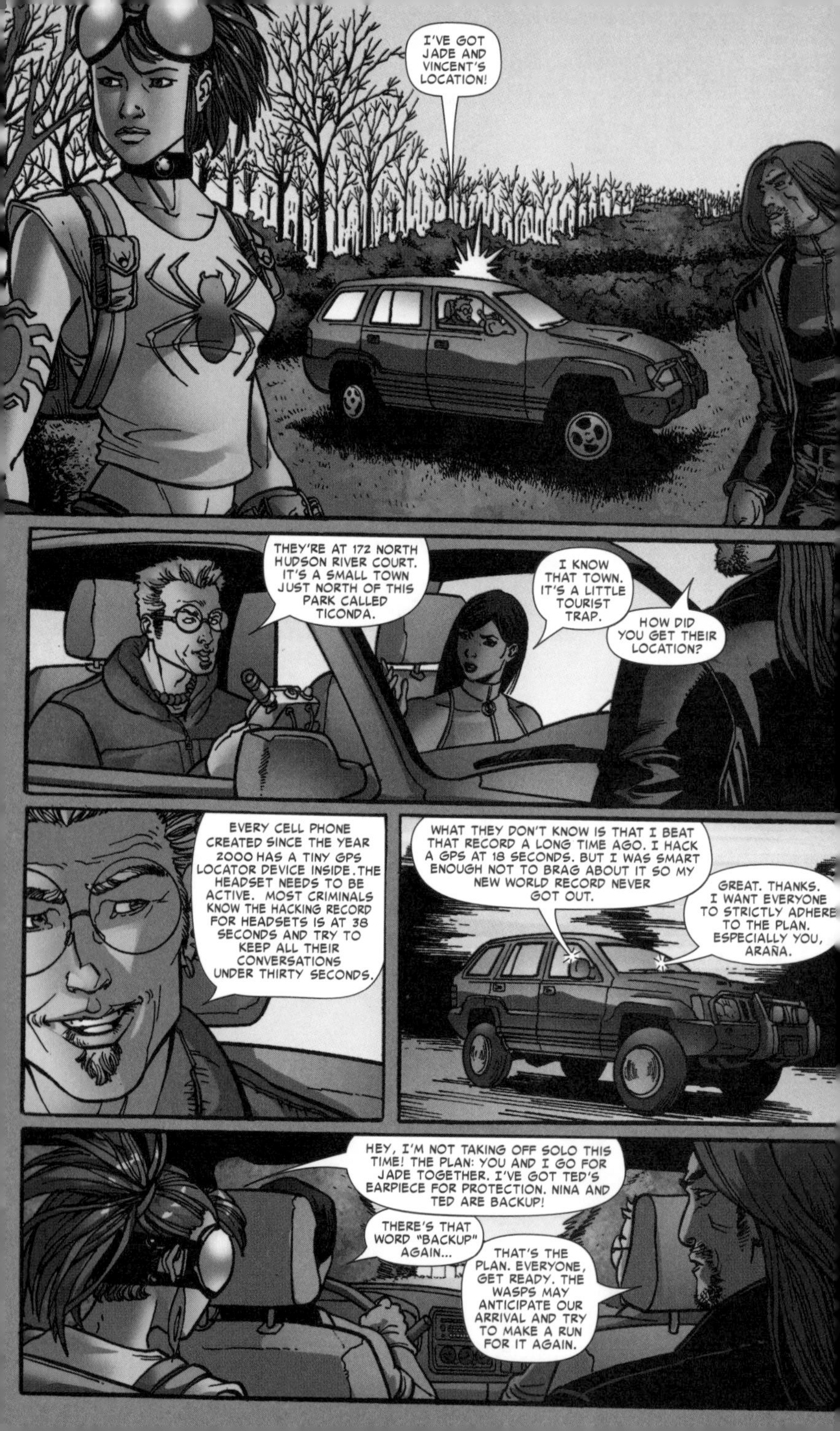
I'VE GOT JADE AND VINCENT'S LOCATION!
THEY'RE AT 172 NORTH HUDSON RIVER COURT. IT'S A SMALL TOWN JUST NORTH OF THIS PARK CALLED TICONDA.
I KNOW THAT TOWN. IT'S A LITTLE TOURIST TRAP.
HOW DID YOU GET THEIR LOCATION?
EVERY CELL PHONE CREATED SINCE THE YEAR 2000 HAS A TINY GPS LOCATOR DEVICE INSIDE. THE HEADSET NEEDS TO BE ACTIVE. MOST CRIMINALS KNOW THE HACKING RECORD FOR HEADSETS IS AT 38 SECONDS AND TRY TO KEEP ALL THEIR CONVERSATIONS UNDER THIRTY SECONDS.
WHAT THEY DON'T KNOW IS THAT I BEAT THAT RECORD A LONG TIME AGO. I HACK A GPS AT 18 SECONDS. BUT I WAS SMART ENOUGH NOT TO BRAG ABOUT IT SO MY NEW WORLD RECORD NEVER GOT OUT.
GREAT. THANKS. I WANT EVERYONE TO STRICTLY ADHERE TO THE PLAN. ESPECIALLY YOU, ARAÑA.
HEY, I'M NOT TAKING OFF SOLO THIS TIME! THE PLAN: YOU AND I GO FOR JADE TOGETHER. I'VE GOT TED'S EARPIECE FOR PROTECTION. NINA AND TED ARE BACKUP!
THERE'S THAT WORD "BACKUP" AGAIN...
THAT'S THE PLAN. EVERYONE, GET READY. THE WASPS MAY ANTICIPATE OUR ARRIVAL AND TRY TO MAKE A RUN FOR IT AGAIN.

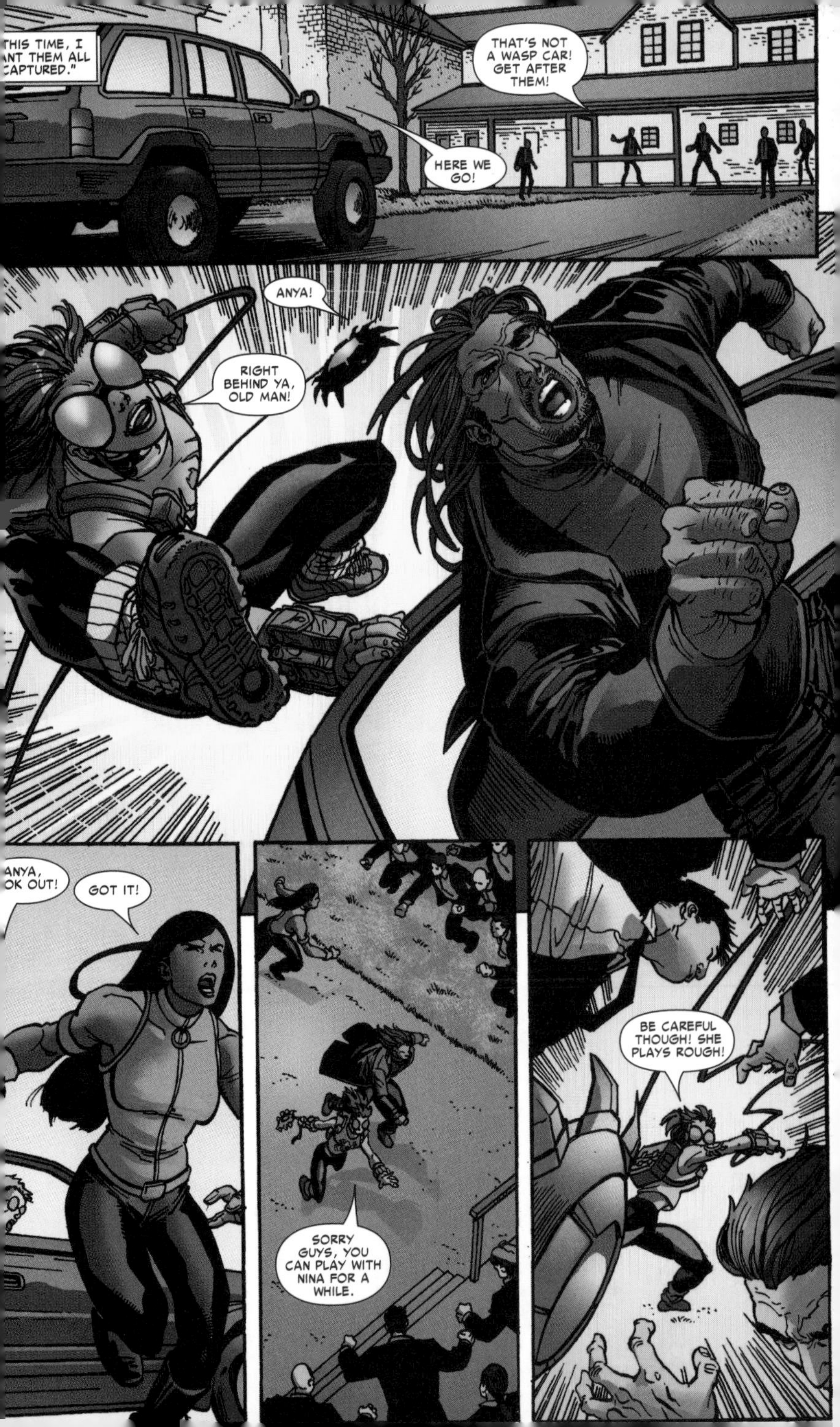
THIS TIME, I
ANT THEM ALL
CAPTURED."
THAT'S NOT A WASP CAR! GET AFTER THEM!
HERE WE GO!
ANYA!
RIGHT BEHIND YA, OLD MAN!
ANYA,
OK OUT!
GOT IT!
SORRY GUYS, YOU CAN PLAY WITH NINA FOR A WHILE.
BE CAREFUL THOUGH! SHE PLAYS ROUGH!

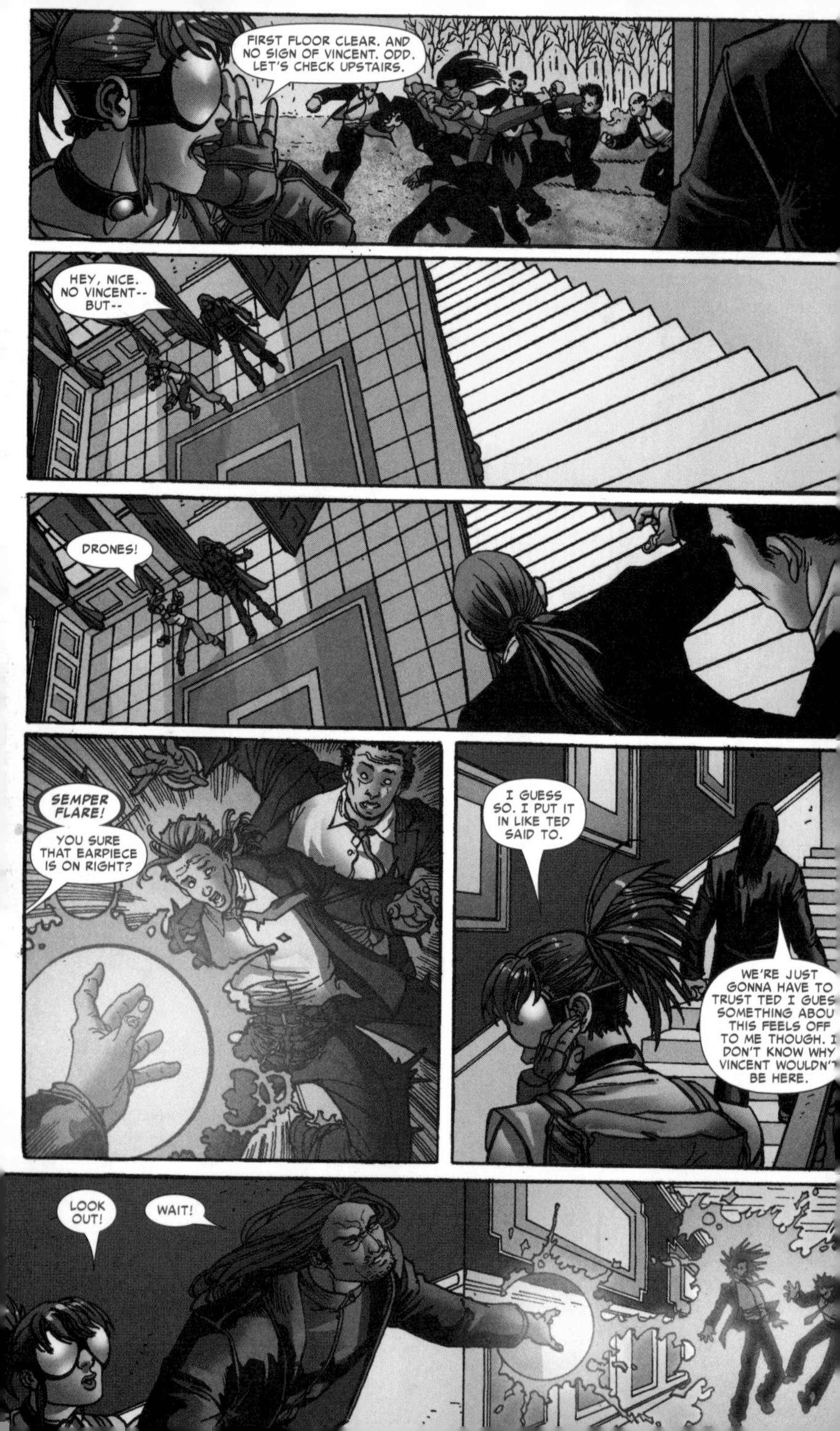
FIRST FLOOR CLEAR. AND NO SIGN OF VINCENT. ODD. LET'S CHECK UPSTAIRS.
HEY, NICE. NO VINCENT-- BUT--
DRONES!
SEMPER FLARE!
YOU SURE THAT EARPIECE IS ON RIGHT?
I GUESS SO. I PUT IT IN LIKE TED SAID TO.
WE'RE JUST GONNA HAVE TO TRUST TED I GUES SOMETHING ABOU THIS FEELS OFF TO ME THOUGH. I DON'T KNOW WHY VINCENT WOULDN'T BE HERE.
LOOK OUT!
WAIT!

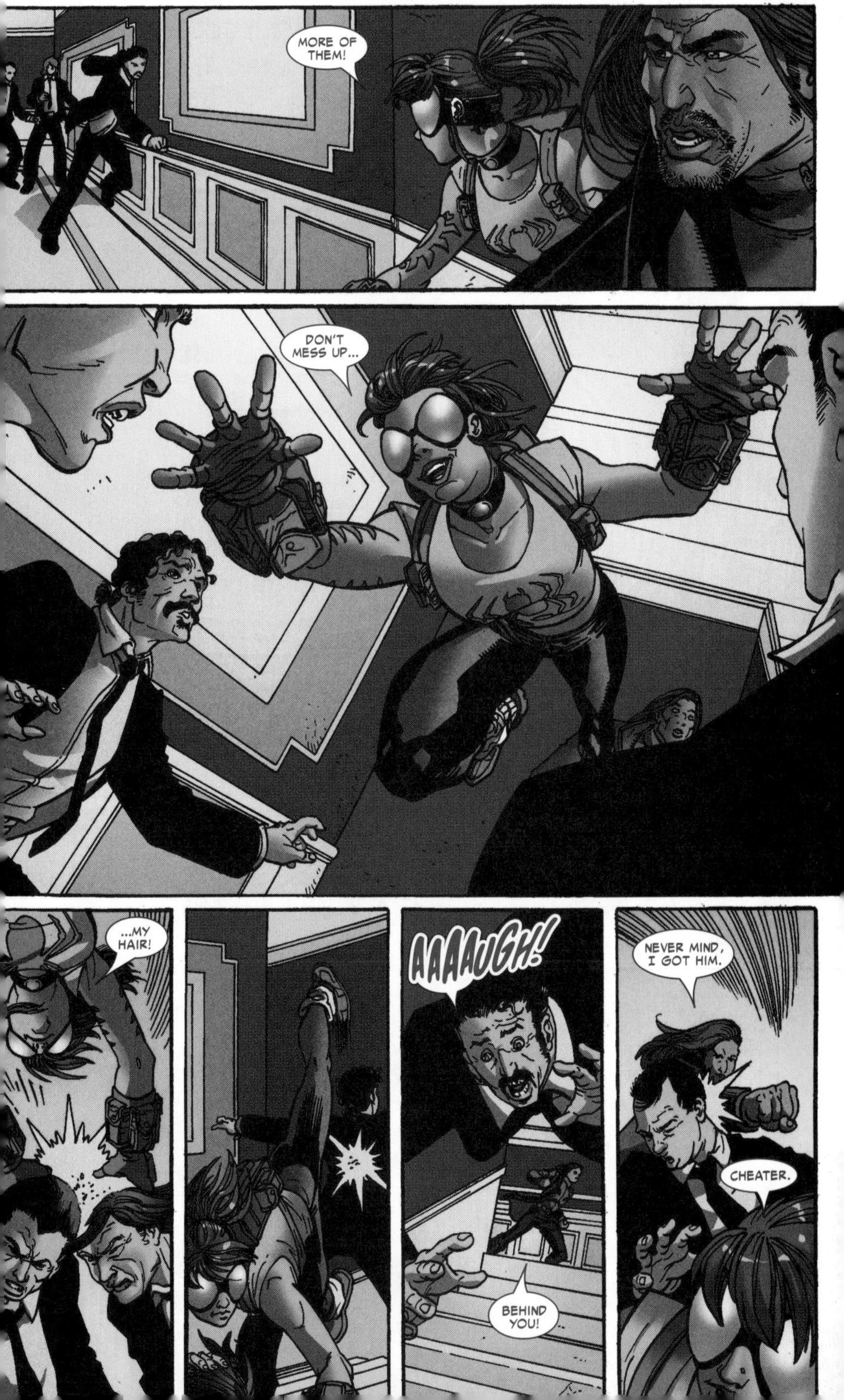
MORE OF THEM!
DON'T MESS UP...
...MY HAIR!
AAAAUGH!
BEHIND YOU!
NEVER MIND, I GOT HIM.
CHEATER.

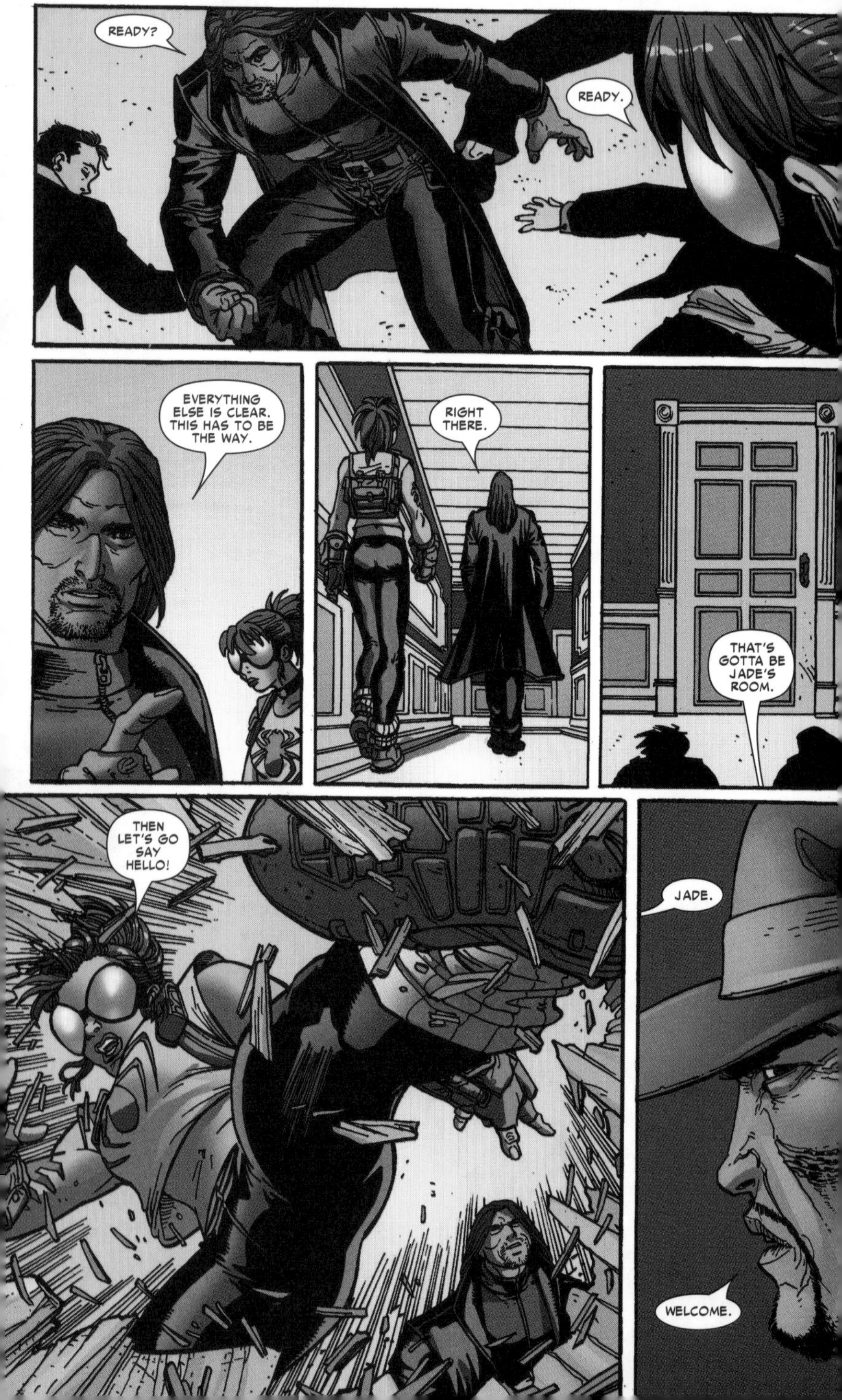
READY?
READY.
EVERYTHING ELSE IS CLEAR. THIS HAS TO BE THE WAY.
RIGHT THERE.
THAT'S GOTTA BE JADE'S ROOM.
THEN LET'S GO SAY HELLO!
JADE.
WELCOME.

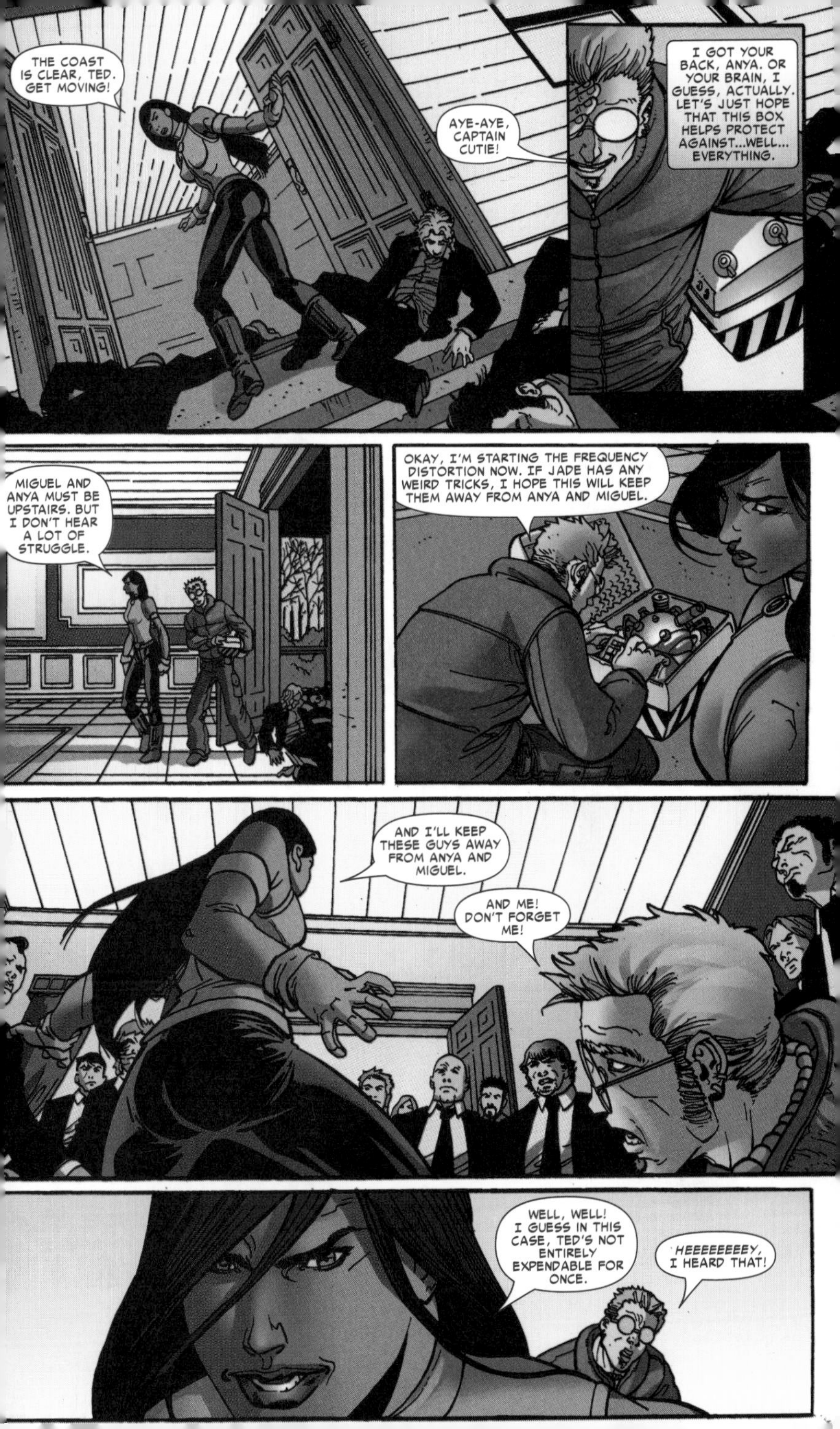
THE COAST IS CLEAR, TED. GET MOVING!
AYE-AYE, CAPTAIN CUTIE!
I GOT YOUR BACK, ANYA. OR YOUR BRAIN, I GUESS, ACTUALLY. LET'S JUST HOPE THAT THIS BOX HELPS PROTECT AGAINST...WELL... EVERYTHING.
MIGUEL AND ANYA MUST BE UPSTAIRS. BUT I DON'T HEAR A LOT OF STRUGGLE.
OKAY, I'M STARTING THE FREQUENCY DISTORTION NOW. IF JADE HAS ANY WEIRD TRICKS, I HOPE THIS WILL KEEP THEM AWAY FROM ANYA AND MIGUEL.
AND I'LL KEEP THESE GUYS AWAY FROM ANYA AND MIGUEL.
AND ME! DON'T FORGET ME!
WELL, WELL! I GUESS IN THIS CASE, TED'S NOT ENTIRELY EXPENDABLE FOR ONCE.
HEEEEEEEEY, I HEARD THAT!

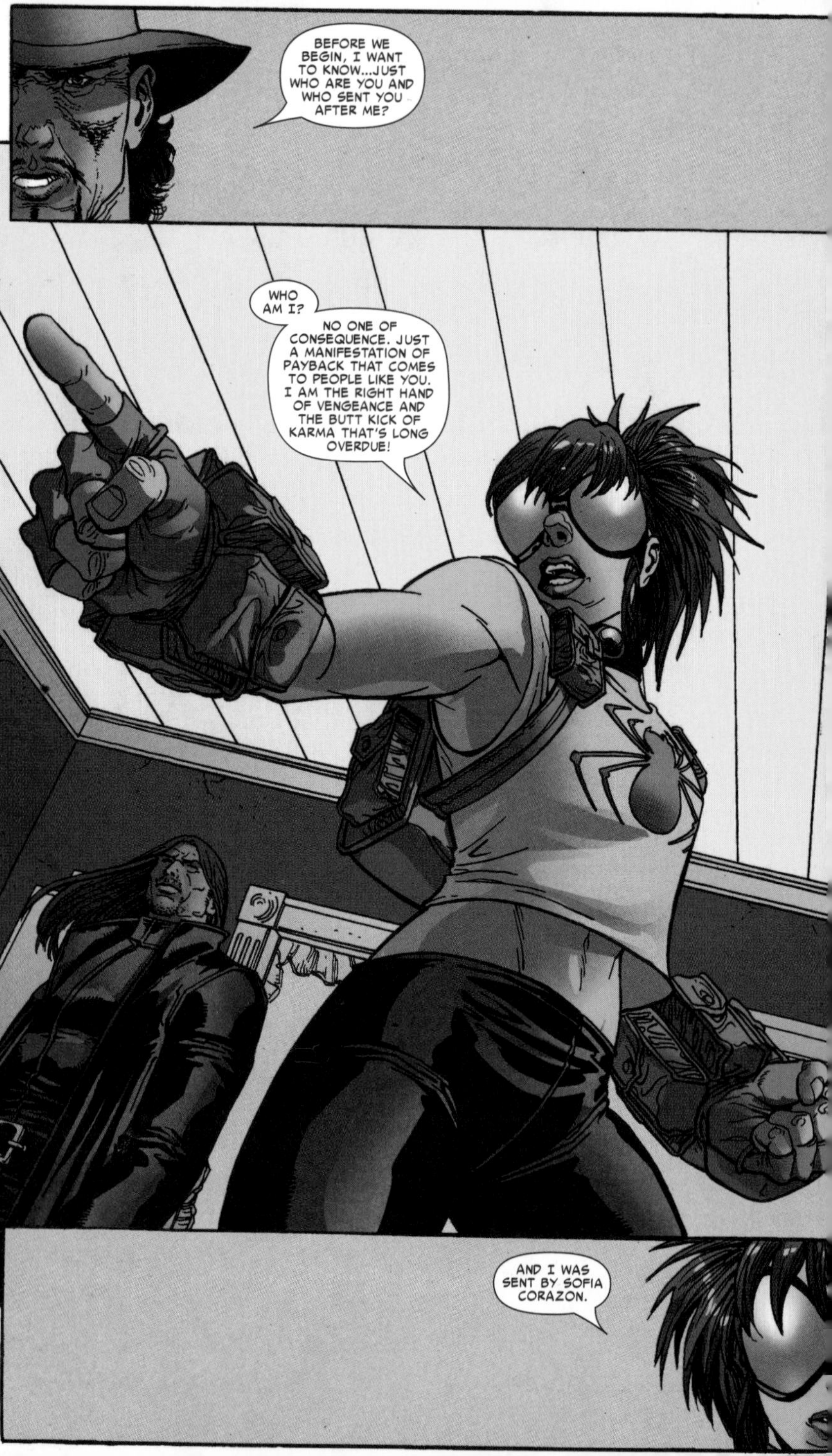
BEFORE WE BEGIN, I WANT TO KNOW...JUST WHO ARE YOU AND WHO SENT YOU AFTER ME?
WHO AM I?
NO ONE OF CONSEQUENCE. JUST A MANIFESTATION OF PAYBACK THAT COMES TO PEOPLE LIKE YOU. I AM THE RIGHT HAND OF VENGEANCE AND THE BUTT KICK OF KARMA THAT'S LONG OVERDUE!
AND I WAS SENT BY SOFIA CORAZON.

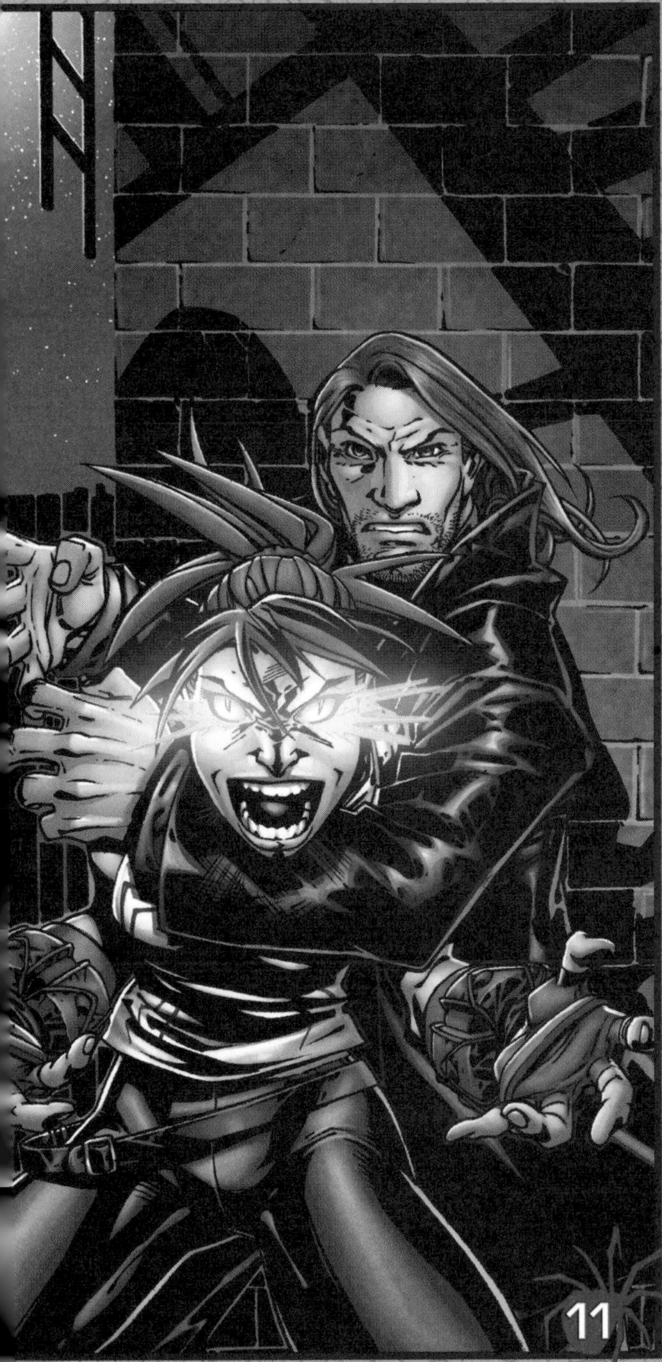

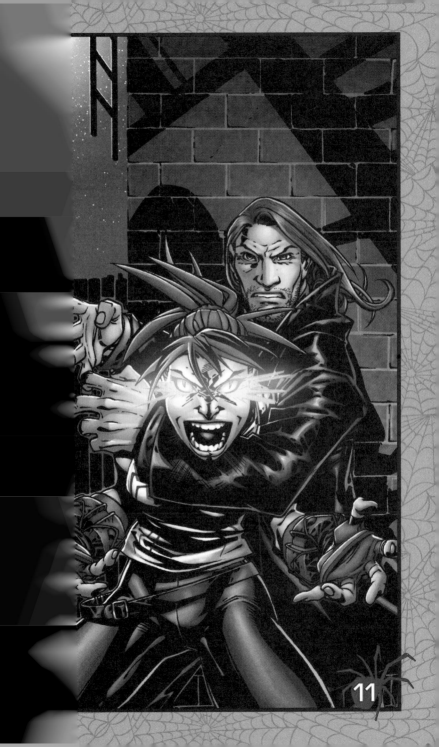

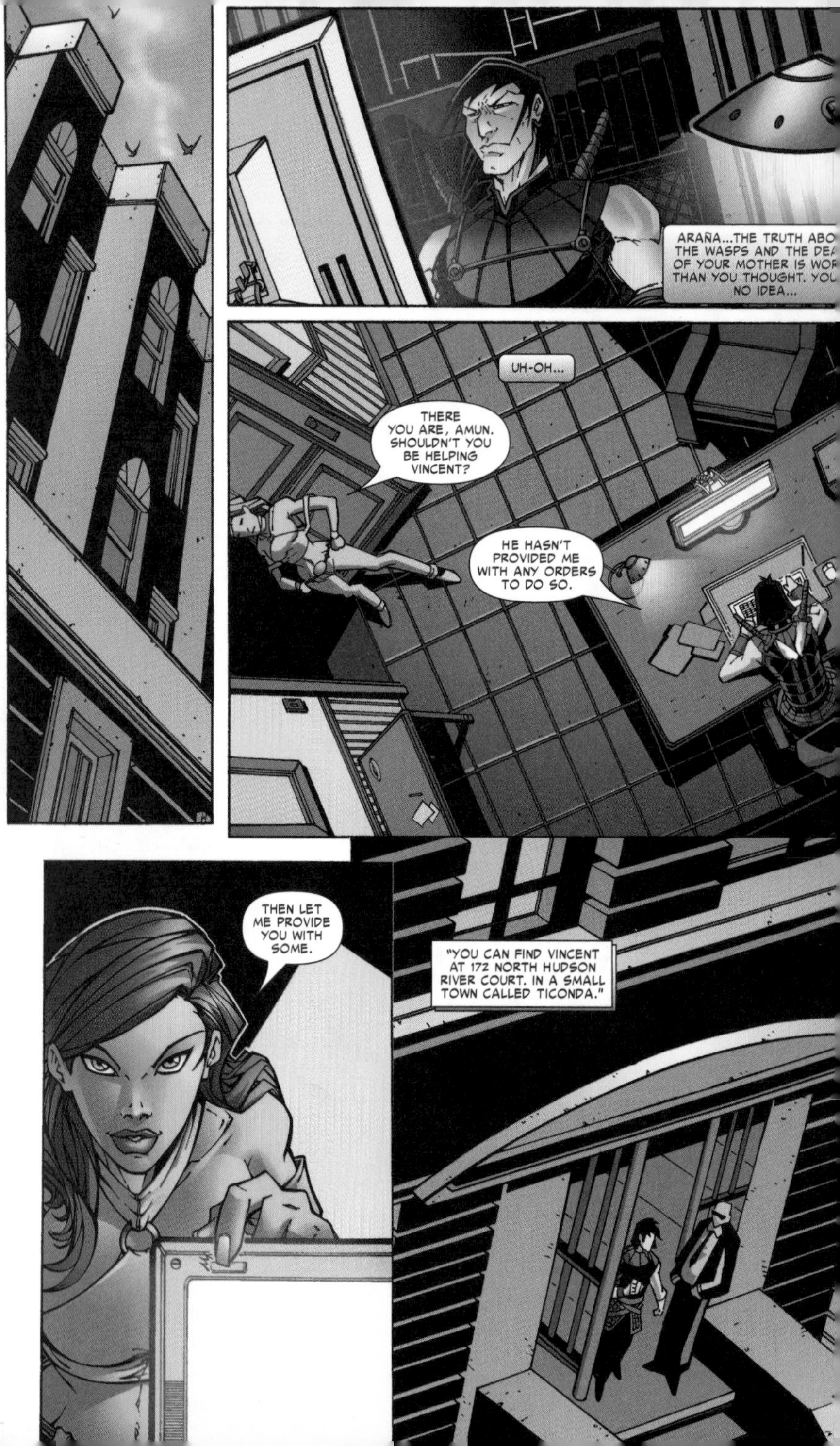

ARAÑA...THE TRUTH ABO THE WASPS AND THE DEA OF YOUR MOTHER IS WOR THAN YOU THOUGHT. YOU NO IDEA...
UH-OH...
THERE YOU ARE, AMUN. SHOULDN'T YOU BE HELPING VINCENT?
HE HASN'T PROVIDED ME WITH ANY ORDERS TO DO SO.
THEN LET ME PROVIDE YOU WITH SOME.
"YOU CAN FIND VINCENT AT 172 NORTH HUDSON RIVER COURT. IN A SMALL TOWN CALLED TICONDA."

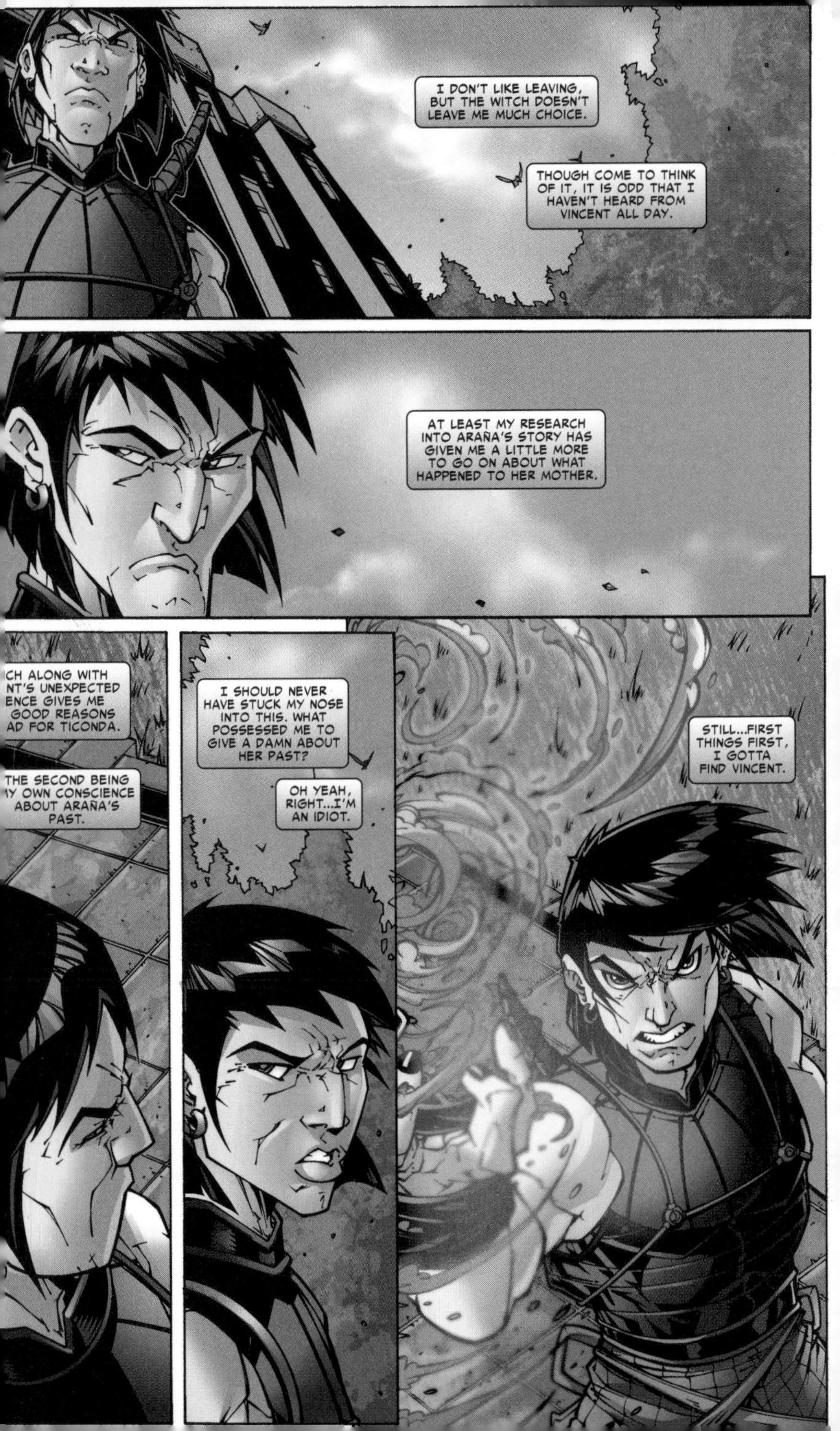
I DON'T LIKE LEAVING, BUT THE WITCH DOESN'T LEAVE ME MUCH CHOICE.
THOUGH COME TO THINK OF IT, IT IS ODD THAT I HAVEN'T HEARD FROM VINCENT ALL DAY.
AT LEAST MY RESEARCH INTO ARAÑA'S STORY HAS GIVEN ME A LITTLE MORE TO GO ON ABOUT WHAT HAPPENED TO HER MOTHER.
CH ALONG WITH NT'S UNEXPECTED ENCE GIVES ME GOOD REASONS AD FOR TICONDA.
THE SECOND BEING Y OWN CONSCIENCE ABOUT ARAÑA'S PAST.
I SHOULD NEVER HAVE STUCK MY NOSE INTO THIS. WHAT POSSESSED ME TO GIVE A DAMN ABOUT HER PAST?
OH YEAH, RIGHT...I'M AN IDIOT.
STILL...FIRST THINGS FIRST, I GOTTA FIND VINCENT.

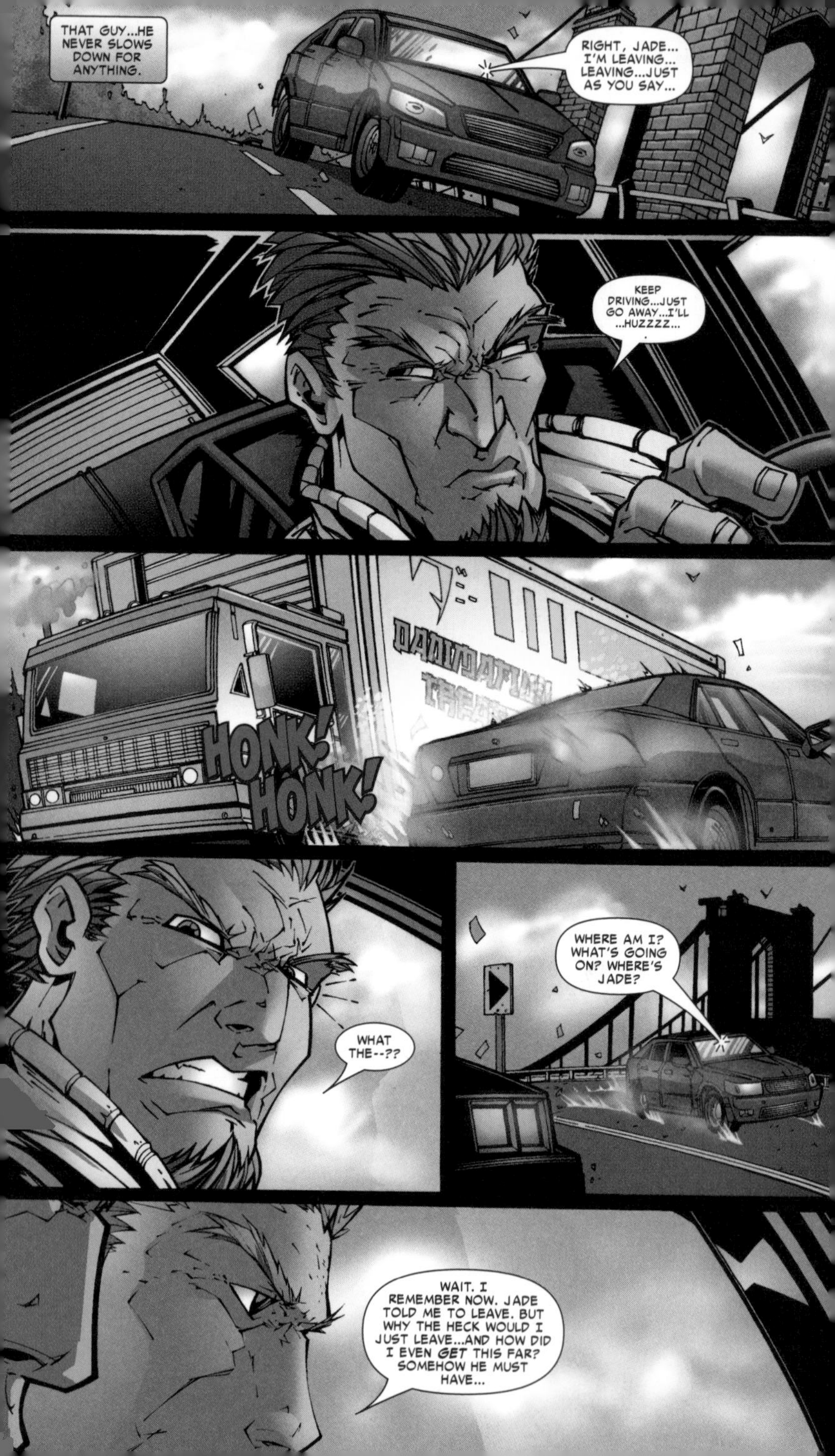
THAT GUY...HE NEVER SLOWS DOWN FOR ANYTHING.
RIGHT, JADE... I'M LEAVING... LEAVING...JUST AS YOU SAY...
KEEP DRIVING...JUST GO AWAY...I'LL ...HUZZZZ... .
HONK! HONK!
WHAT THE--??
WHERE AM I? WHAT'S GOING ON? WHERE'S JADE?
WAIT. I REMEMBER NOW. JADE TOLD ME TO LEAVE. BUT WHY THE HECK WOULD I JUST LEAVE...AND HOW DID I EVEN GET THIS FAR? SOMEHOW HE MUST HAVE...

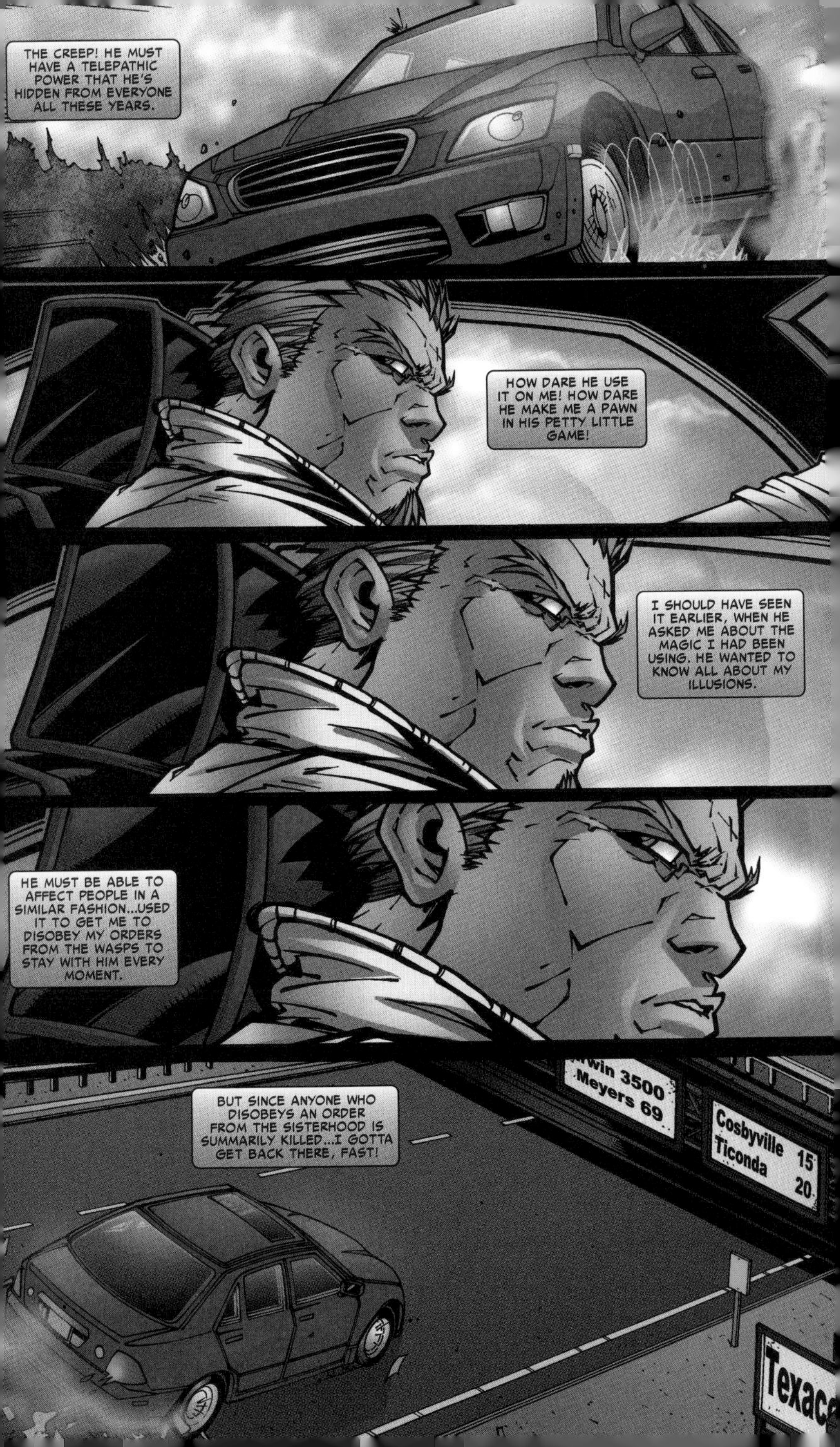
THE CREEP! HE MUST HAVE A TELEPATHIC POWER THAT HE'S HIDDEN FROM EVERYONE ALL THESE YEARS.
HOW DARE HE USE IT ON ME! HOW DARE HE MAKE ME A PAWN IN HIS PETTY LITTLE GAME!
I SHOULD HAVE SEEN IT EARLIER, WHEN HE ASKED ME ABOUT THE MAGIC I HAD BEEN USING. HE WANTED TO KNOW ALL ABOUT MY ILLUSIONS.
HE MUST BE ABLE TO AFFECT PEOPLE IN A SIMILAR FASHION...USED IT TO GET ME TO DISOBEY MY ORDERS FROM THE WASPS TO STAY WITH HIM EVERY MOMENT.
BUT SINCE ANYONE WHO DISOBEYS AN ORDER FROM THE SISTERHOOD IS SUMMARILY KILLED...I GOTTA GET BACK THERE, FAST!
Meyers 69
Cosbyville 15
Ticonda 20

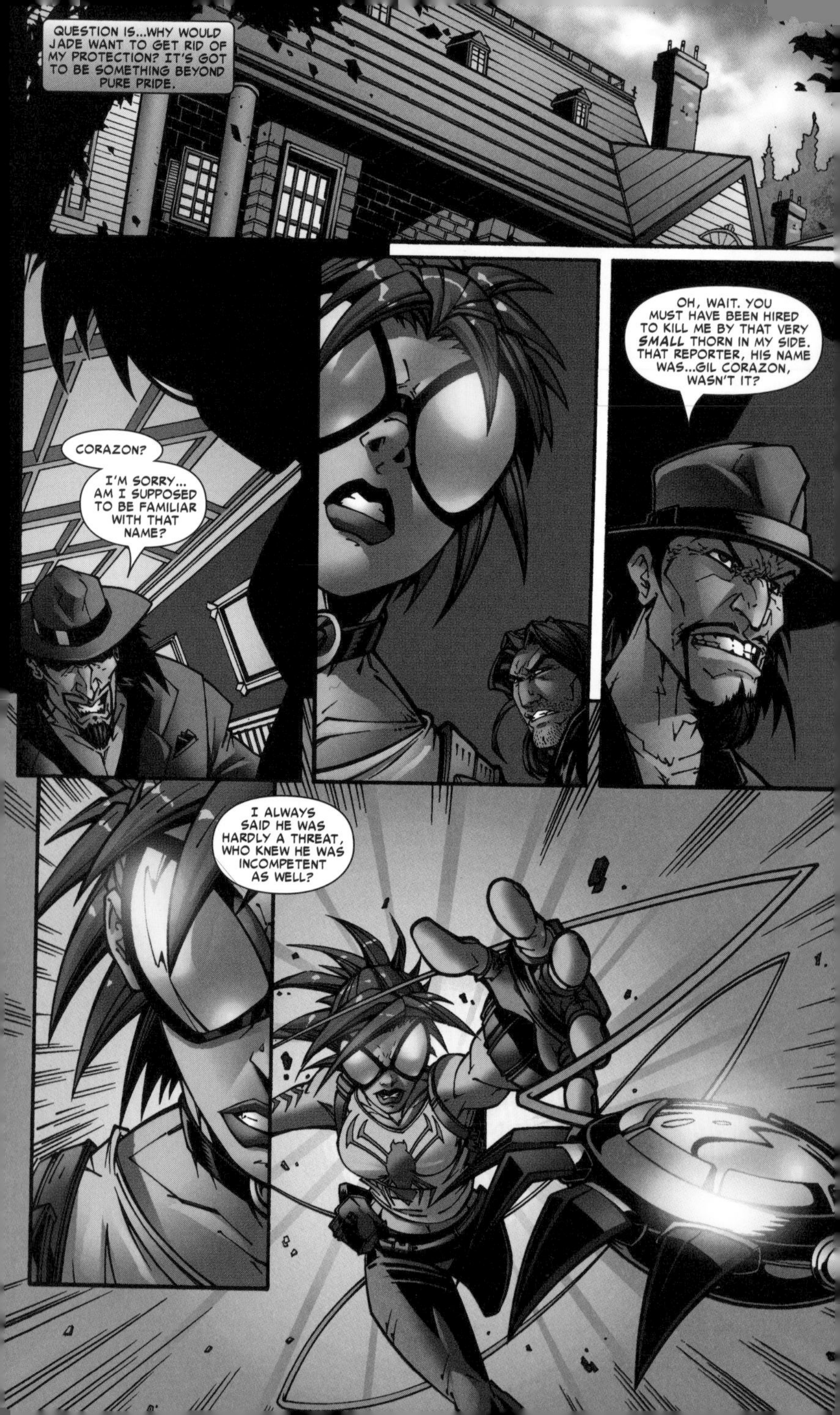
QUESTION IS...WHY WOULD JADE WANT TO GET RID OF MY PROTECTION? IT'S GOT TO BE SOMETHING BEYOND PURE PRIDE.
CORAZON?
I'M SORRY... AM I SUPPOSED TO BE FAMILIAR WITH THAT NAME?
OH, WAIT. YOU MUST HAVE BEEN HIRED TO KILL ME BY THAT VERY SMALL THORN IN MY SIDE. THAT REPORTER, HIS NAME WAS...GIL CORAZON, WASN'T IT?
I ALWAYS SAID HE WAS HARDLY A THREAT, WHO KNEW HE WAS INCOMPETENT AS WELL?

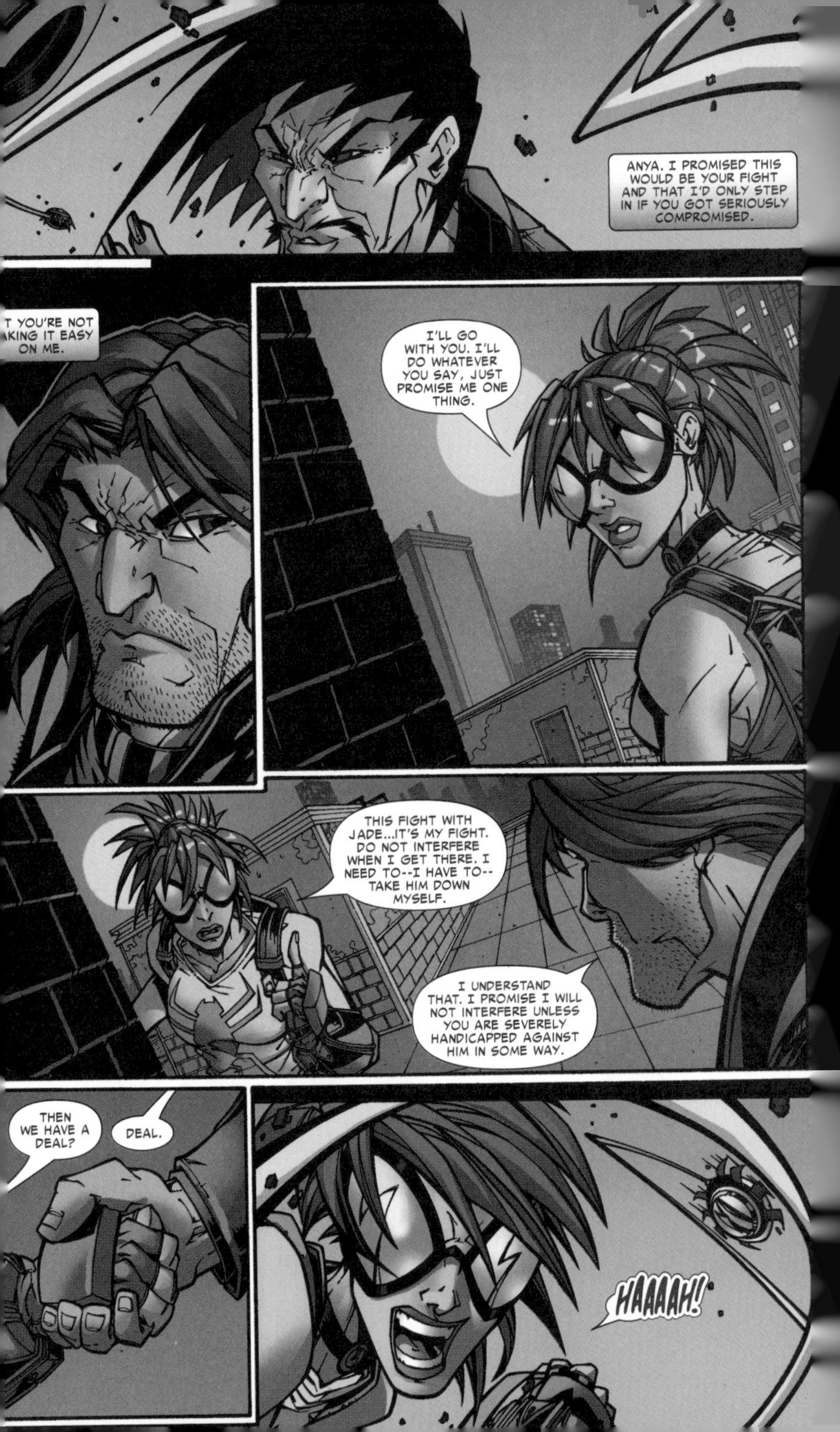
ANYA. I PROMISED THIS WOULD BE YOUR FIGHT AND THAT I'D ONLY STEP IN IF YOU GOT SERIOUSLY COMPROMISED.
T YOU'RE NOT AKING IT EASY ON ME.
I'LL GO WITH YOU. I'LL DO WHATEVER YOU SAY, JUST PROMISE ME ONE THING.
THIS FIGHT WITH JADE...IT'S MY FIGHT. DO NOT INTERFERE WHEN I GET THERE. I NEED TO--I HAVE TO-- TAKE HIM DOWN MYSELF.
I UNDERSTAND THAT. I PROMISE I WILL NOT INTERFERE UNLESS YOU ARE SEVERELY HANDICAPPED AGAINST HIM IN SOME WAY.
THEN WE HAVE A DEAL?
DEAL.
HAAAAH!

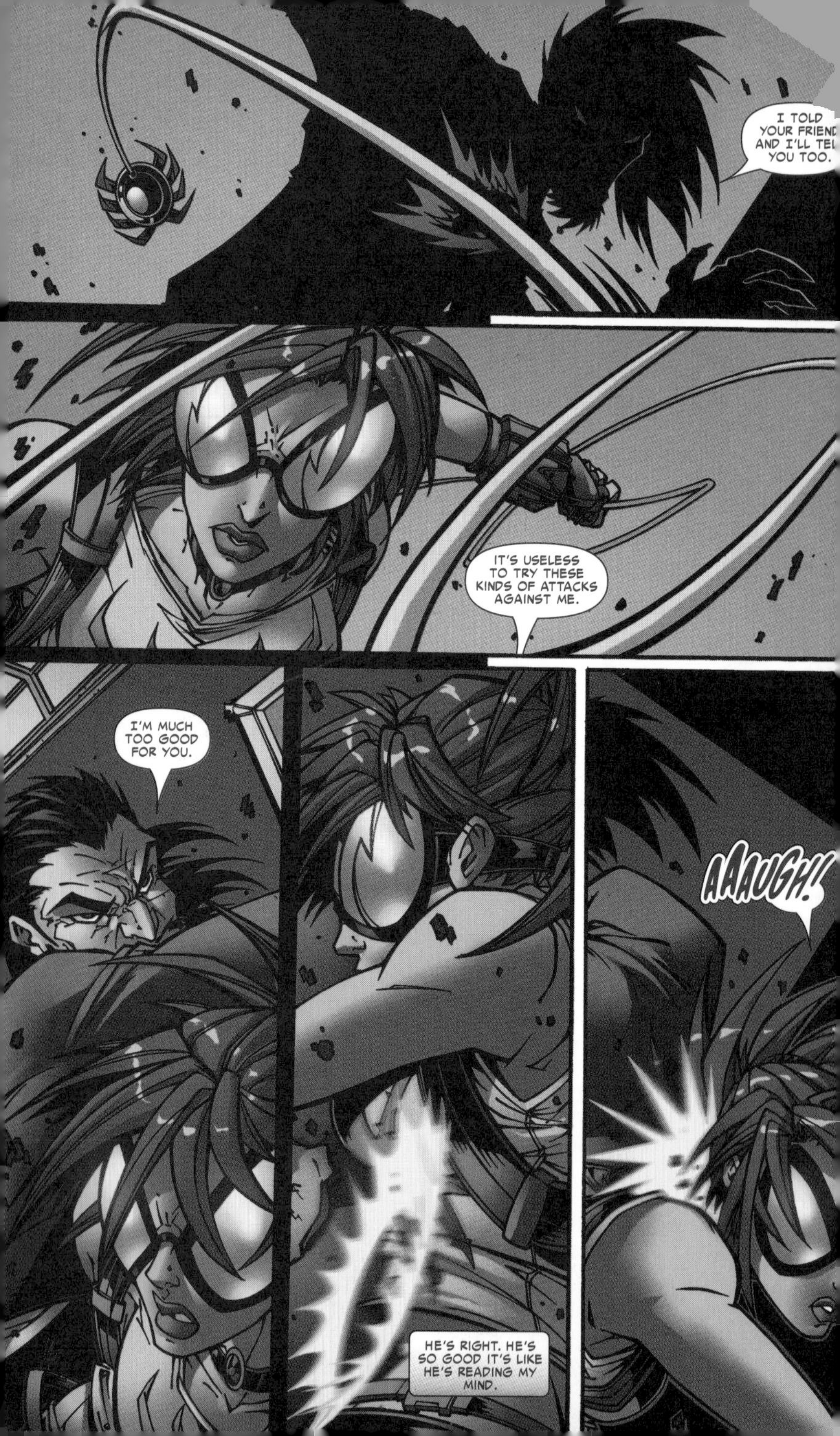
I TOLD YOUR FRIEND AND I'LL TELL YOU TOO.
IT'S USELESS TO TRY THESE KINDS OF ATTACKS AGAINST ME.
I'M MUCH TOO GOOD FOR YOU.
AAAUGH!!
HE'S RIGHT. HE'S SO GOOD IT'S LIKE HE'S READING MY MIND.

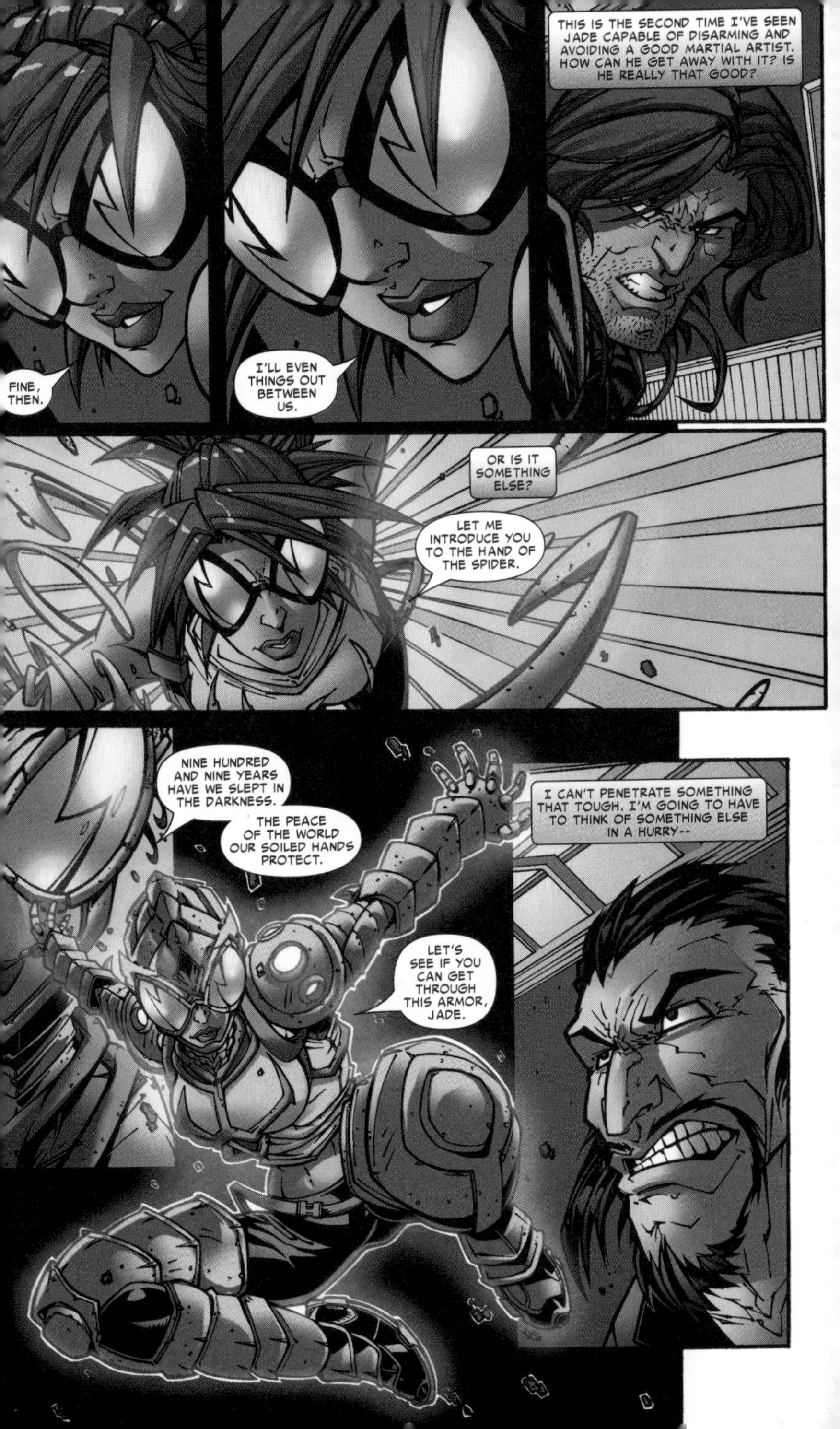
FINE, THEN.
I'LL EVEN THINGS OUT BETWEEN US.
THIS IS THE SECOND TIME I'VE SEEN JADE CAPABLE OF DISARMING AND AVOIDING A GOOD MARTIAL ARTIST. HOW CAN HE GET AWAY WITH IT? IS HE REALLY THAT GOOD?
OR IS IT SOMETHING ELSE?
LET ME INTRODUCE YOU TO THE HAND OF THE SPIDER.
NINE HUNDRED AND NINE YEARS HAVE WE SLEPT IN THE DARKNESS.
THE PEACE OF THE WORLD OUR SOILED HANDS PROTECT.
LET'S SEE IF YOU CAN GET THROUGH THIS ARMOR, JADE.
I CAN'T PENETRATE SOMETHING THAT TOUGH. I'M GOING TO HAVE TO THINK OF SOMETHING ELSE IN A HURRY--

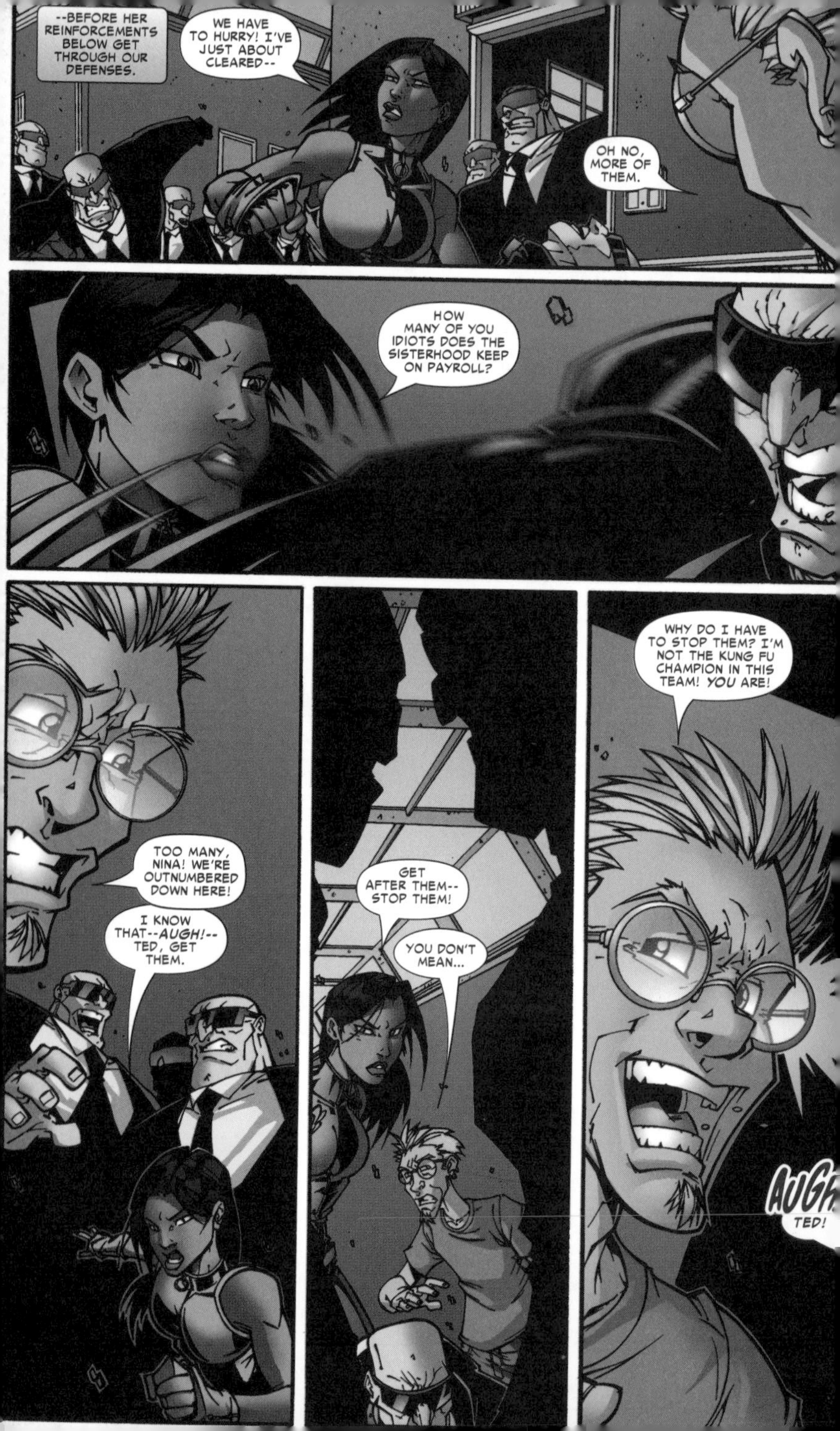
--BEFORE HER REINFORCEMENTS BELOW GET THROUGH OUR DEFENSES.
WE HAVE TO HURRY! I'VE JUST ABOUT CLEARED--
OH NO, MORE OF THEM.
HOW MANY OF YOU IDIOTS DOES THE SISTERHOOD KEEP ON PAYROLL?
TOO MANY, NINA! WE'RE OUTNUMBERED DOWN HERE!
I KNOW THAT--AUGH!-- TED, GET THEM.
GET AFTER THEM-- STOP THEM!
YOU DON'T MEAN...
WHY DO I HAVE TO STOP THEM? I'M NOT THE KUNG FU CHAMPION IN THIS TEAM! YOU ARE!
TED!

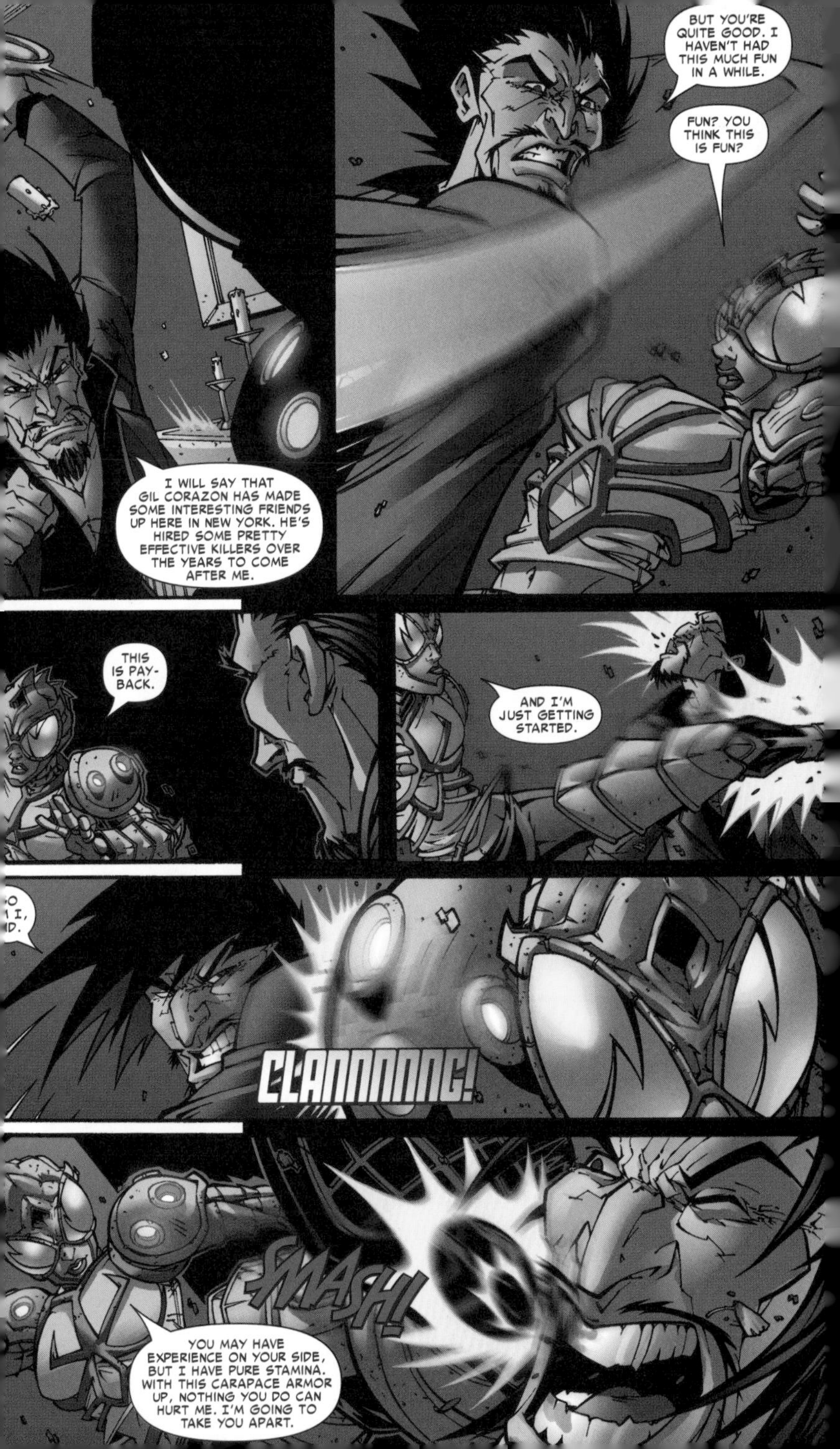
I WILL SAY THAT GIL CORAZON HAS MADE SOME INTERESTING FRIENDS UP HERE IN NEW YORK. HE'S HIRED SOME PRETTY EFFECTIVE KILLERS OVER THE YEARS TO COME AFTER ME.
BUT YOU'RE QUITE GOOD. I HAVEN'T HAD THIS MUCH FUN IN A WHILE.
FUN? YOU THINK THIS IS FUN?
THIS IS PAY-BACK.
AND I'M JUST GETTING STARTED.
CLANNNNNG!
SMASH!
YOU MAY HAVE EXPERIENCE ON YOUR SIDE, BUT I HAVE PURE STAMINA. WITH THIS CARAPACE ARMOR UP, NOTHING YOU DO CAN HURT ME. I'M GOING TO TAKE YOU APART.

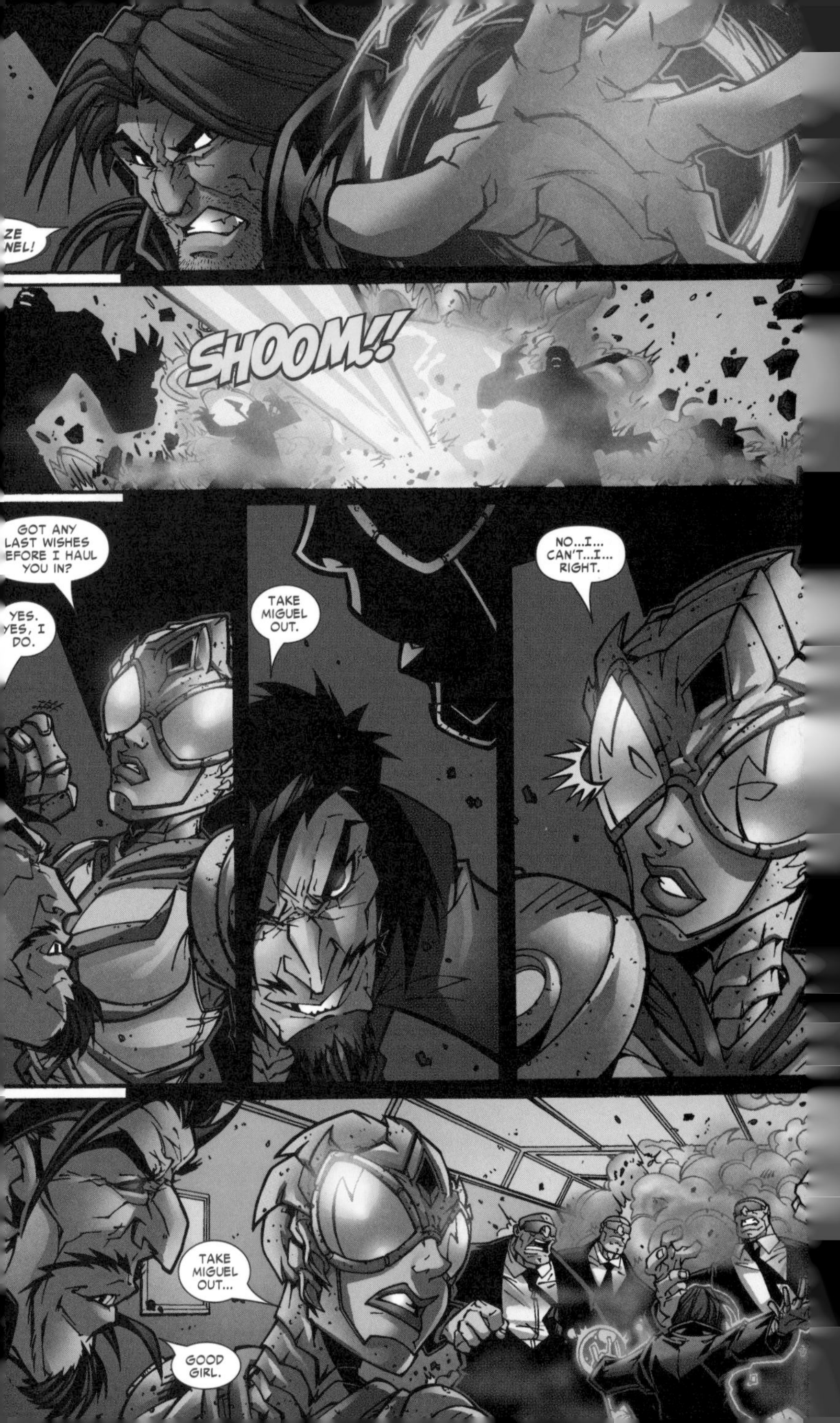
ZE
NEL!
SHOOM!!
GOT ANY LAST WISHES EFORE I HAUL YOU IN?
YES. YES, I DO.
TAKE MIGUEL OUT.
NO...I... CAN'T...I... RIGHT.
TAKE MIGUEL OUT...
GOOD GIRL.

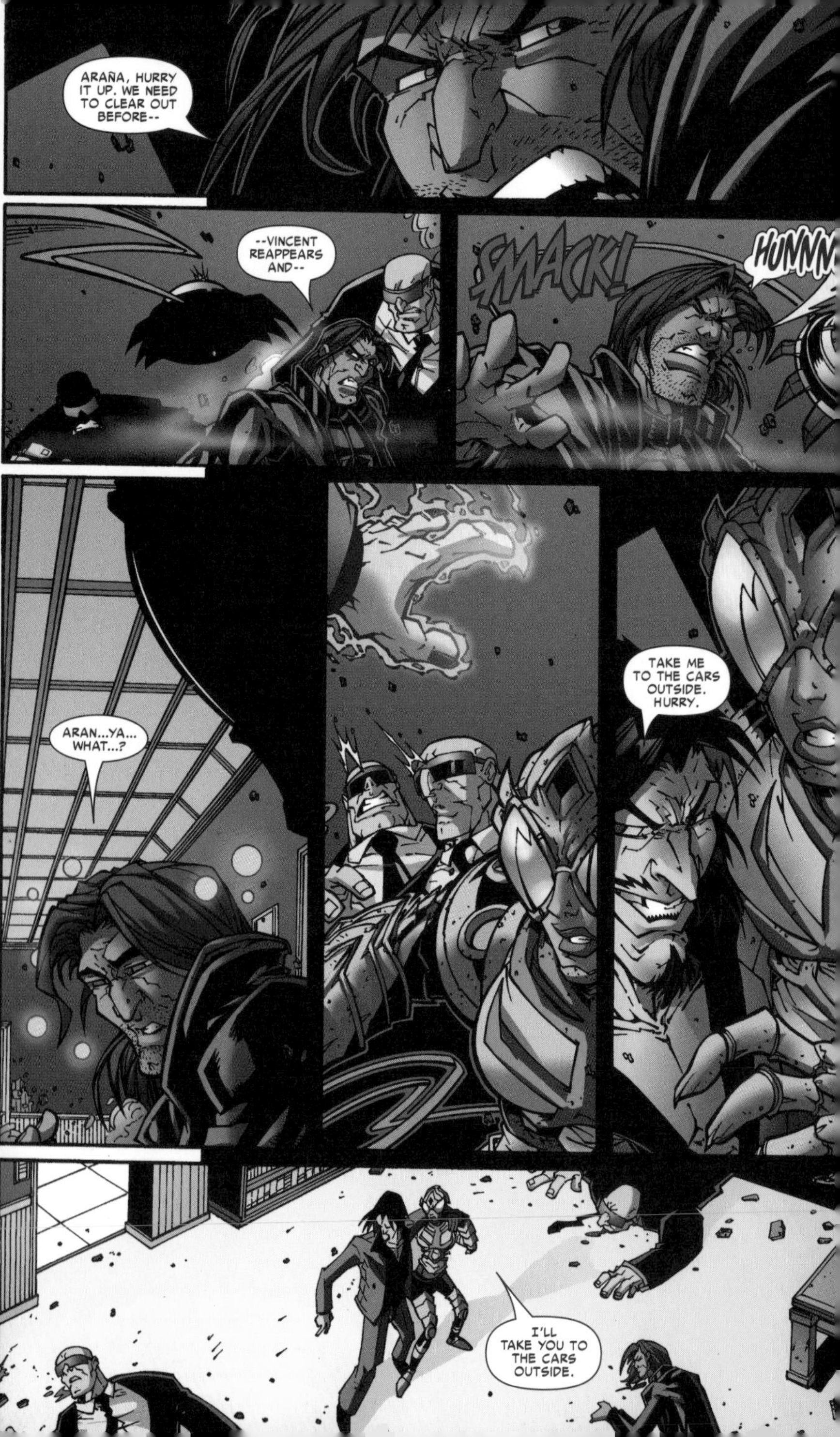
ARAÑA, HURRY IT UP. WE NEED TO CLEAR OUT BEFORE--
--VINCENT REAPPEARS AND--
SMACK!
HUNNN
ARAN...YA... WHAT...?
TAKE ME TO THE CARS OUTSIDE. HURRY.
I'LL TAKE YOU TO THE CARS OUTSIDE.

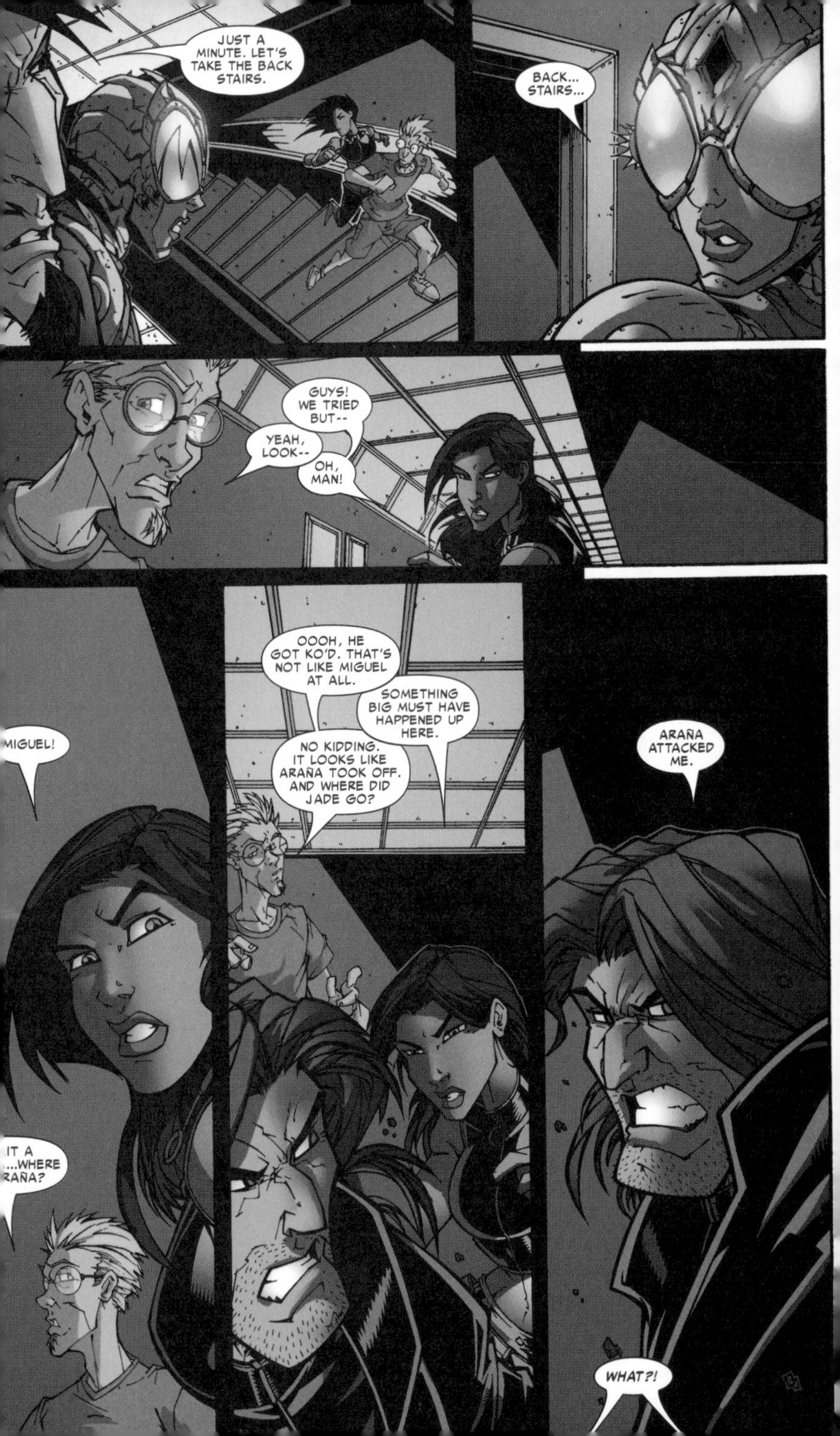
JUST A MINUTE. LET'S TAKE THE BACK STAIRS.
BACK... STAIRS...
GUYS! WE TRIED BUT--
YEAH, LOOK--
OH, MAN!
MIGUEL!
IT A ....WHERE RAÑA?
OOOH, HE GOT KO'D. THAT'S NOT LIKE MIGUEL AT ALL.
SOMETHING BIG MUST HAVE HAPPENED UP HERE.
NO KIDDING. IT LOOKS LIKE ARAÑA TOOK OFF. AND WHERE DID JADE GO?
ARAÑA ATTACKED ME.
WHAT?!

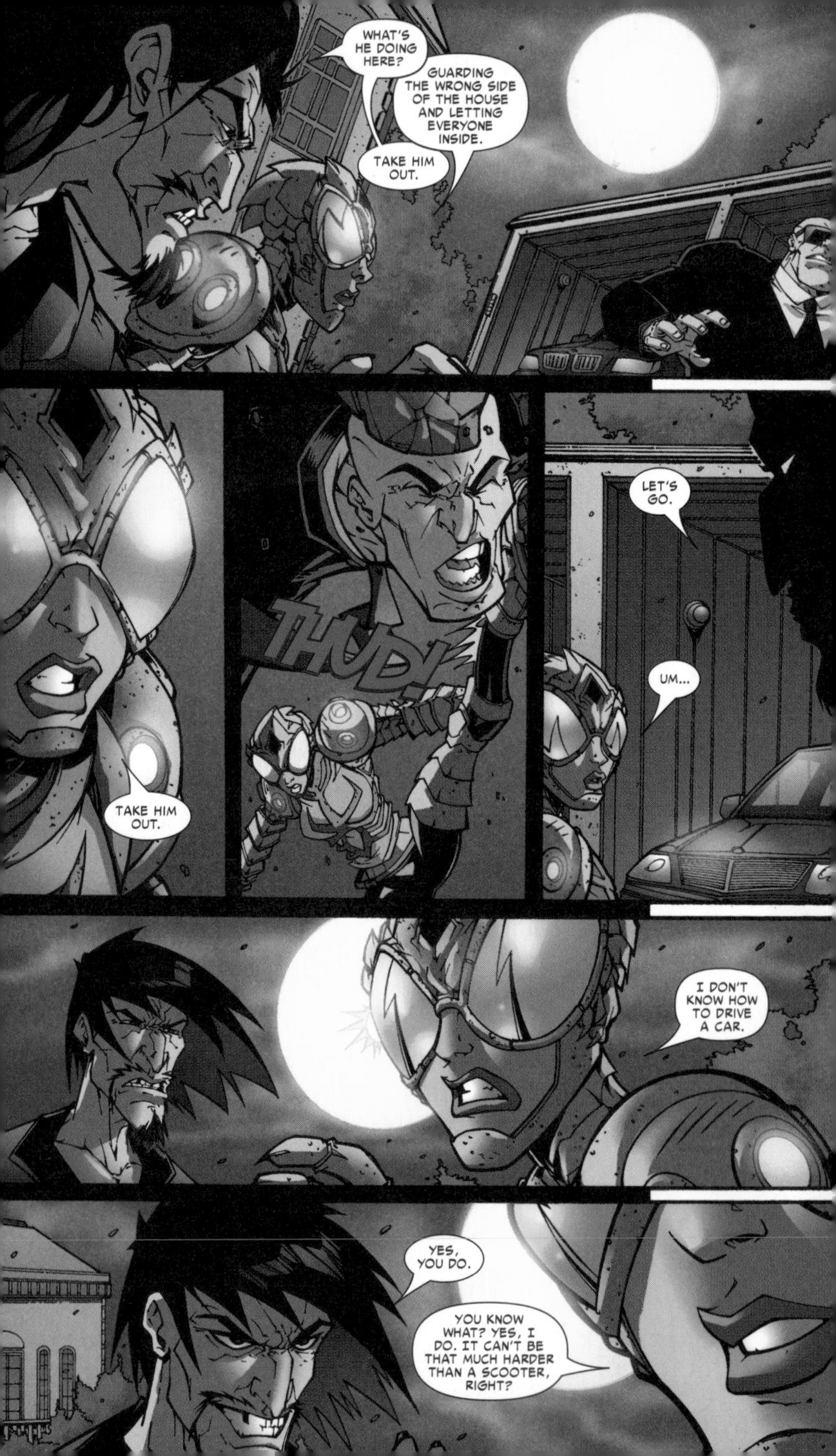
WHAT'S HE DOING HERE?
GUARDING THE WRONG SIDE OF THE HOUSE AND LETTING EVERYONE INSIDE.
TAKE HIM OUT.
TAKE HIM OUT.
THUD!
LET'S GO.
UM...
I DON'T KNOW HOW TO DRIVE A CAR.
YES, YOU DO.
YOU KNOW WHAT? YES, I DO. IT CAN'T BE THAT MUCH HARDER THAN A SCOOTER, RIGHT?

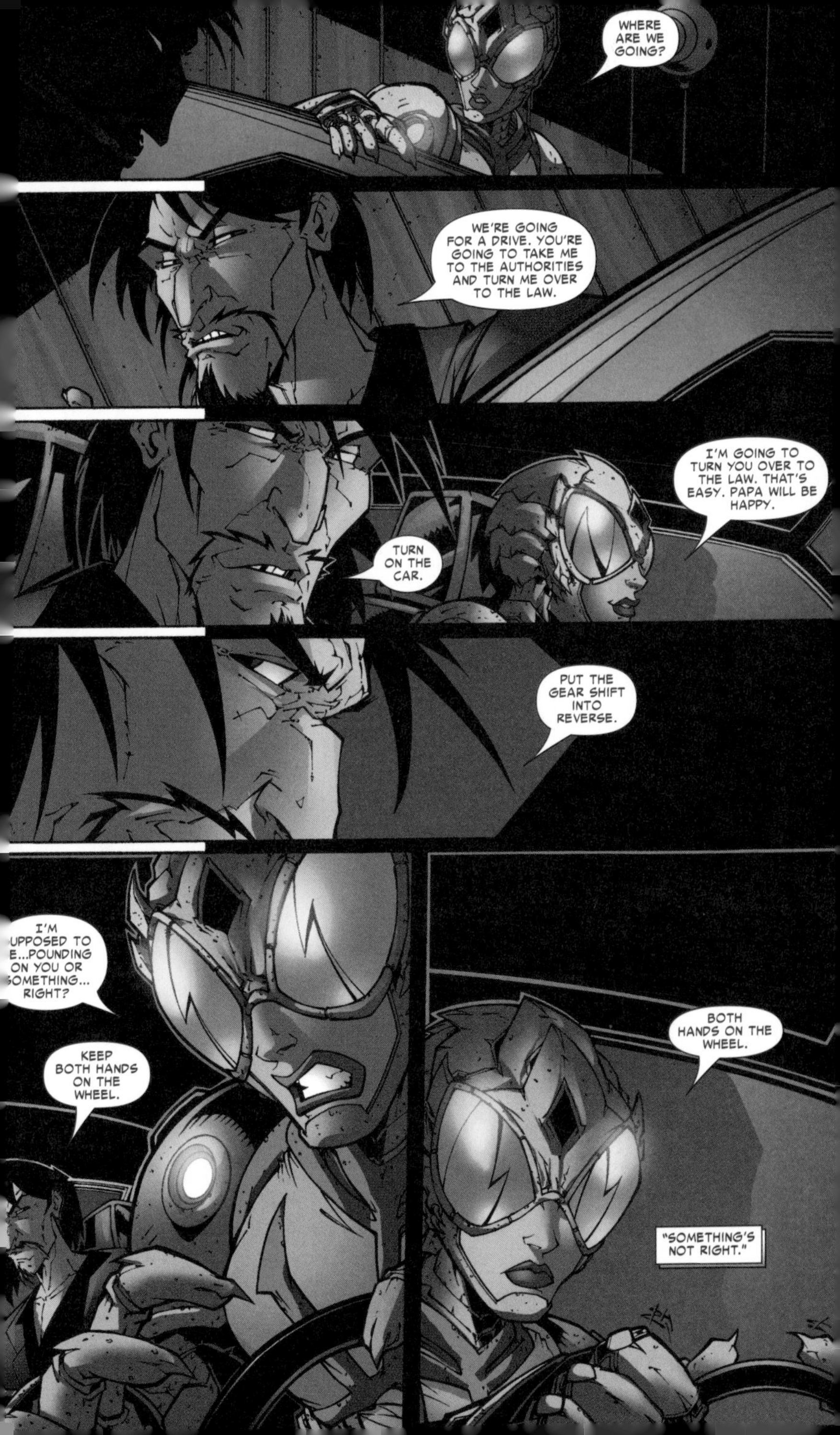
WHERE ARE WE GOING?
WE'RE GOING FOR A DRIVE. YOU'RE GOING TO TAKE ME TO THE AUTHORITIES AND TURN ME OVER TO THE LAW.
I'M GOING TO TURN YOU OVER TO THE LAW. THAT'S EASY. PAPA WILL BE HAPPY.
TURN ON THE CAR.
PUT THE GEAR SHIFT INTO REVERSE.
I'M UPPOSED TO E...POUNDING ON YOU OR OMETHING... RIGHT?
KEEP BOTH HANDS ON THE WHEEL.
BOTH HANDS ON THE WHEEL.
"SOMETHING'S NOT RIGHT."

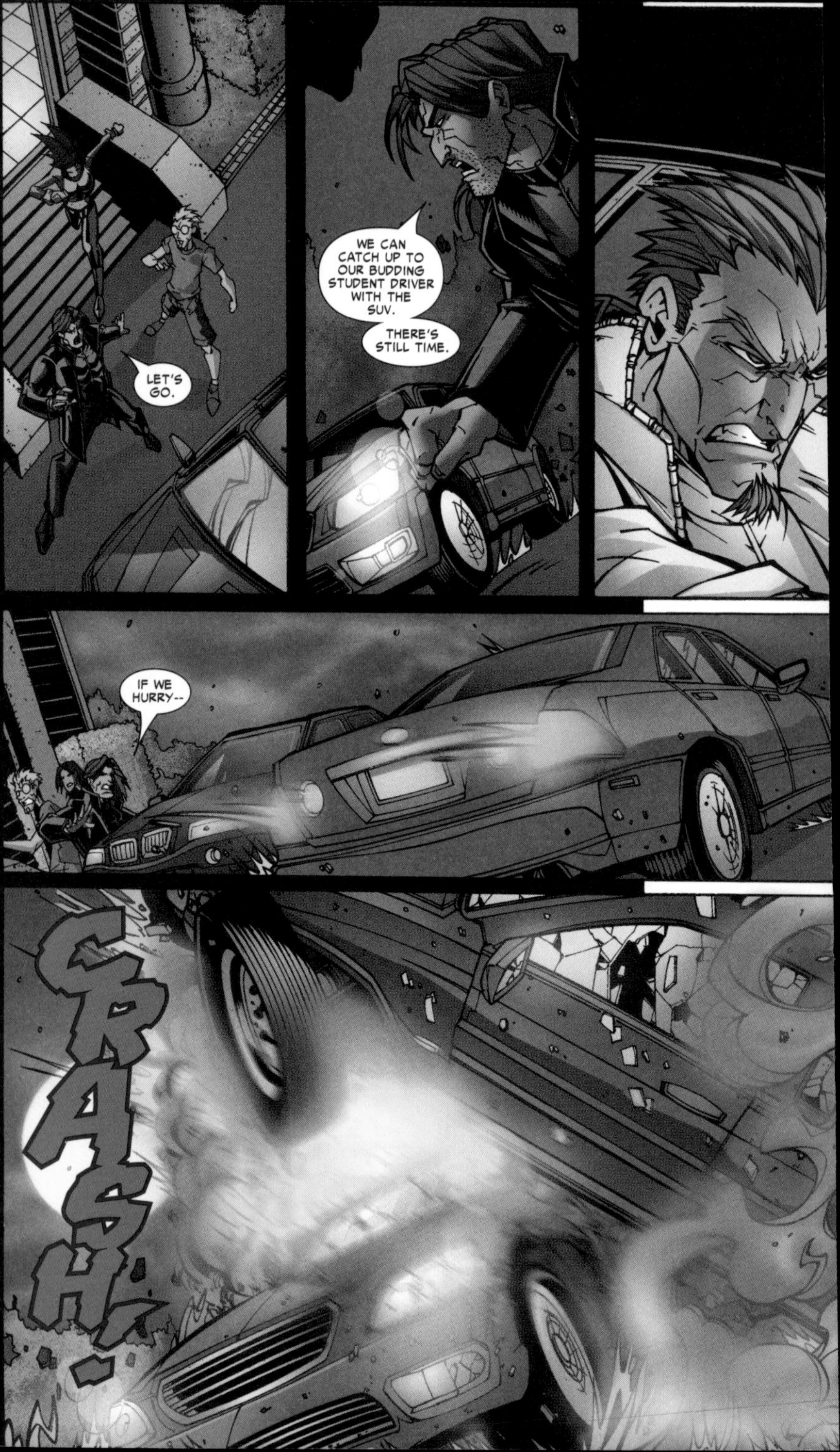
LET'S GO.
WE CAN CATCH UP TO OUR BUDDING STUDENT DRIVER WITH THE SUV.
THERE'S STILL TIME.
IF WE HURRY--
CRASH.

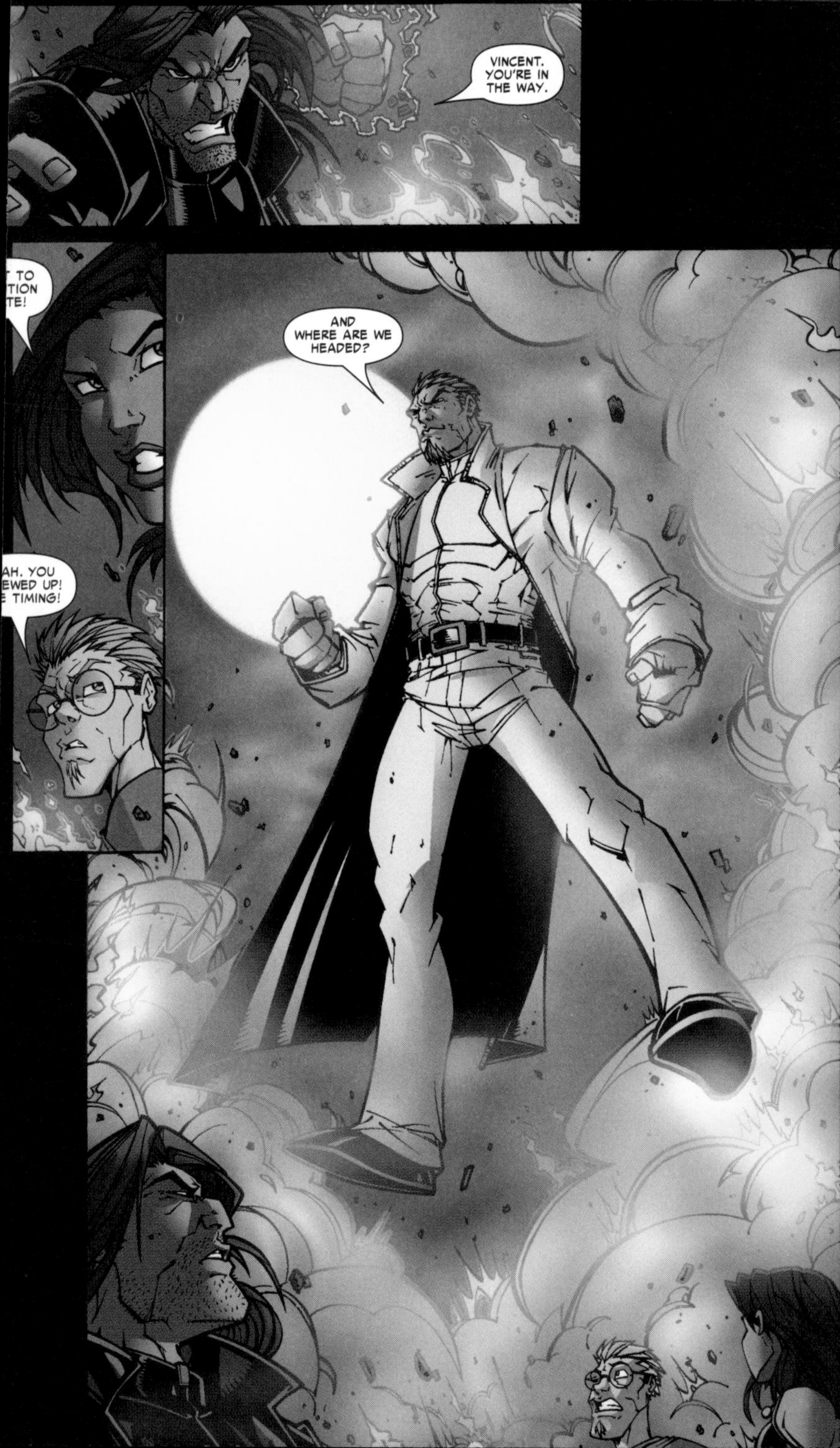
VINCENT. YOU'RE IN THE WAY.
AND WHERE ARE WE HEADED?

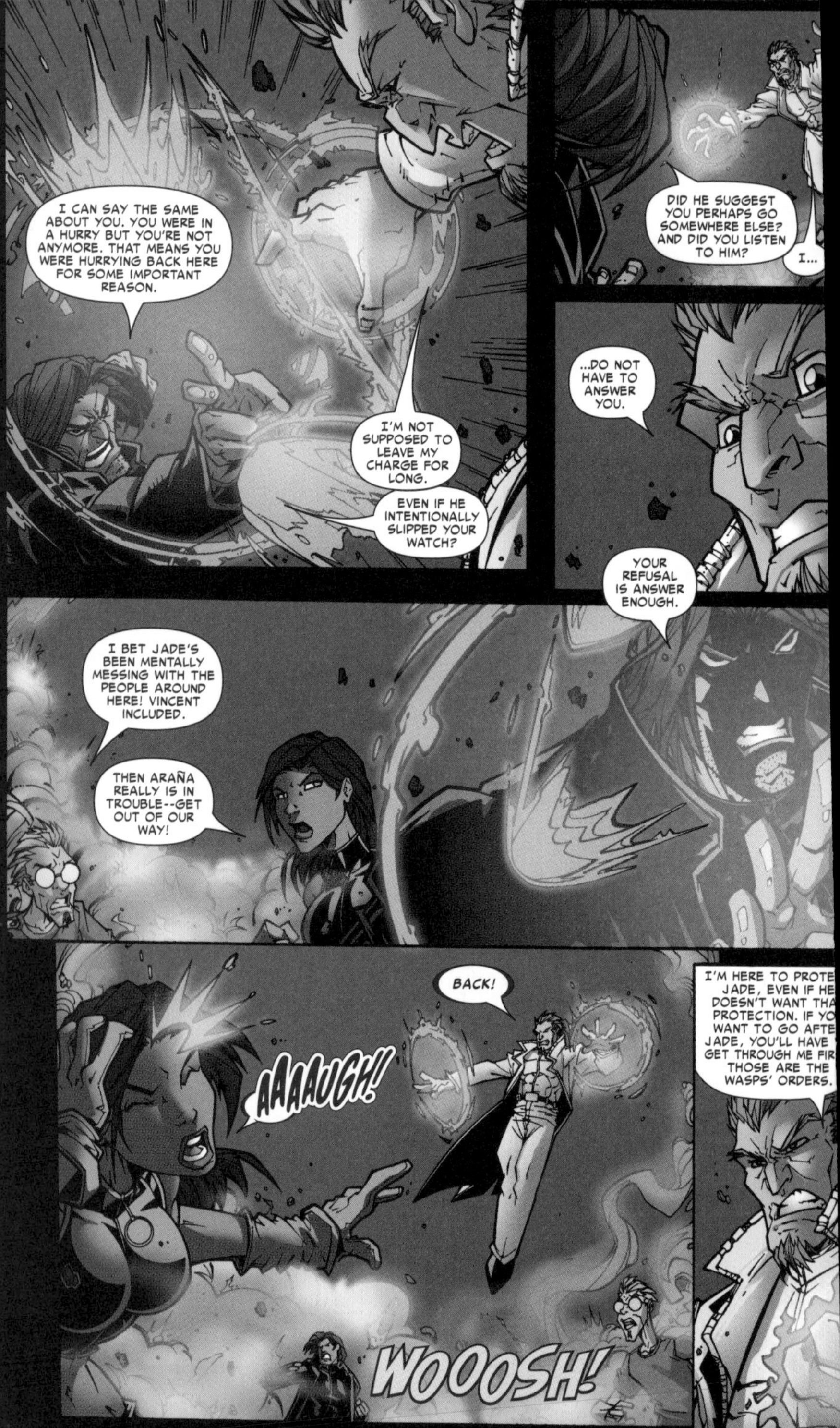

I CAN SAY THE SAME ABOUT YOU. YOU WERE IN A HURRY BUT YOU'RE NOT ANYMORE. THAT MEANS YOU WERE HURRYING BACK HERE FOR SOME IMPORTANT REASON.
I'M NOT SUPPOSED TO LEAVE MY CHARGE FOR LONG.
EVEN IF HE INTENTIONALLY SLIPPED YOUR WATCH?
DID HE SUGGEST YOU PERHAPS GO SOMEWHERE ELSE? AND DID YOU LISTEN TO HIM?
I...
...DO NOT HAVE TO ANSWER YOU.
YOUR REFUSAL IS ANSWER ENOUGH.
I BET JADE'S BEEN MENTALLY MESSING WITH THE PEOPLE AROUND HERE! VINCENT INCLUDED.
THEN ARAÑA REALLY IS IN TROUBLE--GET OUT OF OUR WAY!
BACK!
AAAAUGH!!
I'M HERE TO PROTE JADE, EVEN IF HE DOESN'T WANT THA PROTECTION. IF YO WANT TO GO AFTE JADE, YOU'LL HAVE GET THROUGH ME FIR THOSE ARE THE WASPS' ORDERS.
WOOOSH!

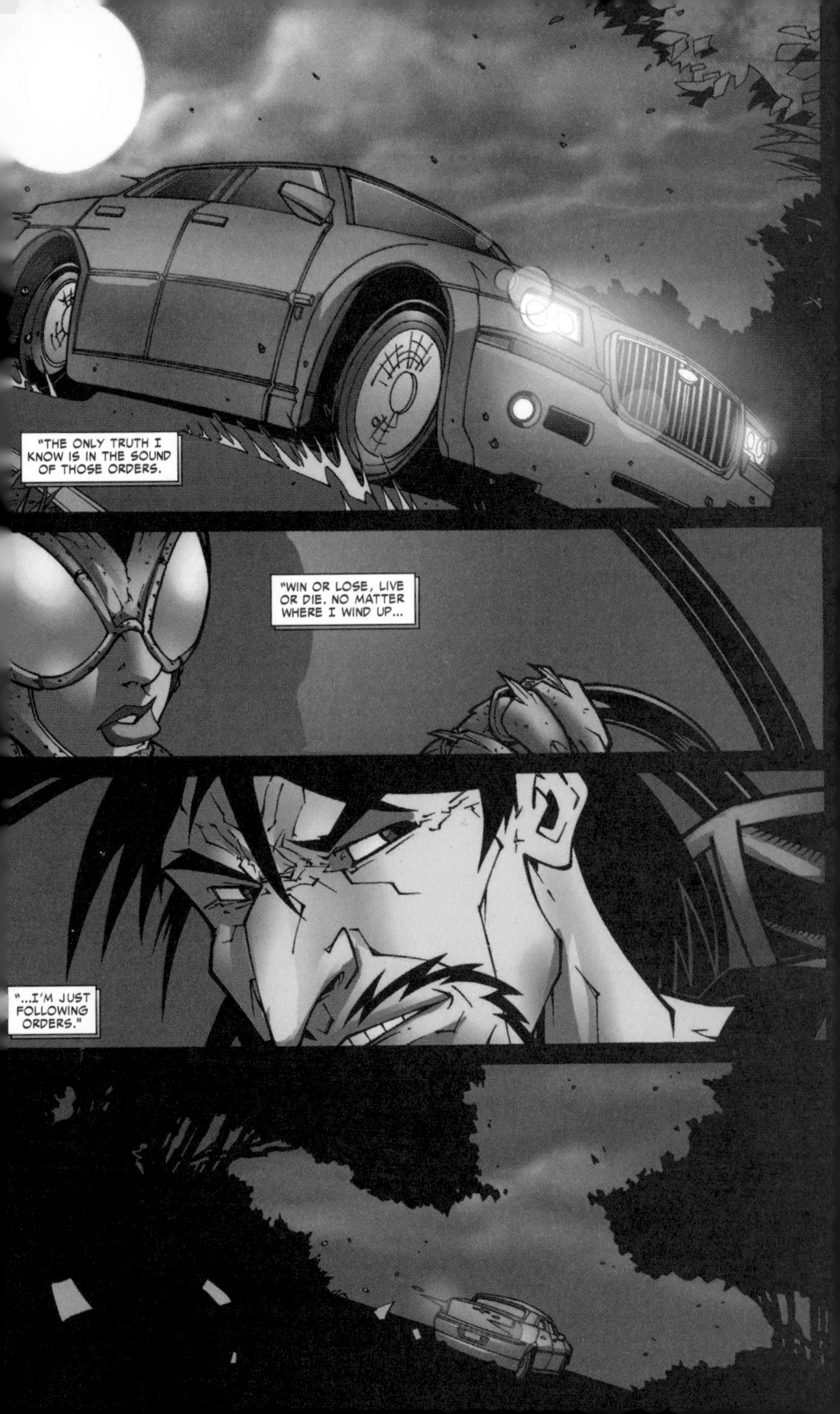
"THE ONLY TRUTH I KNOW IS IN THE SOUND OF THOSE ORDERS.
"WIN OR LOSE, LIVE OR DIE. NO MATTER WHERE I WIND UP...
"...I'M JUST FOLLOWING ORDERS."

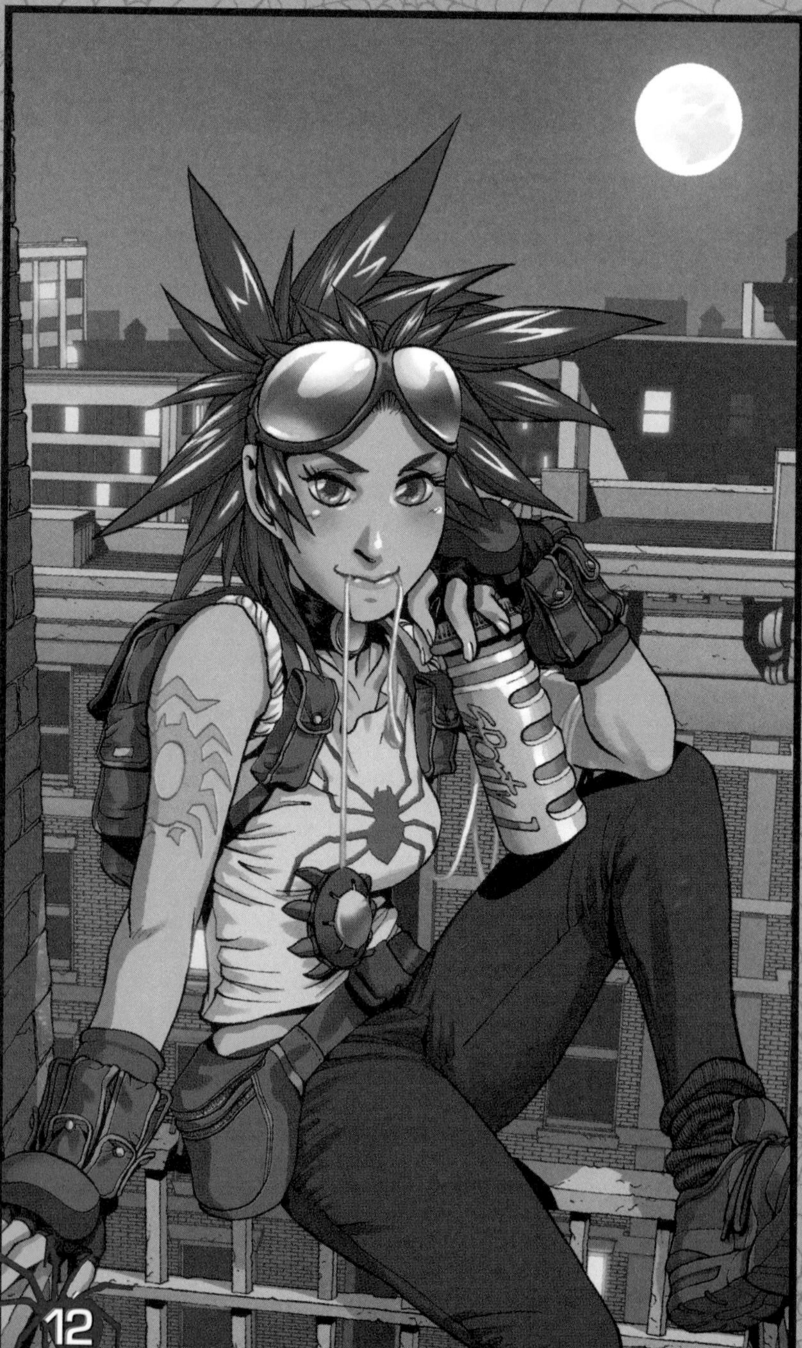

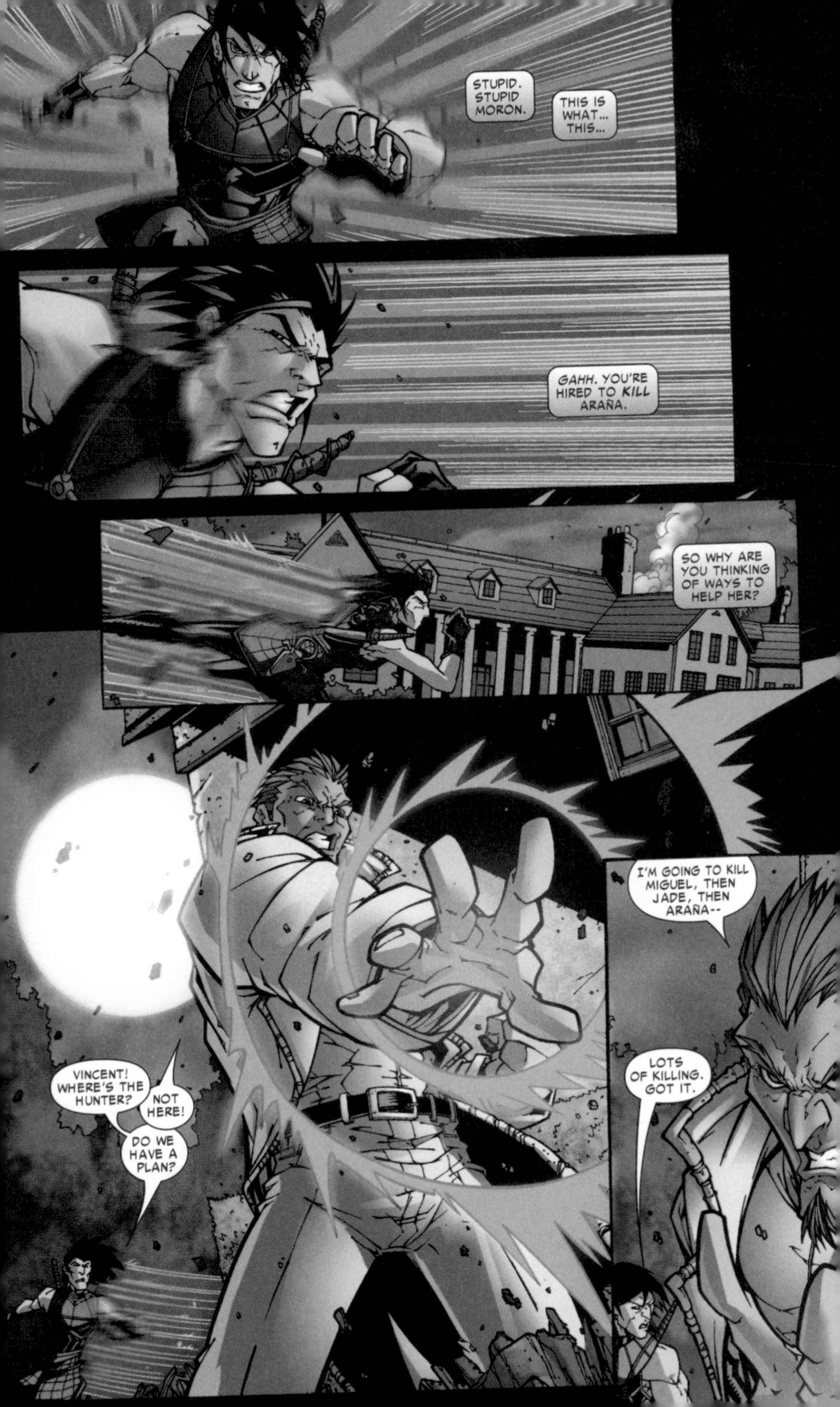
STUPID. STUPID MORON.
THIS IS WHAT... THIS...
GAHH. YOU'RE HIRED TO KILL ARAÑA.
SO WHY ARE YOU THINKING OF WAYS TO HELP HER?
I'M GOING TO KILL MIGUEL, THEN JADE, THEN ARAÑA--
LOTS OF KILLING. GOT IT.
VINCENT! WHERE'S THE HUNTER?
NOT HERE!
DO WE HAVE A PLAN?

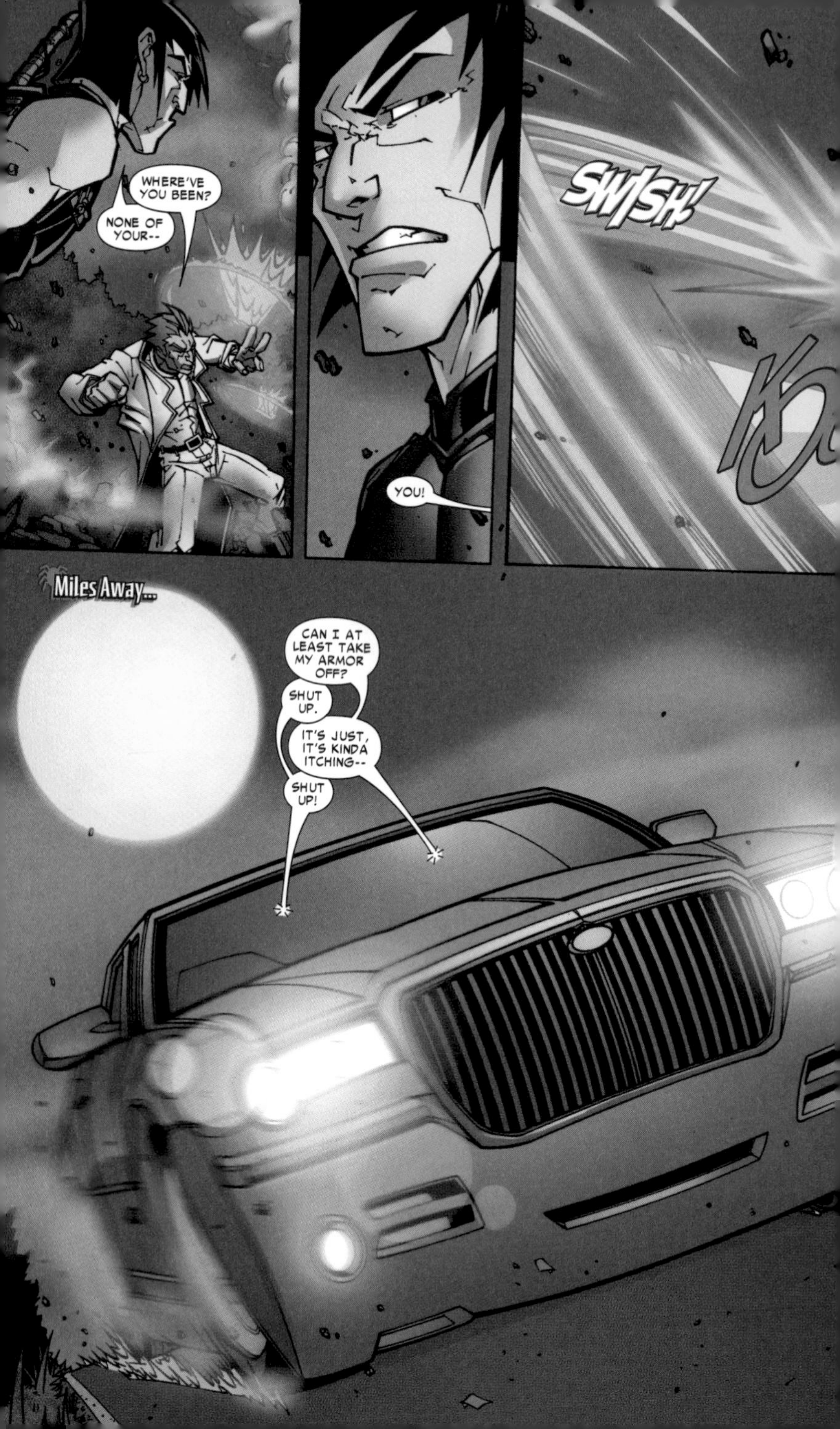
WHERE'VE YOU BEEN?
NONE OF YOUR--
YOU!
SWISH!
Miles Away...
CAN I AT LEAST TAKE MY ARMOR OFF?
SHUT UP.
IT'S JUST, IT'S KINDA ITCHING--
SHUT UP!

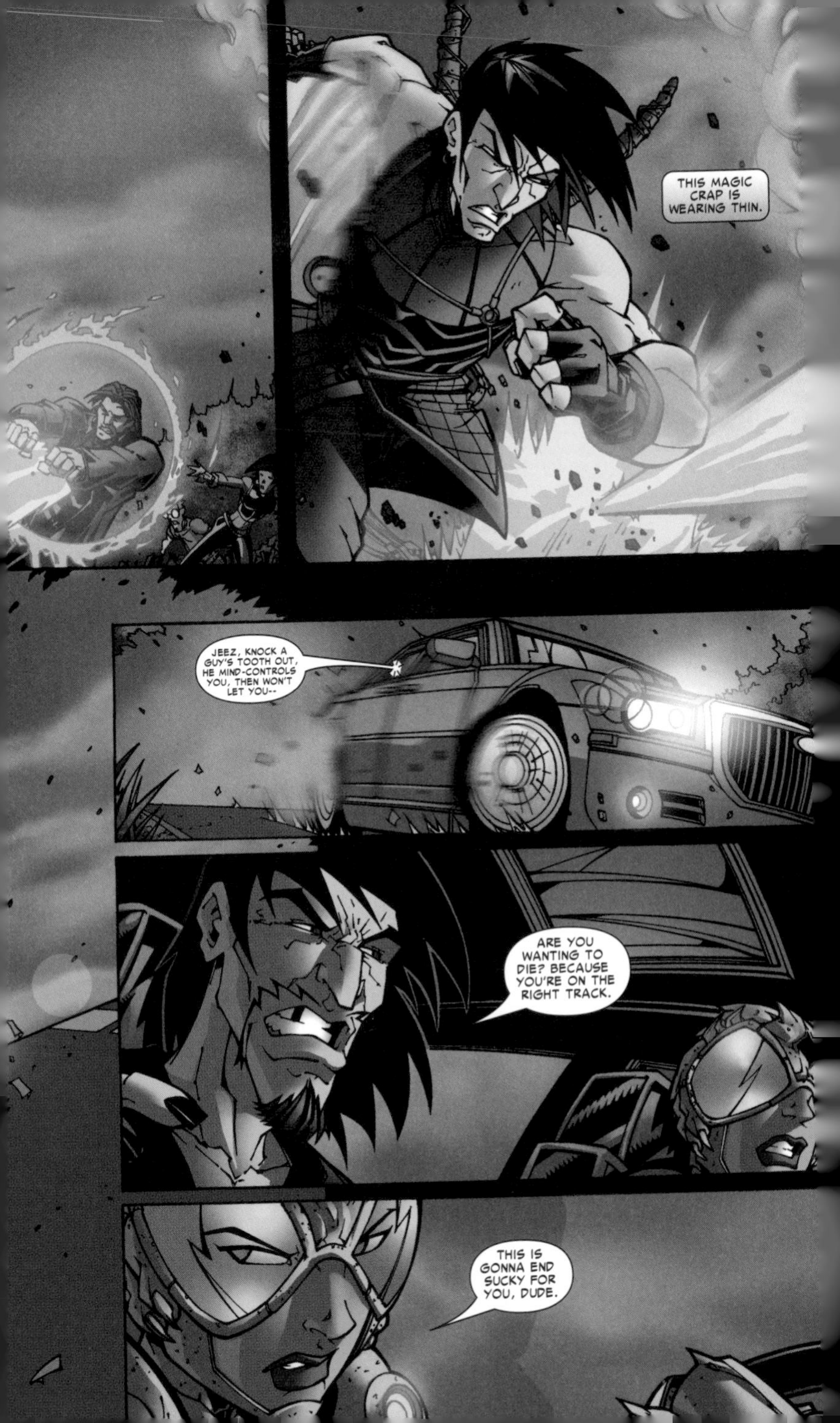
THIS MAGIC CRAP IS WEARING THIN.
JEEZ, KNOCK A GUY'S TOOTH OUT, HE MIND-CONTROLS YOU, THEN WON'T LET YOU--
ARE YOU WANTING TO DIE? BECAUSE YOU'RE ON THE RIGHT TRACK.
THIS IS GONNA END SUCKY FOR YOU, DUDE.

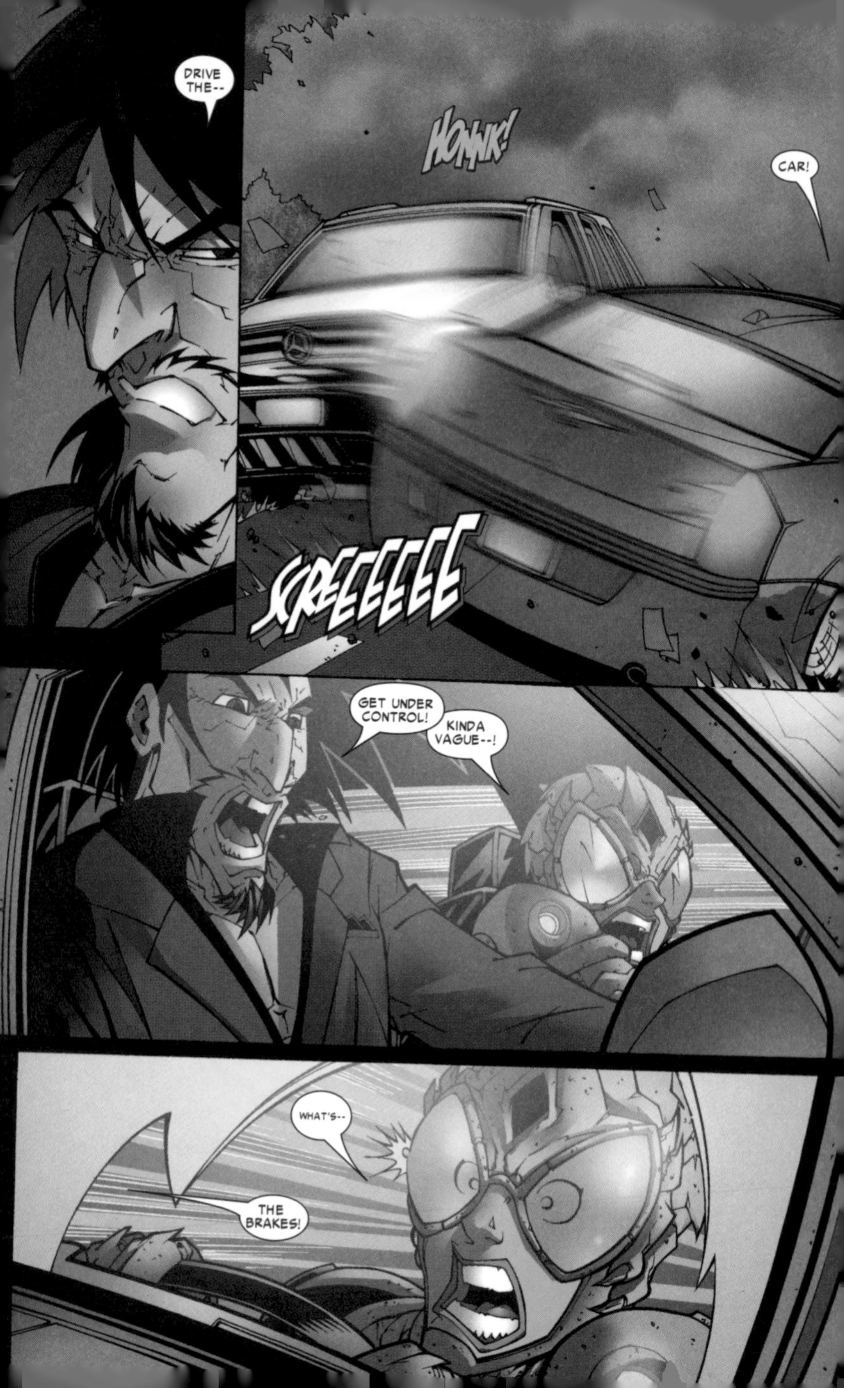
DRIVE THE--
HONNK!
CAR!
SCREEEEEEE
GET UNDER CONTROL!
KINDA VAGUE--!
WHAT'S--
THE BRAKES!

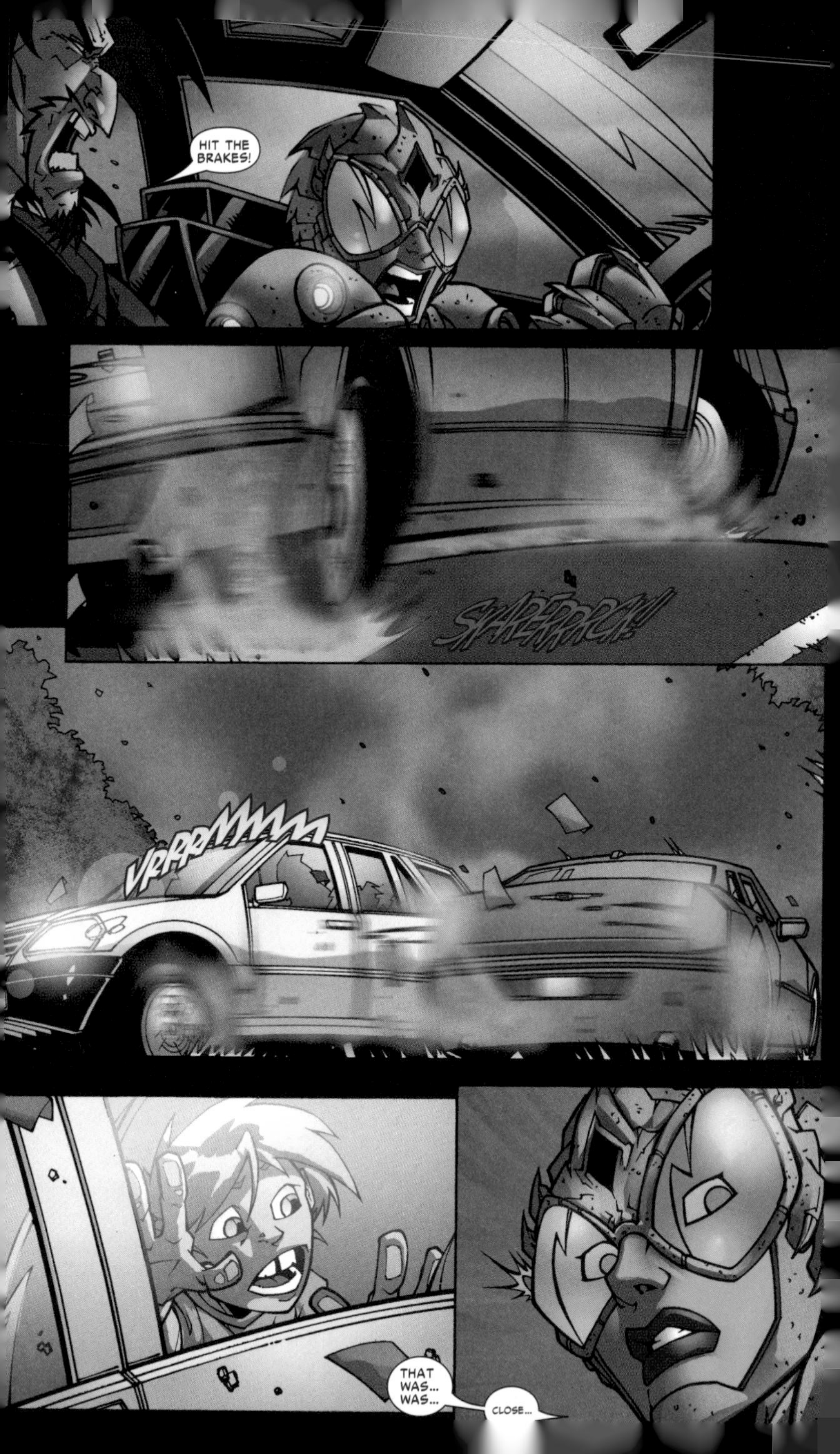
HIT THE BRAKES!
THAT WAS... WAS...
CLOSE...

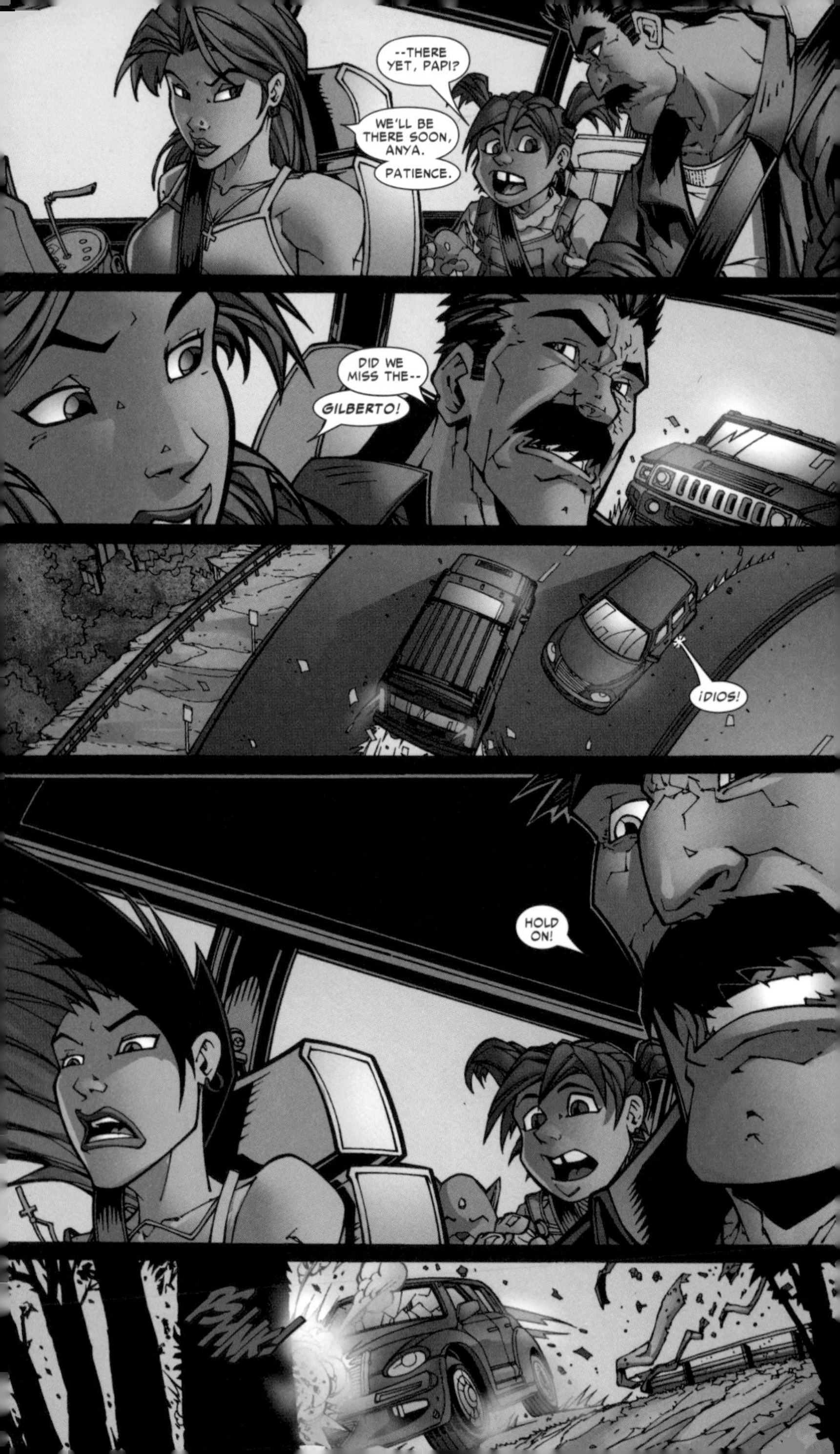
--THERE YET, PAPI?
WE'LL BE THERE SOON, ANYA.
PATIENCE.
DID WE MISS THE--
GILBERTO!
¡DIOS!
HOLD ON!

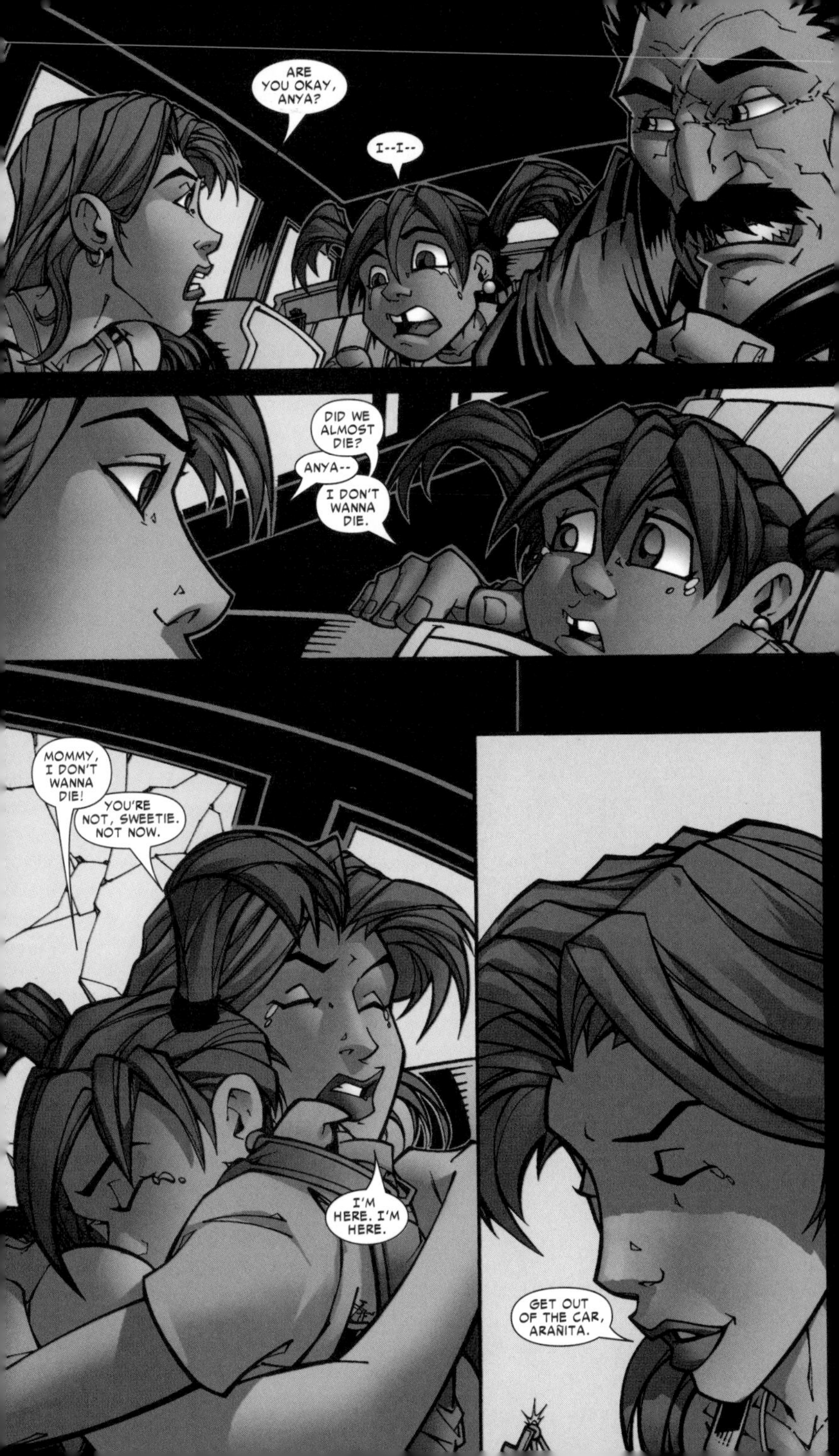
ARE YOU OKAY, ANYA?
I--I--
DID WE ALMOST DIE?
ANYA--
I DON'T WANNA DIE.
MOMMY, I DON'T WANNA DIE!
YOU'RE NOT, SWEETIE. NOT NOW.
I'M HERE. I'M HERE.
GET OUT OF THE CAR, ARAÑITA.

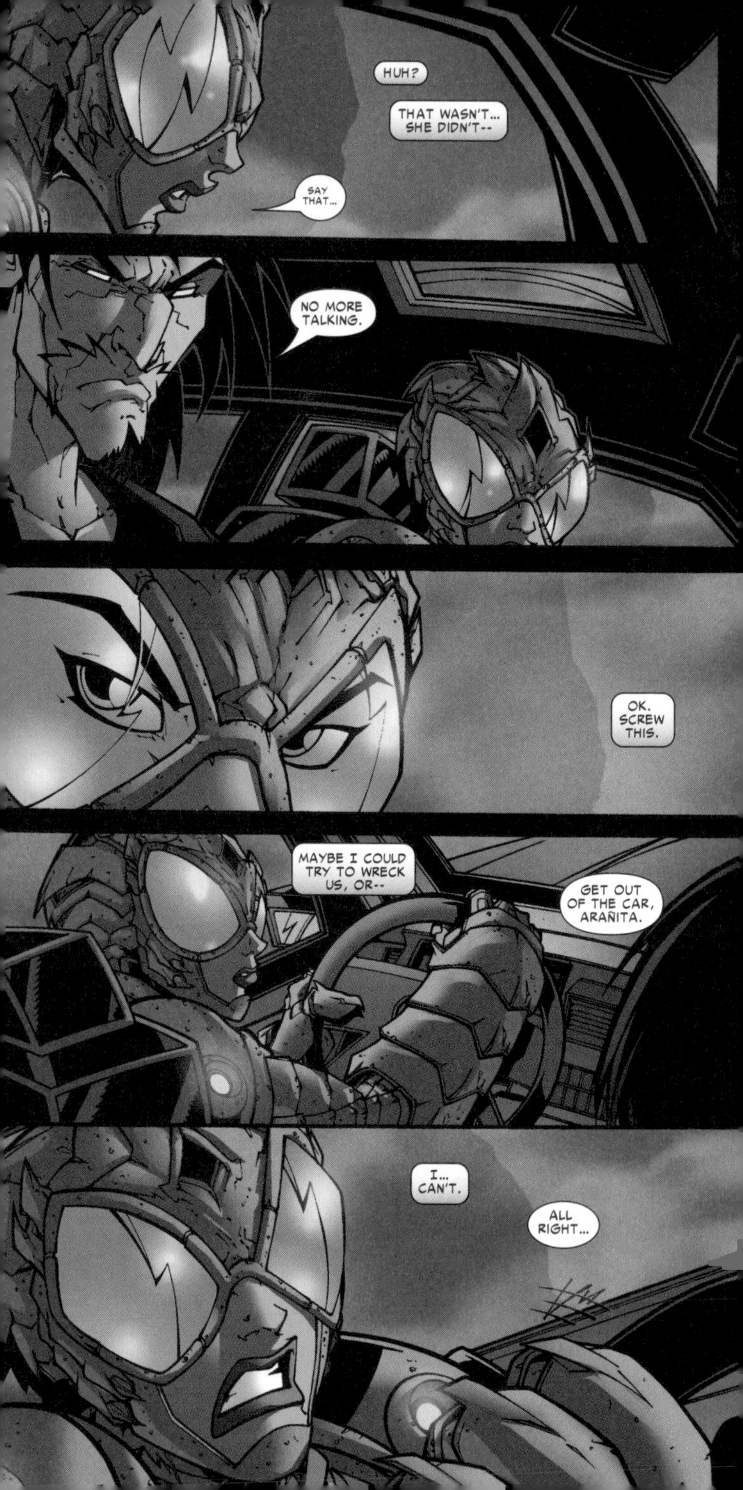
HUH?
THAT WASN'T... SHE DIDN'T--
SAY THAT...
NO MORE TALKING.
OK. SCREW THIS.
MAYBE I COULD TRY TO WRECK US, OR--
GET OUT OF THE CAR, ARAÑITA.
I... CAN'T.
ALL RIGHT...

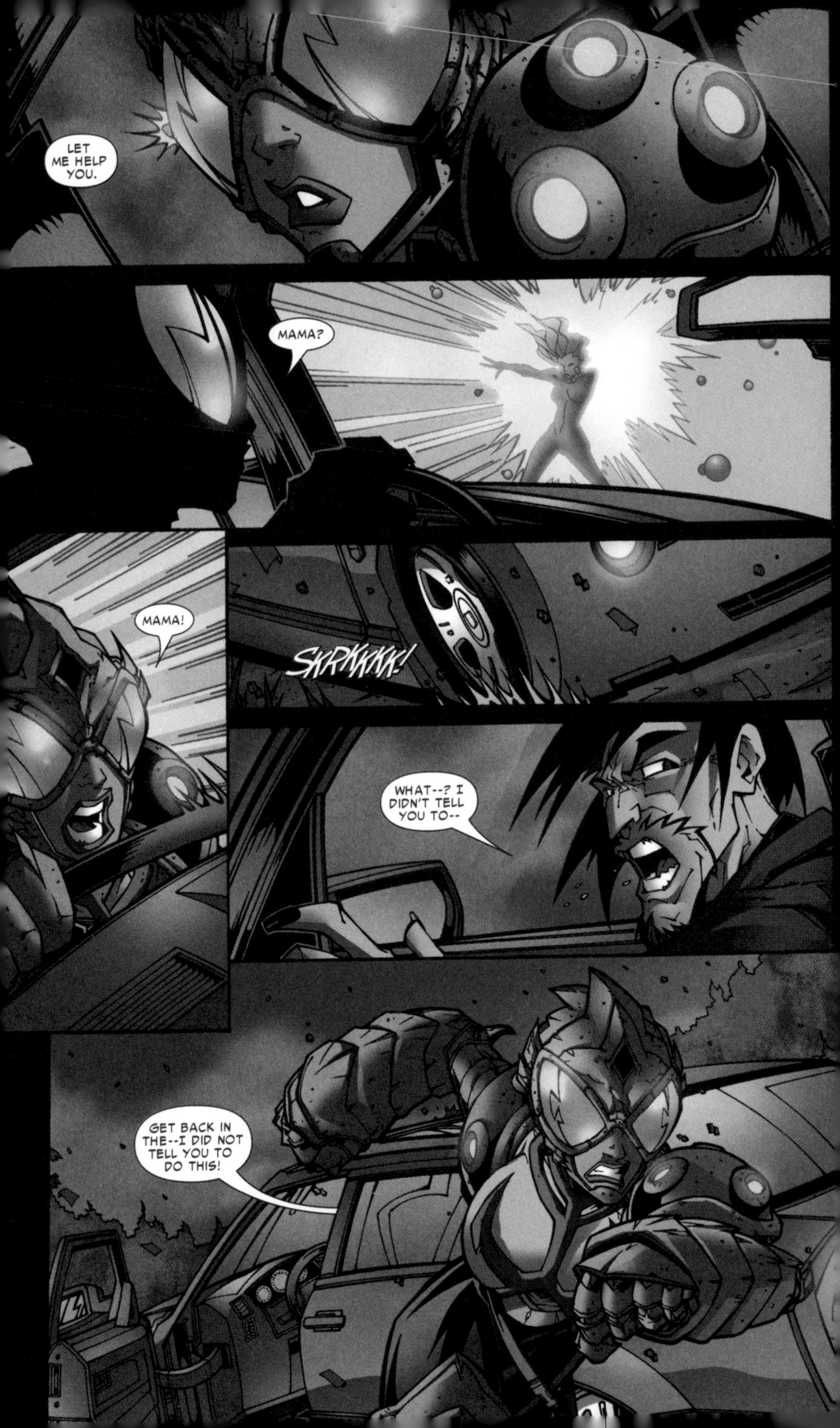
LET ME HELP YOU.
MAMA?
MAMA!
SKRKKKK!
WHAT--? I DIDN'T TELL YOU TO--
GET BACK IN THE--I DID NOT TELL YOU TO DO THIS!

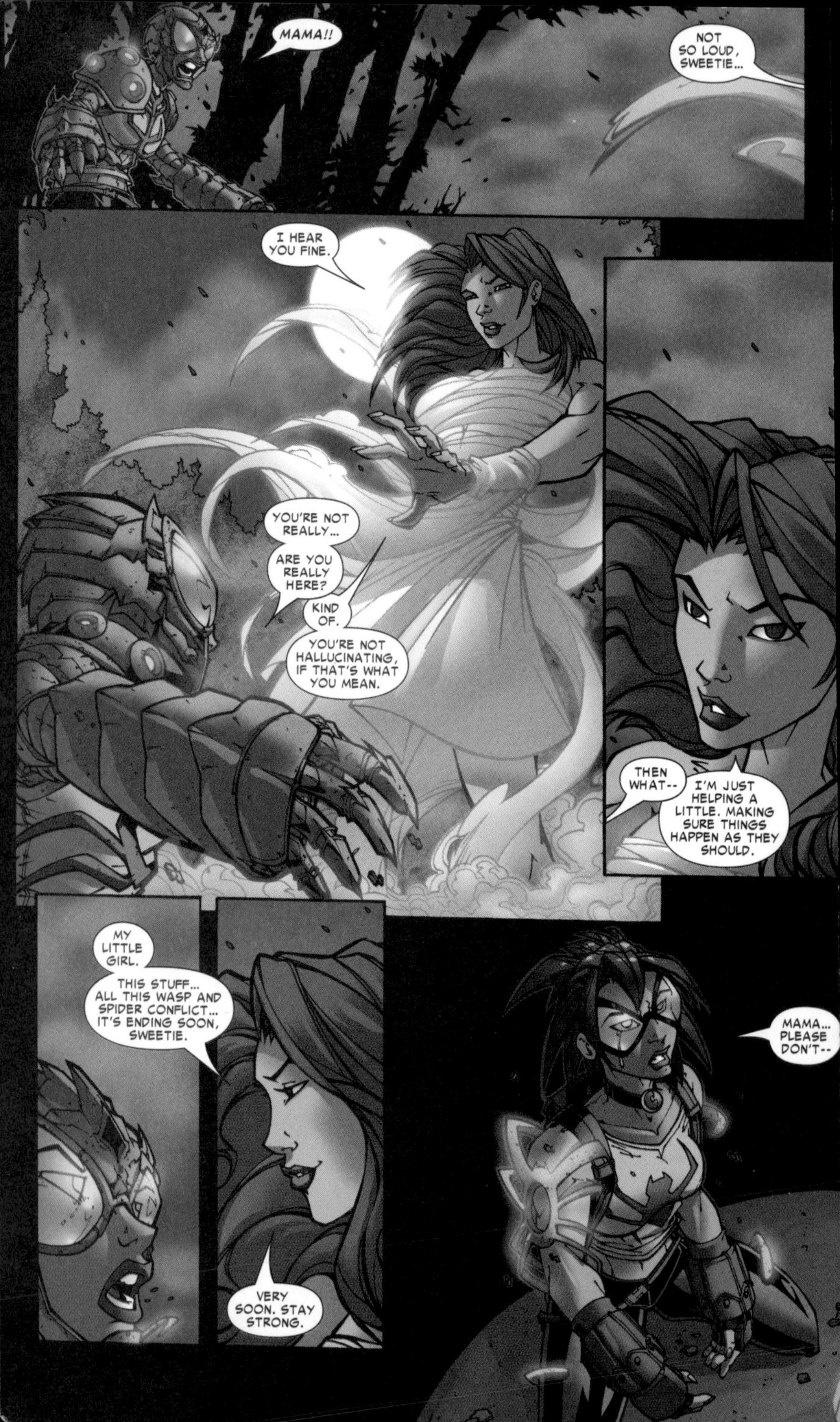
MAMA!!
NOT SO LOUD, SWEETIE...
I HEAR YOU FINE.
YOU'RE NOT REALLY...
ARE YOU REALLY HERE?
KIND OF.
YOU'RE NOT HALLUCINATING, IF THAT'S WHAT YOU MEAN.
THEN WHAT--
I'M JUST HELPING A LITTLE. MAKING SURE THINGS HAPPEN AS THEY SHOULD.
MY LITTLE GIRL.
THIS STUFF... ALL THIS WASP AND SPIDER CONFLICT... IT'S ENDING SOON, SWEETIE.
VERY SOON. STAY STRONG.
MAMA... PLEASE DON'T--

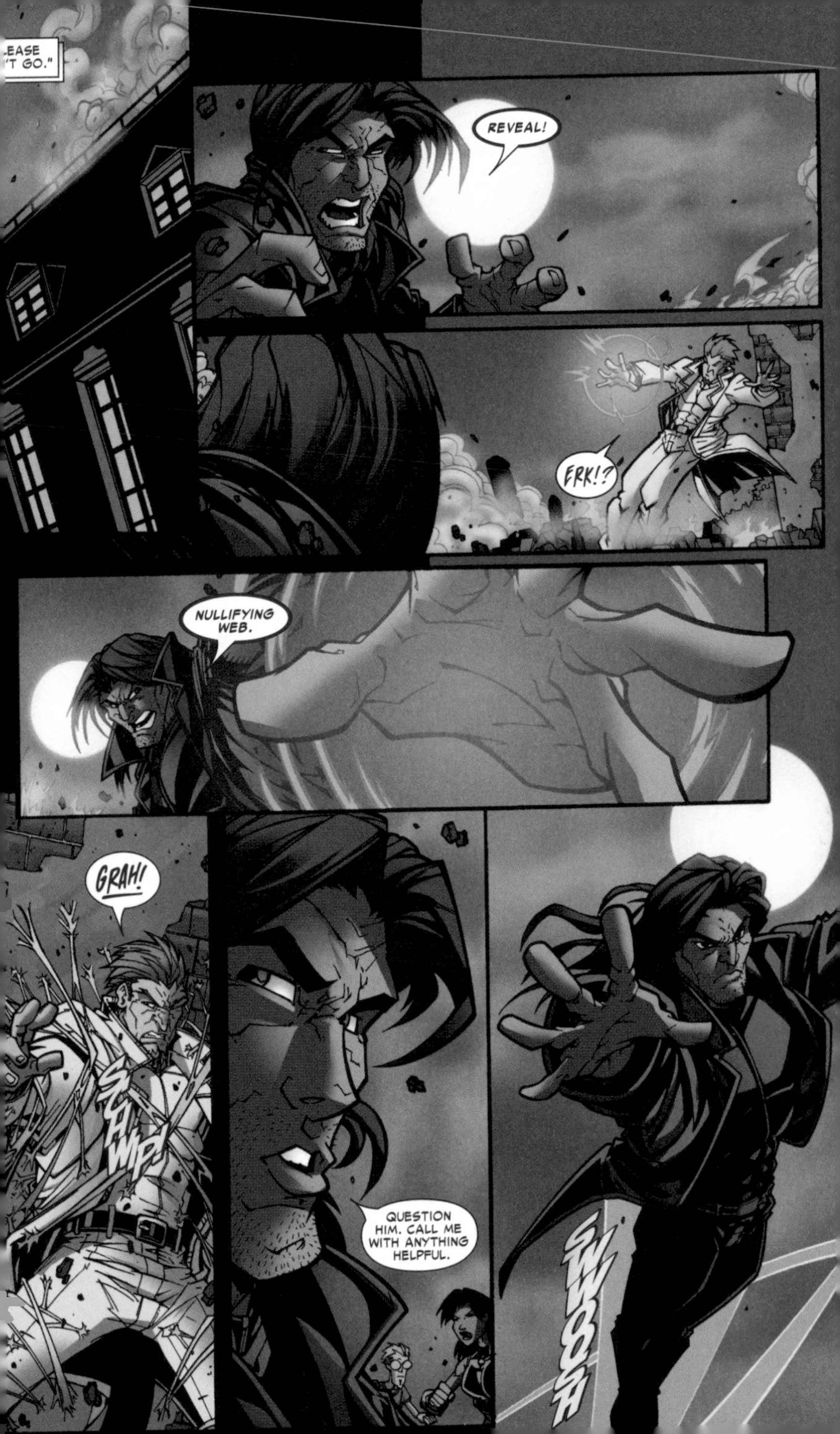

"...LEASE ...'T GO."
REVEAL!
ERK!?
NULLIFYING WEB.
GRAH!
SHOMP!
QUESTION HIM. CALL ME WITH ANYTHING HELPFUL.
SWOOSH

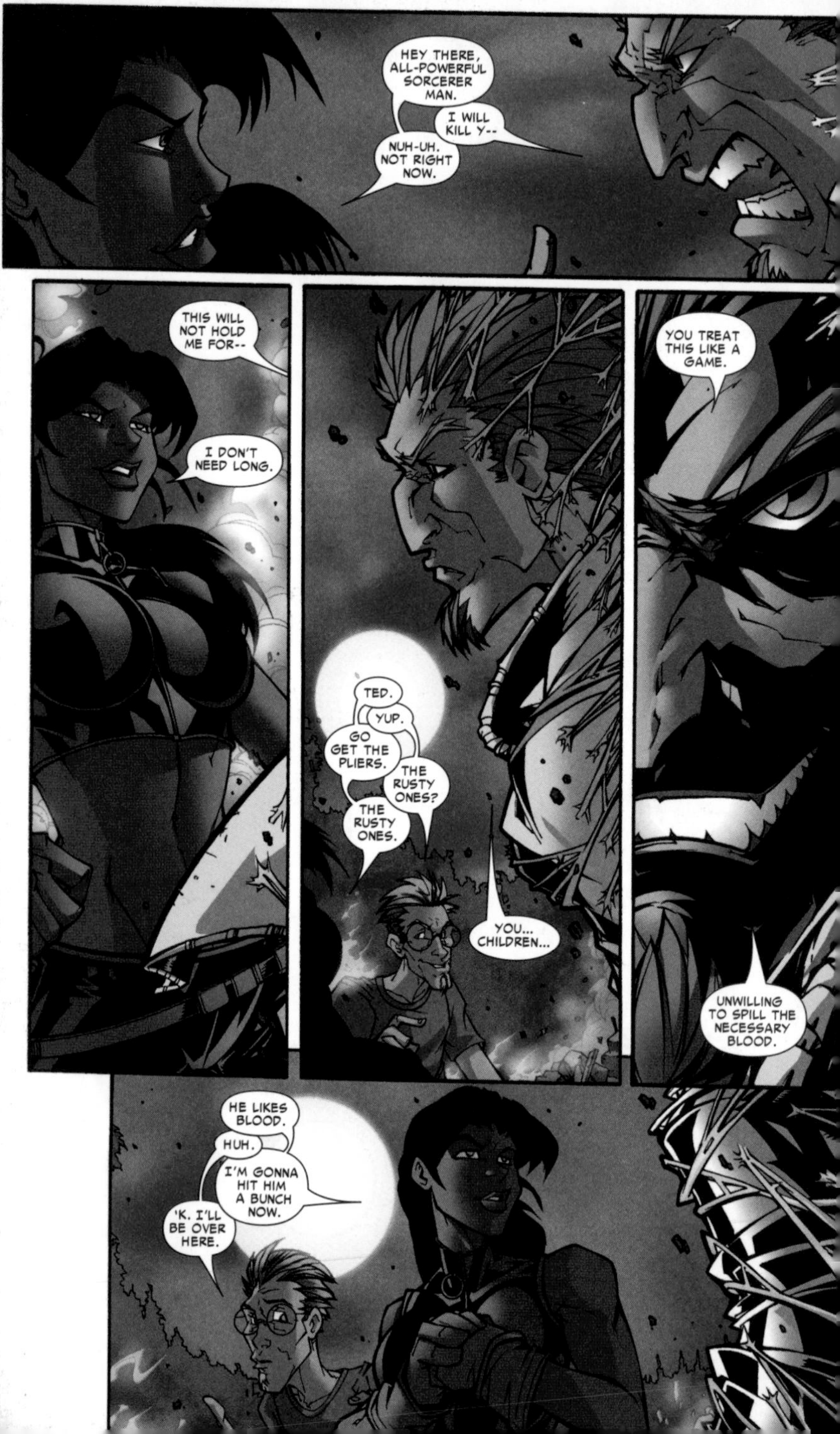
HEY THERE, ALL-POWERFUL SORCERER MAN.
I WILL KILL Y--
NUH-UH. NOT RIGHT NOW.
THIS WILL NOT HOLD ME FOR--
I DON'T NEED LONG.
TED.
YUP.
GO GET THE PLIERS.
THE RUSTY ONES?
THE RUSTY ONES.
YOU... CHILDREN...
YOU TREAT THIS LIKE A GAME.
UNWILLING TO SPILL THE NECESSARY BLOOD.
HE LIKES BLOOD.
HUH.
I'M GONNA HIT HIM A BUNCH NOW.
'K. I'LL BE OVER HERE.

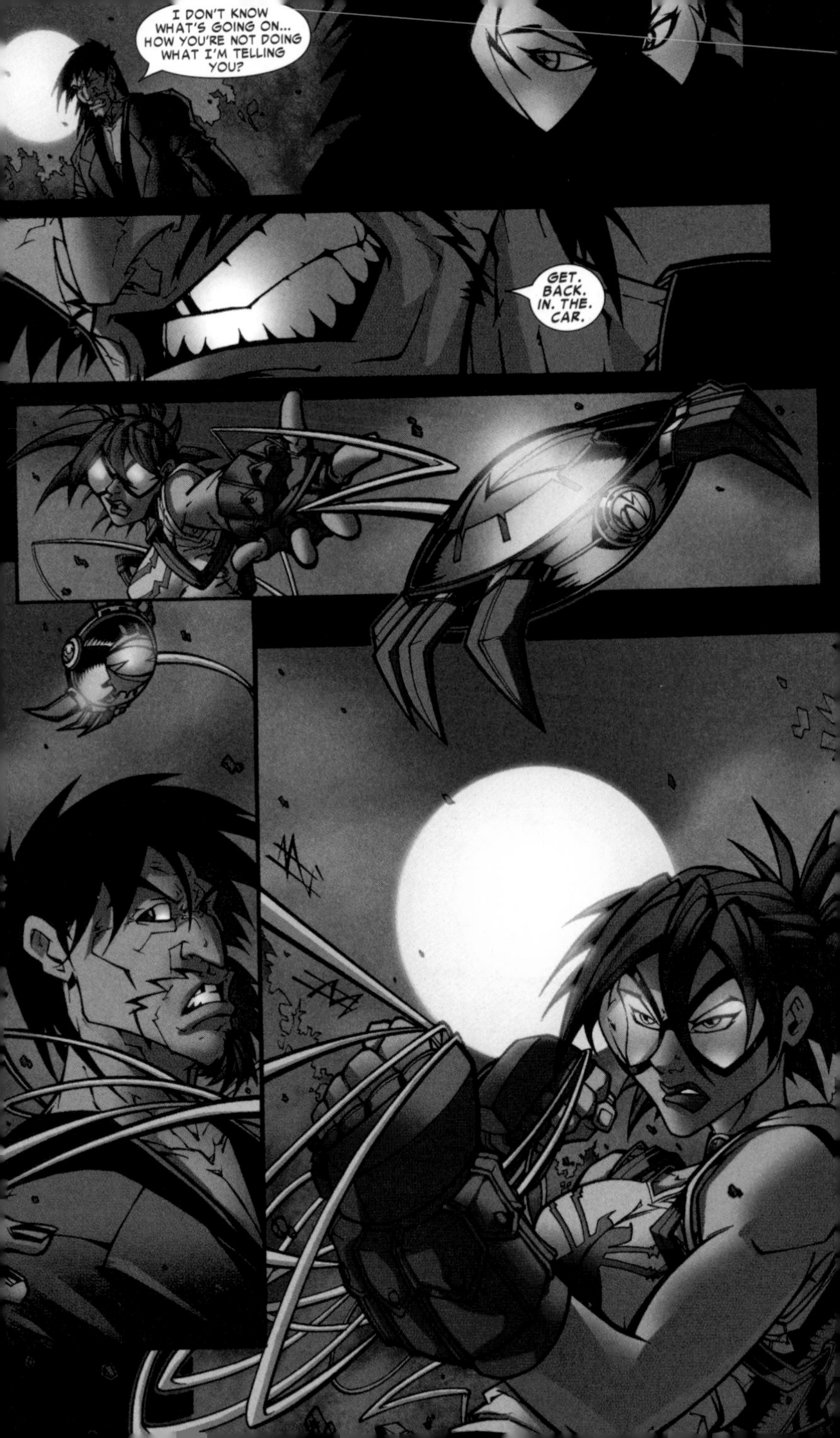
I DON'T KNOW WHAT'S GOING ON... HOW YOU'RE NOT DOING WHAT I'M TELLING YOU?
GET. BACK. IN. THE. CAR.

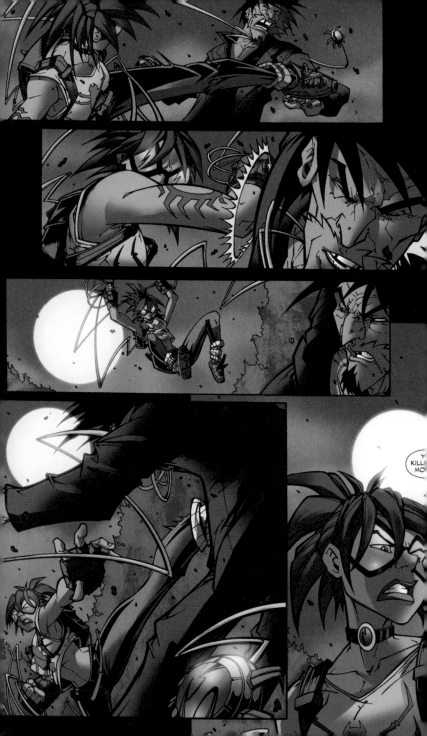

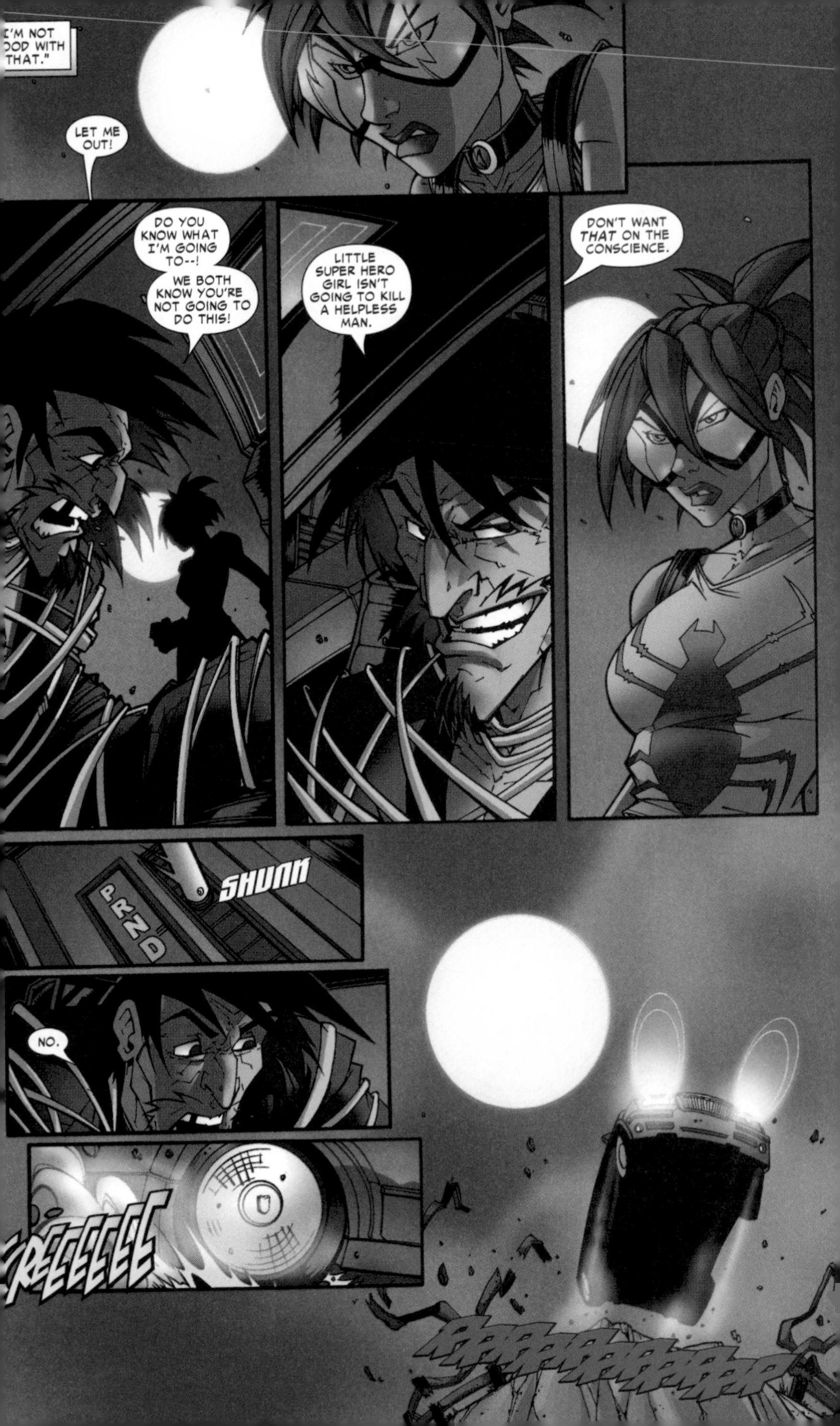
"I'M NOT GOOD WITH THAT."
LET ME OUT!
DO YOU KNOW WHAT I'M GOING TO--!
WE BOTH KNOW YOU'RE NOT GOING TO DO THIS!
LITTLE SUPER HERO GIRL ISN'T GOING TO KILL A HELPLESS MAN.
DON'T WANT THAT ON THE CONSCIENCE.
P R N D
SHUNK
NO.
REEEEEEE

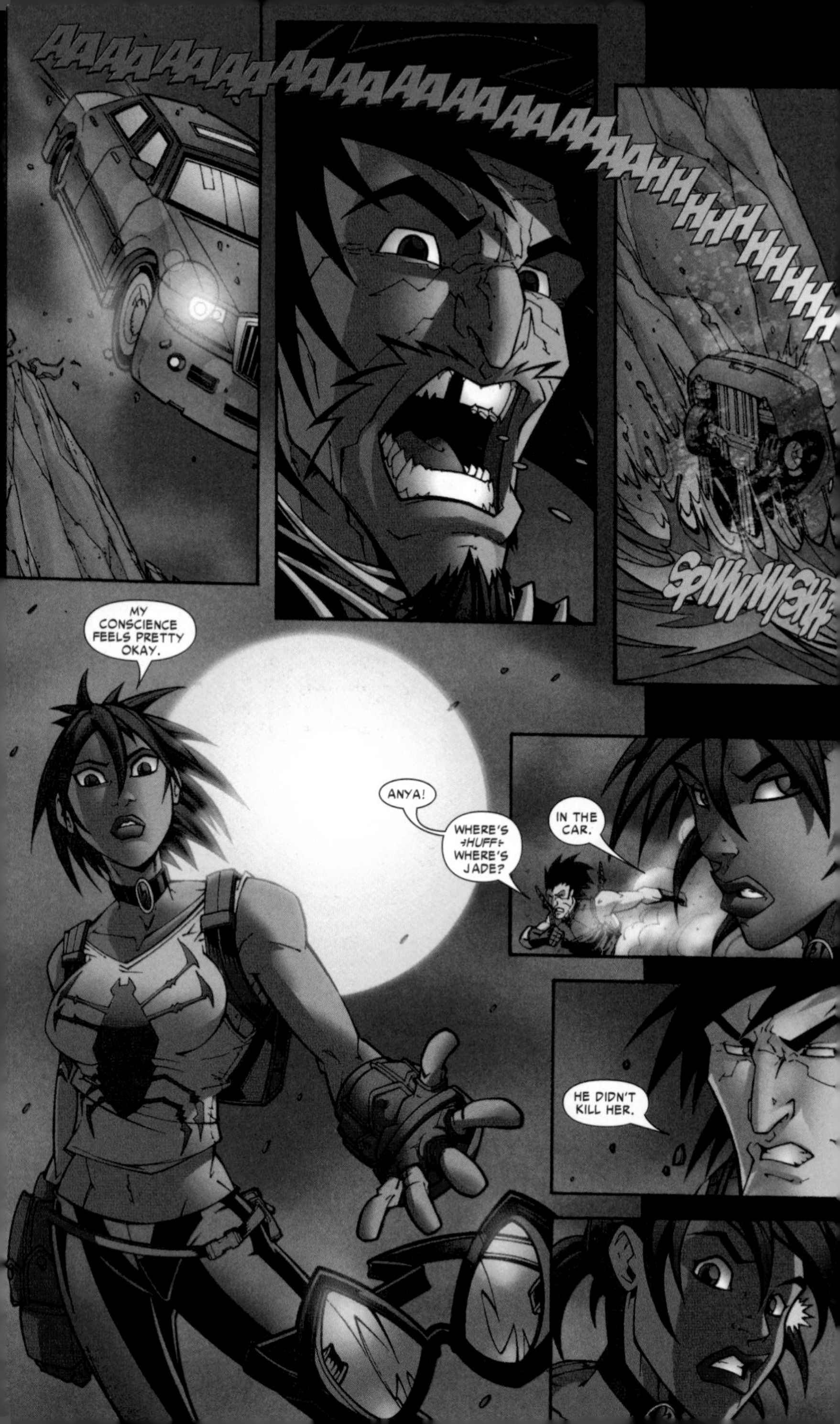
AAAAAAAAAAAAAAAAAAAAAAAAAAAHHHHHHHHHHHH
SPWWWISHH
MY CONSCIENCE FEELS PRETTY OKAY.
ANYA!
WHERE'S -HUFF- WHERE'S JADE?
IN THE CAR.
HE DIDN'T KILL HER.

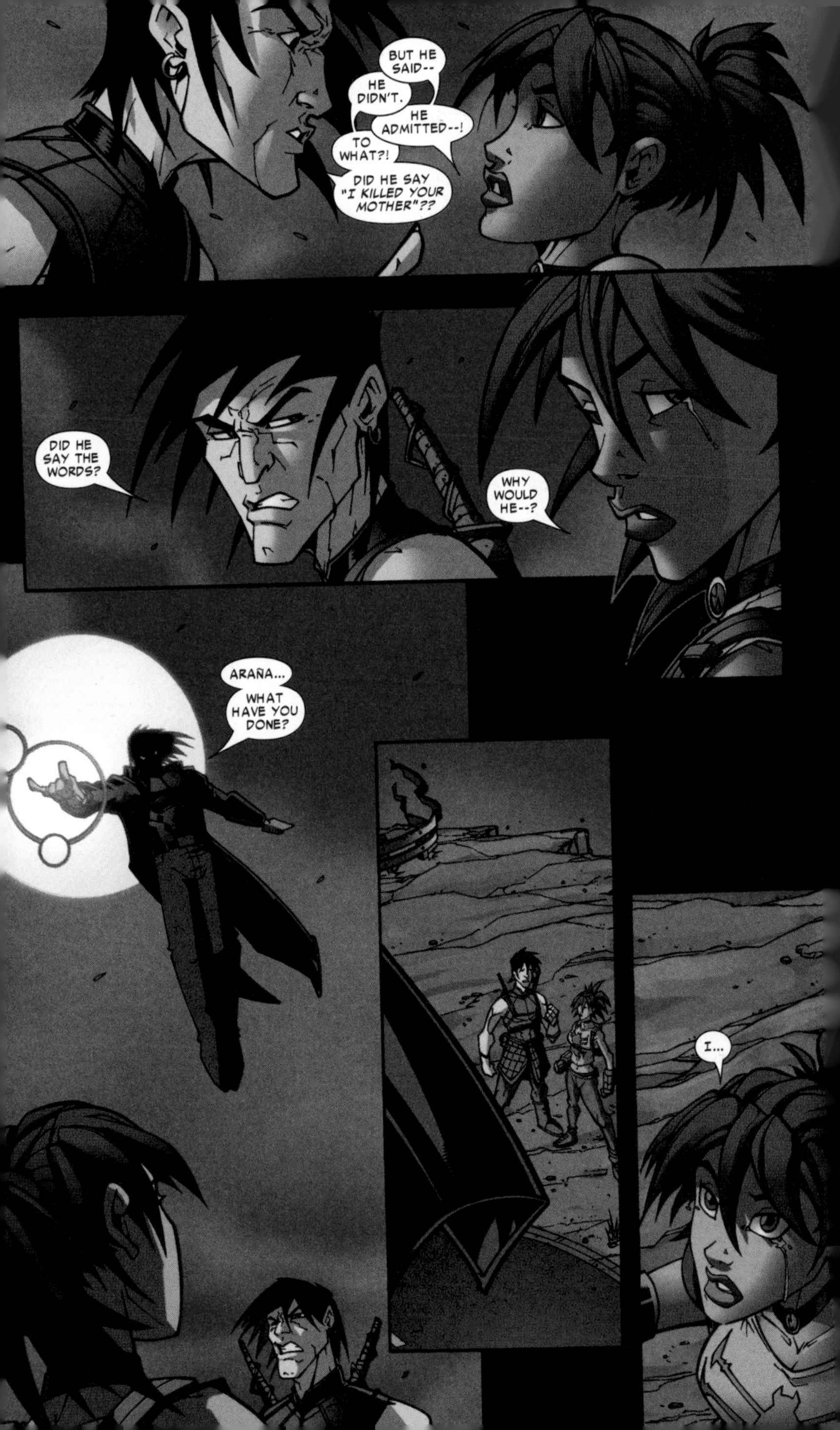
BUT HE SAID--
HE DIDN'T.
HE ADMITTED--!
TO WHAT?!
DID HE SAY "I KILLED YOUR MOTHER"??
DID HE SAY THE WORDS?
WHY WOULD HE--?
ARAÑA... WHAT HAVE YOU DONE?
I...

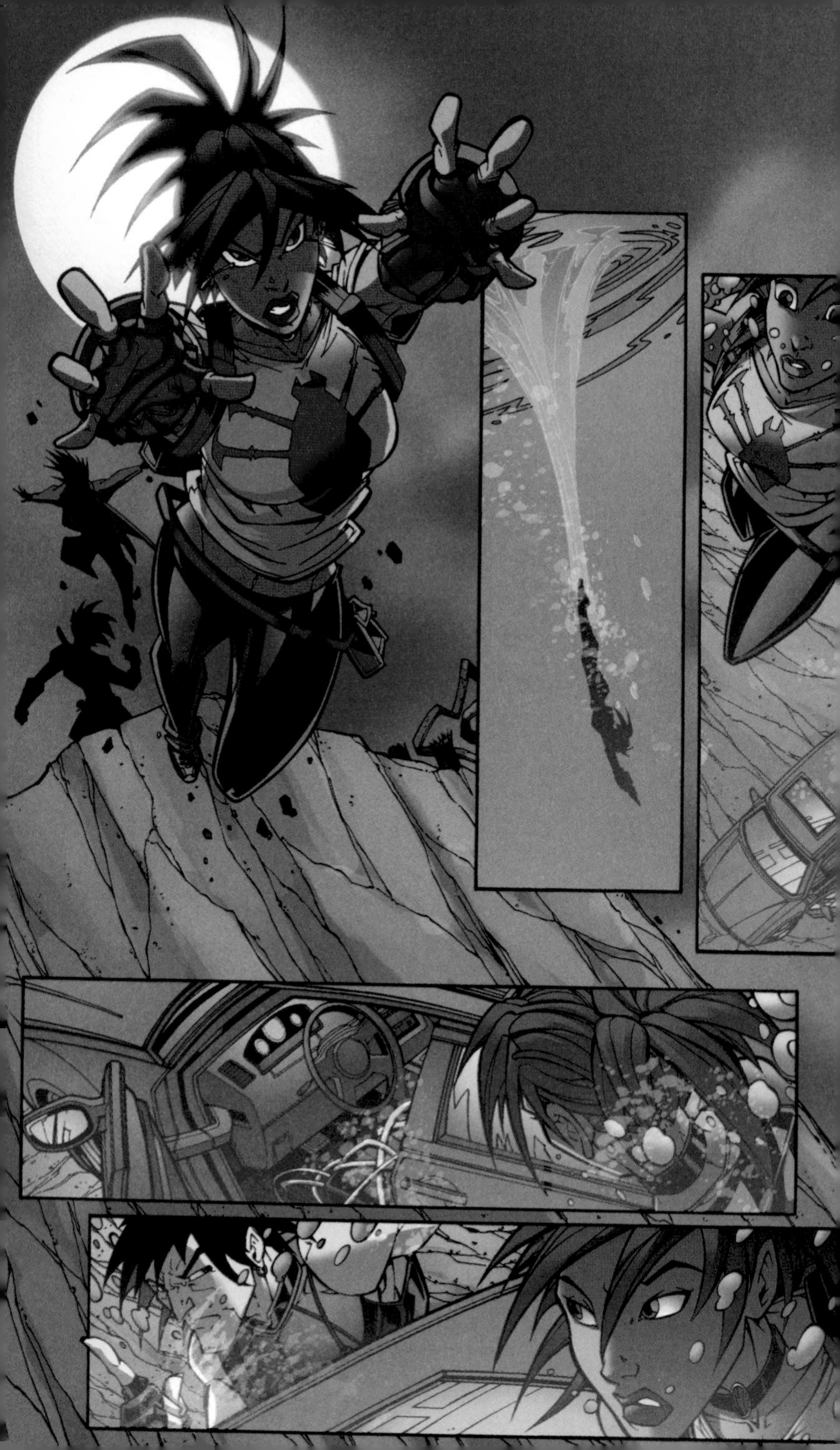

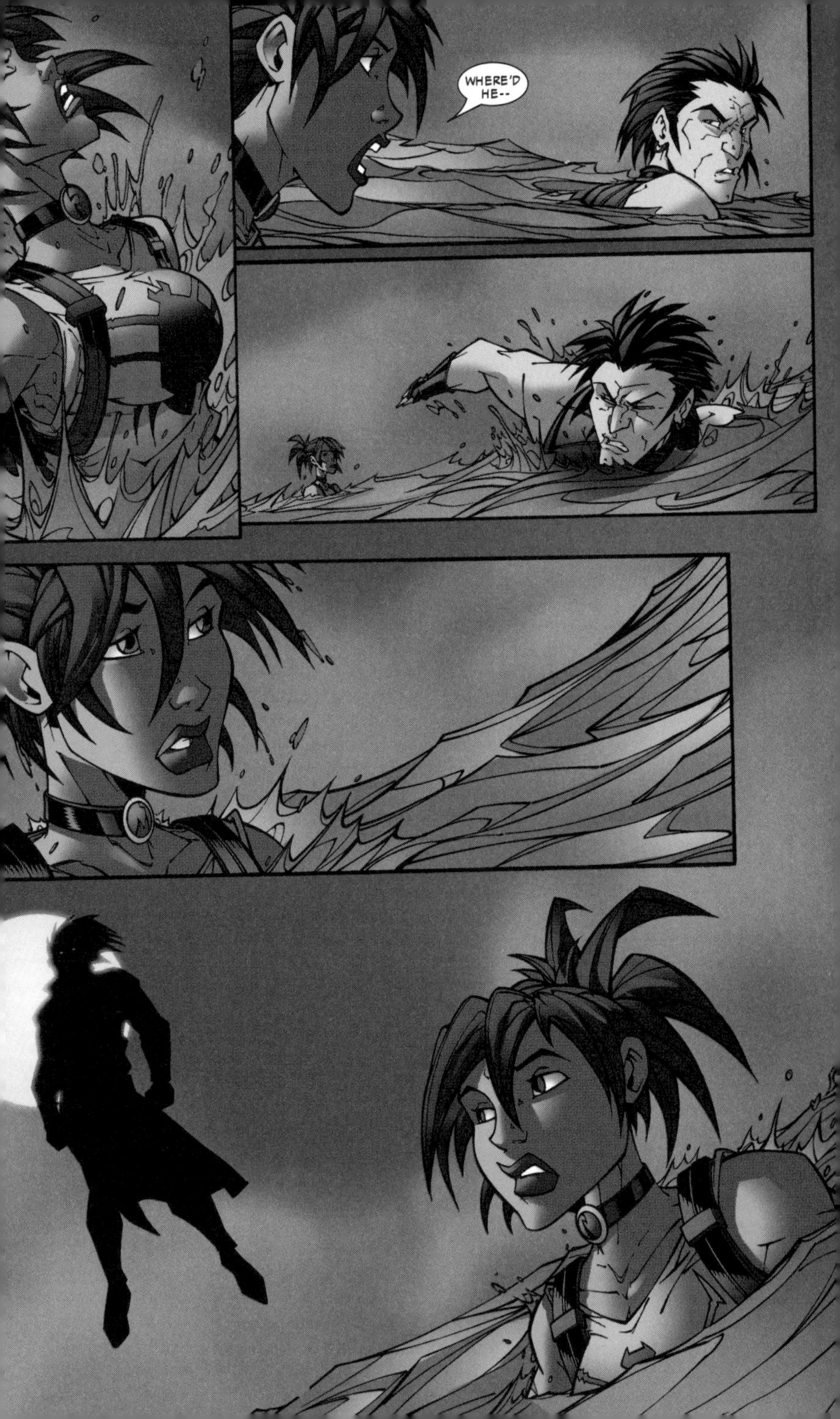
WHERE'D HE--

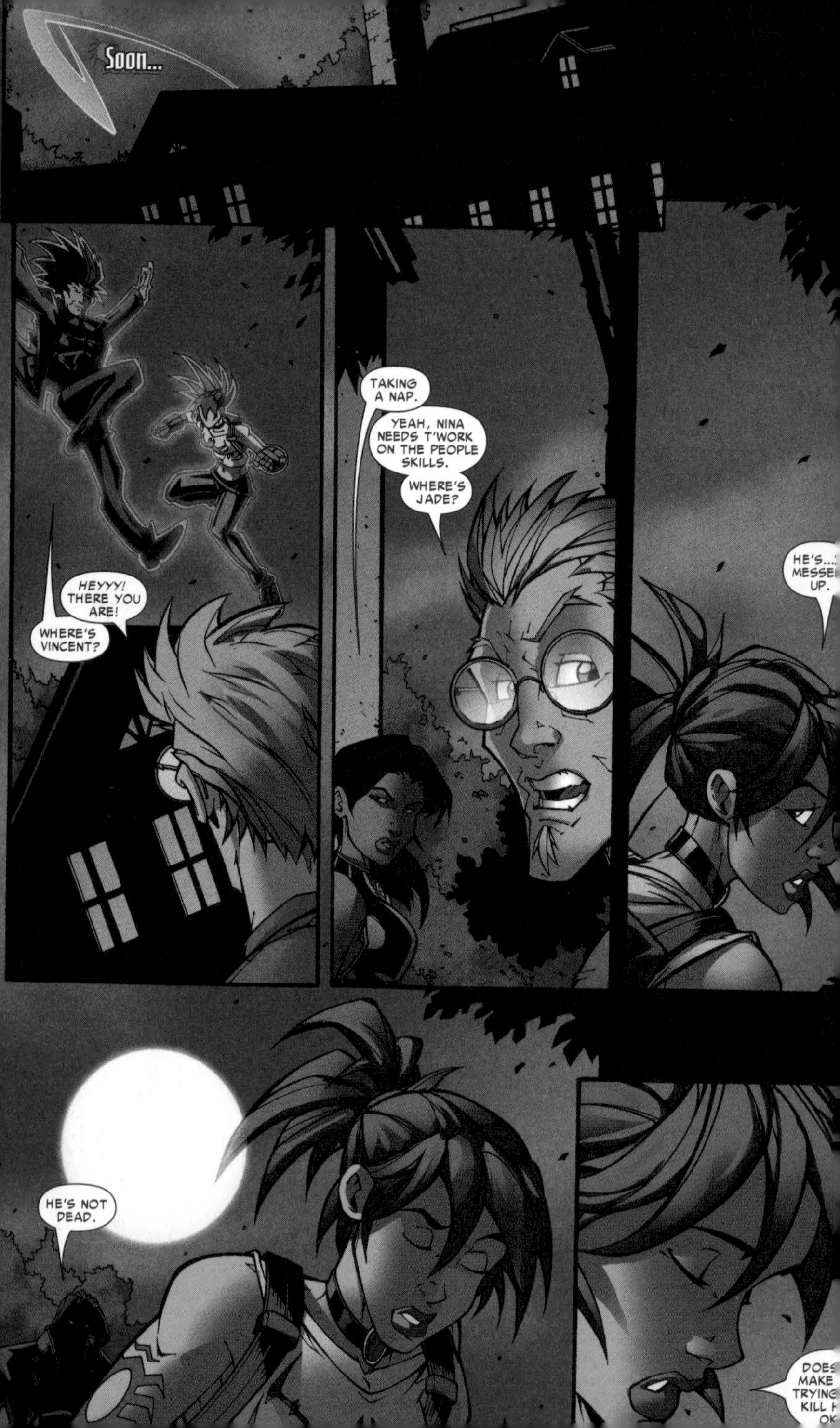
Soon...
HEYYY! THERE YOU ARE!
WHERE'S VINCENT?
TAKING A NAP.
YEAH, NINA NEEDS T'WORK ON THE PEOPLE SKILLS.
WHERE'S JADE?
HE'S... MESSE UP.
HE'S NOT DEAD.
DOES MAKE TRYING KILL OK

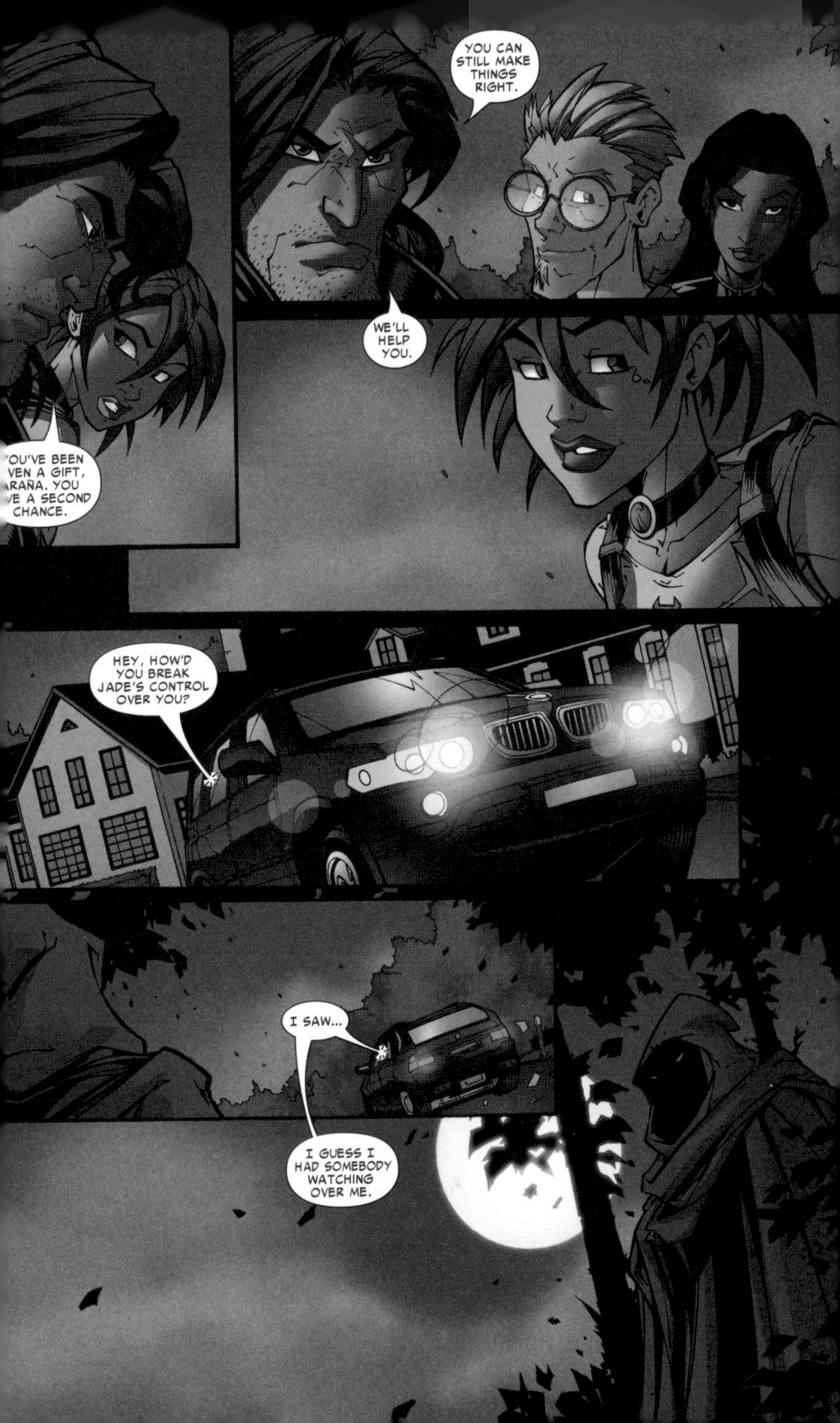

YOU CAN STILL MAKE THINGS RIGHT.
WE'LL HELP YOU.
OU'VE BEEN VEN A GIFT, ARAÑA. YOU VE A SECOND CHANCE.
HEY, HOW'D YOU BREAK JADE'S CONTROL OVER YOU?
I SAW...
I GUESS I HAD SOMEBODY WATCHING OVER ME.

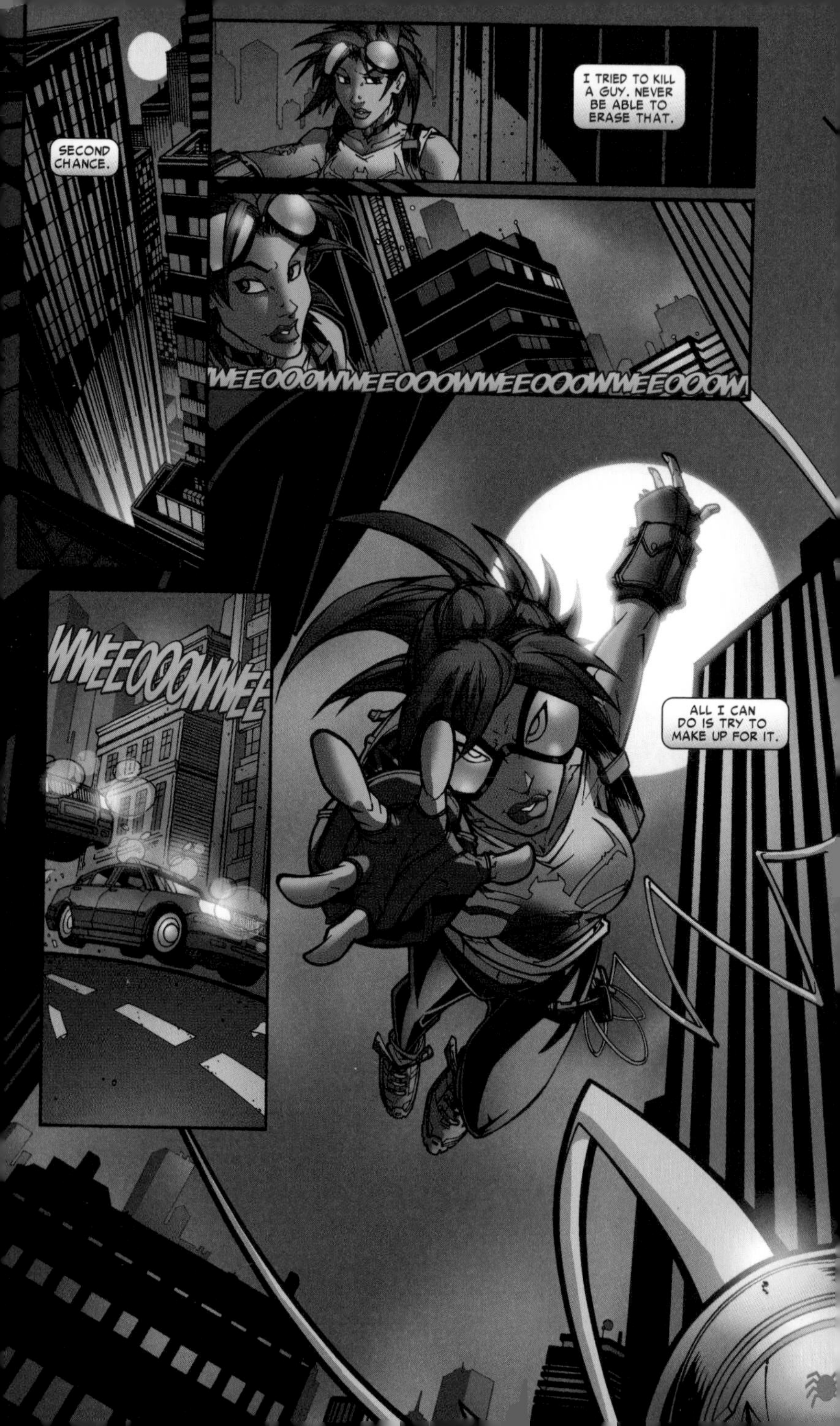

SECOND CHANCE.
I TRIED TO KILL A GUY. NEVER BE ABLE TO ERASE THAT.
WEEOOOWWEEOOOWWEEOOOWWEEOOOW
WWEEOOOWWEE
ALL I CAN DO IS TRY TO MAKE UP FOR IT.